Fraudster

Kevin Trudeau

Editor: Clarence R. Keeler

Title: Fraudster

Subtitle: Kevin Trudeau

Editor: Clarence R. Keeler

Created on: 2015-09-01 13:53 (UTC)

ISBN: 978-3-86898-008-0

Produced by: PediaPress GmbH, Moritz-Hilf-Str. 26, 65549 Limburg, Germany, http://pediapress.com/

The content within this book was generated collaboratively by volunteers. Please be advised that nothing found here has necessarily been reviewed by people with the expertise required to provide you with complete, accurate or reliable information. Some information in this book may be misleading or simply wrong. PediaPress does not guarantee the validity of the information found here. If you need specific advice (for example, medical, legal, financial, or risk management) please seek a professional who is licensed or knowledge-able in that area.

Sources, licenses and contributors of the articles and images are listed in the section entitled "References". Parts of the books may be licensed under the GNU Free Documentation License. A copy of this license is included in the section entitled "GNU Free Documentation License"

All third-party trademarks used belong to their respective owners.

Create your own custom Wikipedia-Book at http://pediapress.com

collection id: 7fac9adef85a4eff2a51e45b2821e
pdf writer version: 0.10.2 mwlib version: 0.15.14

Contents

Articles 1

Preface 1
Kevin Trudeau 3
MegaMemory 19
Natural Cures "They" Don't Want You to Know About 19
The Weight-Loss Cure "They" Don't Want You to Know About . . 23
Quackery 26
International Pool Tour 46
Ed Foreman 52
Greg Caton 56
Reno R. Rolle 60
Ronald Hoffman 61
Robert Barefoot 63
Donald Barrett 64
Leigh Valentine 66
Infomercial 68
Big Pharma conspiracy theory 82
Tammy Faye Messner 84
Nancy Valen 92
Federal Trade Commission 96
Food and Drug Administration 106
Pharmaceutical industry 129
Alternative medicine 151
Fraud 207

Appendix **223**

References 223

Article Sources and Contributors 241

Image Sources, Licenses and Contributors 243

Article Licenses **245**

Index **247**

Preface

It has been my express pleasure to edit the information contained in this book. We now live in the ultimate information age. There are so many sources. The Internet has made the media and the marketplace global. Of particular dislike are criminals who commit fraud by utilizing the various forms of available media. This is done to release false, misleading often dangerous information to an unsuspecting global public, for their own profit. Especially heinous are criminals who focus on fraudulent health/medical information and so called"cures" for serious illnesses. Such criminals futher victimize the ill and are a threat to global public health. It is ever my hope that this book will inform and inspire readers to seek correct information by doing their own research. As always, "Knowledge is Power." Clarence R. Keeler

Kevin Trudeau

Kevin Trudeau	
	Trudeau in 2005
Born	Kevin Mark Trudeau February 6, 1963 Lynn, Massachusetts, US
Occupation	Author, radio and television personality
Known for	Promoting alternative medicine Founding the International Pool Tour
Criminal charge	Fraud, larceny and contempt of court Regulatory settlements with the FTC and eight state Attorneys-General for false claims and misleading representations

Kevin Mark Trudeau (/truːˈdoʊ/; born February 6, 1963) is an American author, radio personality, infomercial host, salesman and convicted fraudster who has promoted various unsubstantiated health, diet and financial remedies. Several of his books, including *Natural Cures "They" Don't Want You to Know About*, allege that both the U.S. Food and Drug Administration and the pharmaceutical industry value profit over treatments or cures. He is currently incarcerated at Federal Prison Camp Montgomery, near Montgomery, Alabama, and is scheduled for release on July 18, 2022.

Trudeau's activities have been the subject of both criminal and civil action. He was convicted of larceny and credit card fraud in the early 1990s, and in 1998 he was sued by U.S. Federal Trade Commission (FTC) for making false or misleading claims in infomercials promoting his book *The Weight-Loss Cure "They" Don't Want You to Know About*. In 2004, he settled that action, by agreeing to pay a $500,000 fine and consenting to a lifetime ban on promoting products other than his books (which are protected by the First Amendment) via infomercials.[1] On November 29, 2011, the Seventh Circuit Court of Appeals upheld a $37.6 million fine levied against him for violating that 2004 settlement. Additionally, on remand, the district court modified its final order, requiring that he post a $2 million bond before engaging in future infomercial advertising. In April 2013 he was reported to have filed for bankruptcy to avoid fines and stay further Federal prosecution.

In 2013, he was twice briefly jailed for continued failure to pay fines related to his conviction, pleading poverty while continuing to live a lavish lifestyle. In November 2013, Trudeau was convicted of criminal contempt and incarcerated;[2] and on March 17, 2014, Trudeau was sentenced to 10 years in federal prison.[3]

Despite his imprisonment, infomercials for (and featuring) Trudeau continue to air on US television stations.[4]

Early life

Trudeau grew up in Lynn, Massachusetts, the adopted son of Robert and Mary Trudeau. He attended St. Mary's High School in Lynn, where he was voted "Most Likely to Succeed" by the class of 1981.

Career

After being incarcerated for fraud in the early 1990s, Trudeau joined a multi-level marketing firm, Nutrition for Life. The firm was successful until the Attorney General of Illinois charged that it was running a pyramid scheme. Trudeau and Nutrition for Life settled cases brought by the state of Illinois, and seven other U.S. states, for US$185,000.Wikipedia:Please clarify

Next, Trudeau produced and appeared in a series of late-night television infomercial broadcasts throughout North America. They promoted a range of products, including health aids, dietary supplements (such as coral calcium), baldness remedies, addiction treatments, memory-improvement courses, reading-improvement programs and real estate investment strategies. The FTC took regulatory action against Trudeau, alleging that his broadcasts contained unsubstantiated claims and misrepresentations. In 1998, he was fined. In 2004, he settled a contempt-of-court action arising out of the same cases by agreeing to a settlement that included both payment of a $2 million fine and a ban on further use of infomercials to promote any product other than publications protected by the First Amendment.

In 2004, Trudeau began writing books and promoting them with infomercials on U.S. television. The first book he published was a medical guide titled

Natural Cures "They" Don't Want You to Know About, which was published in 2005. The book was criticized for containing no natural cures. Trudeau said he was not able to include them because of threats by the FTC.[5] The book became a bestseller selling 5 million copies.[6]

Two years later, Trudeau published a second medical book titled *More Natural Cures Revealed: Previously Censored Brand Name Products That Cure Disease* (ISBN 0-9755995-4-2). According to Trudeau, the book identifies brand name products that will cure myriad illnesses. Trudeau's books claim that animals in the wild rarely develop degenerative conditions like cancer or Alzheimer's disease, and that many diseases are caused not by viruses or bacteria, but rather by an imbalance in vital energy. Science writer Christopher Wanjek critiqued and rejected many of these claims in his July 25, 2006 LiveScience.com health column.

Trudeau went on to publish *The Weight-Loss Cure "They" Don't Want You to Know About* and *Debt Cures "They" Don't Want You to Know About*. His writing has been commercially successful. In September 2005, *Natural Cures* was listed in the *New York Times* as the number-one-selling nonfiction book in the United States for 25 weeks. It has sold more than five million copies.

Trudeau launched a self-titled Internet radio talk show in February 2009 which also aired on several small radio stations consisting of mostly brokered programming.

Personal Life

Trudeau has been married at least three times. Little is known about his first marriage, to Oleksandra Polozhentseva, a Ukrainian immigrant. His second union, in 2007, to Kristine Dorow, a Norwegian student whom he met in London, ended in annulment after four months. In 2008 he married Natalya Babenko, another Ukrainian, who currently runs several of his former companies. She has returned to her home in Kiev, according to Trudeau.[7]

Publications

Natural Cures "They" Don't Want You to Know About

Main article: Natural Cures "They" Don't Want You to Know About

In 2004, Trudeau self-published the book 'Natural Cures "They" Don't Want You to Know About', which aimed to provide natural cures and medical advice. The natural cures discussed in the book were for a variety of diseases. The advice centered on various forms of alternative medicine. Trudeau made a number of outstanding claims in the book that received widespread media attention. This included that the sun does not cause cancer, sunscreen is one of the major causes of skin cancer and that AIDS is a hoax.

In the year of the book's launch, Trudeau featured in a 30-minute infomercial, in which he advertised the book. A number of Internet watchdogs were said to have analyzed the transcript, with Quackwatch concluding that the claims were misleading.

After the release of the book a natural cure for Diabetes included in the book was disputed by its purported source. The book refers to research carried out on a natural cure for diabetes at the University of Calgary. When questioned about the natural remedy, the University told ABC News "there have been no human studies conducted at the University of Calgary in the past 20 years on herbal remedies for diabetes."

Rose Shapiro published a book titled *Suckers: How Alternative Medicine Makes Fools of Us All*, in which she was critical of Trudeau's theories in his book.

After Trudeau's book achieved quick initial sales during 2005, the New York State Consumer Protection Board issued a warning saying that his book contains no actual cures. CPB Chairman Teresa A. Santiago stated that the book contents were merely "speculation". Throughout the book, readers are told that the cures they are looking for, in many cases, are available if they spend more money and subscribe to Trudeau's newsletter or his website. Both cost $71.40 per year or $499 for a "lifetime membership", an offer which was criticized by the Board. What appeared to be a back cover endorsement from former FDA commissioner Herbert Ley—who died three years before the book was written—was actually a 35-year-old quote from a *New York Times* interview.[8]

More Natural Cures Revealed

Following *Natural Cures 'They" Don't Want You to Know About*, Trudeau released a second medical guide two years later. His second book was self-published as well and titled *More Natural Cures Revealed: Previously Censored Brand Name Products That Cure Disease*.

The book is a similar publication to his first, where he purports to explain why drug and food companies hide the truth about how their products can cause disease. In *More Natural Cures Revealed*, Trudeau writes that workers at the FDA and FTC want to censor him and, figuratively, burn his books. Though the book received negative comments from some reviewers, it received average ratings on both Amazon and GoodReads.com.

The Weight Loss Cure "They" Don't Want You to Know About

Main article: The Weight-Loss Cure "They" Don't Want You to Know About

In April 2007, Trudeau released *The Weight Loss Cure "They" Don't Want You to Know About*. The book describes a weight loss plan originally proposed by British endocrinologist ATW Simeons in the 1950s involving injections of human chorionic gonadotropin. The diet was criticized in 1962 by the *Journal of the American Medical Association* as hazardous to human health and a waste of money. In 1976, the FTC ordered clinics and promoters of the Simeons Diet and hCG to inform prospective patients that there had not been "substantial evidence" to conclude hCG offered any benefit above that achieved on a restricted calorie diet. Clinical research trials published by the Journal of the American Medical Association and the American Journal of Clinical Nutrition have shown that hCG is ineffective as a weight-loss aid, citing "no statistically significant difference in the means of the two groups" and that hCG "does not appear to enhance the effectiveness of a rigidly imposed regimen for weight reduction."

The FTC has filed a contempt-of-court action against Trudeau alleging that the alleged misrepresentations in the book violate a 2004 consent order.

Debt Cures "They" Don't Want You to Know About

Debt Cures was published in 2007 and has been marketed on television. Chuck Jaffee, a columnist at CBS MarketWatch, stated: "Truth be told, most of the information [in the book] is readily available in personal finance columns you can find online or in books that are readily available in your local library." Trudeau says that if readers disagree with items on their credit reports, they can dispute them as identity theft; this was the "magic cure" of the book's title.

Trudeau routinely mentions esteemed names throughout his books to extend himself creditability, such as Hazel Valera, Executive Director of the California-based non-profit organization Clear Credit Exchange, Harvard Law Professor, Elizabeth Warren, and Robert Hinsley of Consumers Defense, yet none of the mentioned were ever interviewed by Trudeau.

Your Wish Is Your Command

Published in 2009, the product says it gives tools on how to use the Law of Attraction to manifest readers' desires. The packaging also says it contains key links to using the Law of Attraction that are missing in other publications. Among the claims made in the related infomercial is Trudeau's assertion to have virtually flunked out of high school.[9] He also says he was "taken in" by a mysterious group called "The Brotherhood" that taught him the secrets that he is now widely announcing in his book. There is also an invitation to join the now defunct "Global Information Network," an "exclusive group of highly influential, affluent, and freedom-orientated [sic] people" (see below). The group operated out of the country of Nevis and employed the Law of Attraction as its principal wealth generator, a concept regarded by most in the scientific community as at best pseudoscience.[10,11]

Media interviews

Trudeau has been interviewed by CNN's Paula Zahn, Matt Lauer of NBC's *Today Show*, and Harry Smith of CBS's *The Early Show*.[12] Trudeau was also the subject of investigative reports done by *Inside Edition*, ABC's *20/20*[13] and *Dateline NBC*.[14] The *20/20* segment highlighted a *Nightline* interview with Jake Tapper in which Trudeau misrepresented the money he was forced to pay to the government, the charges filed against him and the reason the government did not follow through with charges, and claiming ignorance when the claims made in his book were called false by Tapper. Trudeau was interviewed by Jacques Peretti for the fourth episode of the series *The Men Who Made Us Thin* on BBC2.

Infomercials

At one time, Trudeau was a prolific producer of infomercials. He consented to an FTC ban applying to everything except publications that the FTC concluded would infringe upon his First Amendment rights. All of his subsequent infomercials advertised his books *Natural Cures 'They" Don't Want You To Know About* and *The Weight Loss Cure*. Notable co-hosts included Leigh Valentine (former wife of televangelist Robert Tilton)[15] and the late Tammy Faye Messner (the former Tammy Faye Bakker).

Pharmaceutical companies

Trudeau says that pharmaceutical companies "don't want us to get well" because curing disease is not nearly as profitable as treating it in perpetuity. According to Trudeau, the corporate profit motive overrides the human desire to truly help people.

Trudeau says that natural treatments cannot be patented and are not profitable enough to justify spending hundreds of millions of dollars in testing, so they will always lack FDA approval. Trudeau uses herpes as an example, saying that people with herpes must buy an expensive drug for the rest of their lives.

He says that if there were a cheap, easy cure for herpes, the FDA and pharmaceutical companies would not want the population to know about it because corporate profits would suffer.

He cites the number of advertisements on television for prescription drugs and points out that prescription drugs should be advertised to doctors, not to the general public.

He states in one infomercial that there are twelve known cures for cancer but that they are being kept from the general public by the FDA, the FTC, and the pharmaceutical companies. He also says that the FDA and the FTC are two of the most corrupt organizations in America and that there is a long list of chemical ingredients that are secretly not required to be on the FDA ingredients label that are damaging to human health.

Trudeau offers a conspiracy theory, saying that the drug industry and the FDA work with each other to effectively deceive the public by banning all-natural cures in order to protect the profits of the drug industry. Trudeau says that FDA commissioners who leave the FDA to work for large drug companies are paid millions of dollars. In any other industry, according to Trudeau, this would be called "bribery," a "conflict of interest" or "payoffs." Trudeau also says in his infomercials that the food industry includes chemicals (such as MSG and aspartame) to get people "addicted to food" and to "make people obese."

Trudeau has also declared that he will lead a crusade against the FDA and the FTC and will make an effort to sue companies who promote false claims in advertising, such as leading pharmaceutical companies.

References to scientific studies

One of the major complaints about Trudeau's infomercials is that he makes only vague references to scientific studies, making them impossible to crosscheck for accuracy. The same criticism exists for the anecdotal evidence he presents in the infomercials.[16] He does not mention names of people who have been cured by his methods. For example, he tells a story in an infomercial about "a friend from England" who came to his house and complained of heartburn. He also references a study done on the antidepressant qualities of St. John's Wort compared to two prescription medications. He claims that the media reported St. John's Wort was "proven ineffective in study."

The infomercials suggest that referencing studies to substantiate claims will be addressed further in the book, but this is not the case. Readers of his book are often referred to his fee-based subscription website to find Trudeau's suggested natural cures.Wikipedia:Please clarify

Newspaper articles

A pair of 2005 Associated Press articles by Candice Choi on the infomercials elaborated on the success and problems of the programs. Choi says that by repeatedly mentioning government sanctions against him, Trudeau "anticipated any backlash with his cuckoo conspiracy theory" and can partially deflect any criticism of him or his infomercials. Trudeau's use of the word "cure" is an issue for regulators. Also, bookstores are polled on their decisions to sell or not sell a successful and controversial self-published book.

Additional marketing ventures

Audio tapes: "Mega Memory"

Trudeau says he adapted techniques used to improve the memory of the blind and the mentally challenged to create *Mega Memory* and *Advanced Mega Memory* audio tapes. His promotion of memory-enhancing products was ended by the intervention of the Federal Trade Commission which alleged that the claims made by Trudeau were false and programs involved would not enable users to achieve a "photographic memory," as the advertising claimed.

Trudeau used research that Dr. Michael Van Masters conducted with the State School for the Blind in Muskogee, Oklahoma, in 1975 as the basis of the *Mega Memory* products. Trudeau was selling automobiles at Neponset Lincoln Mercury in the Dorchester neighborhood of Boston in 1982 when he first met Van Masters. Shortly after meeting Van Masters, Kevin joined Van Masters in the memory business in Chicago. Wikipedia:Citation needed

Non-surgical face lift

In addition to *Natural Cures*, Trudeau also hosted an infomercial that features the "Perfect Lift" non-surgical face lift. In the United Kingdom, this infomercial was found to violate the ITC advertising rules.

In 2008, Trudeau began airing another infomercial, for a product called Firmalift, with Leigh Valentine.

Trudeau partners with Donald Barrett and ITV Direct

On September 11, 2006, Donald Barrett and ITV Direct, a direct marketing company based in Beverly, Massachusetts, announced that they had partnered with Trudeau to market both of his *Natural Cures* books.[17] Trudeau also worked with ITV to create ITV Ventures, a new MLM group based out of ITV's home office.[18] As of December 2006, ITV Direct has pulled all information concerning both this partnership and Trudeau's books from its corporate website; however, the infomercials have continued to run as of April 14, 2008.

Figure 1: *IPT Starship Stage for TV rounds and finals at North American Championship held in Las Vegas, Nevada, July 2006*

International Pool Tour

Main article: International Pool Tour

In 2005, Trudeau founded the International Pool Tour (IPT). His goal was to transform billiards into a "major league" sport with aggressive promotion and the largest purses ever offered. The initial three events in 2005 and early 2006 were successful, but at the fourth, the IPT World Open tournament in Reno, Nevada, promoters announced that they did not have sufficient funds on hand to cover the purse. Winners were assured that they would receive their prizes in small installments, but most were never paid. The Reno fiasco marked the demise not only of IPT, but of professional pool competitions as a whole. As one commentator put it, "The pool hustler wasn't murdered by any single suspect, but the last man holding the knife was Kevin Trudeau."

Legal proceedings

In connection with his promotional activities he has had a felony conviction and has been an unsuccessful defendant in several Federal Trade Commission (FTC) lawsuits. Trudeau has been charged several times by agencies of the United States government for making claims without evidence. In these cases

Trudeau signed a consent decree in which he did not plead guilty but did agree to stop making the claims and to pay a fine. Trudeau subsequently began to sell books, which are protected by the First Amendment.

Trudeau was convicted of fraud and larceny in the early 1990s. The FTC has sued him repeatedly and keeps an extensive record of its conflicts with him. A court order currently restricts his ability to promote and sell any product or service; however, he is permitted to promote books and other publications due to free-speech protection under the First Amendment as long as they are not used to promote or sell products or services and do not contain misrepresentations. On November 19, 2007, a court found Trudeau in contempt of that court order for making deceptive claims about his book *The Weight Loss Cure 'They" Don't Want You to Know About*. In August 2008, he was fined more than $5 million[19] and banned from infomercials for three years for continuing to make fraudulent claims pertaining to the book. The amount of the monetary damages was later increased to $37 million.

1990–1991: Larceny and credit card fraud

In 1990, Trudeau posed as a doctor in order to deposit $80,000 in false checks, and in 1991 he pleaded guilty to larceny. That same year, Trudeau faced federal charges of credit card fraud after he stole the names and Social Security numbers of eleven customers of a mega memory product and charged $122,735.68 on their credit cards.[20] He spent two years in federal prison because of this conviction. Later, in an interview, he explained his crimes as:

> "... *youthful indiscretions and not as bad as they sound, and besides, both were partly the fault of other people, and besides, he has changed. The larceny he explains as a series of math errors compounded by the 'mistake' of a bank official. As for why the bank thought he was a doctor, that was just a simple misunderstanding, because he jokingly referred to himself as a 'doctor in memory'. He still can't quite believe he was prosecuted for the larceny charges. 'Give me a break,' he says.*"

1996: SEC and various states

Trudeau began working for Nutrition For Life, a multi-level marketing program, in the mid-1990s. In 1996, his recruitment practices were cited by the states of Illinois and Michigan, as well as the U.S. Securities and Exchange Commission. Illinois sued Trudeau and Jules Leib, his partner, accusing them of operating an illegal pyramid scheme. They settled with Illinois and seven other states for $185,000 after agreeing to change their tactics. Michigan forbade him from operating in the state.[21] A class action lawsuit was filed by stockholders of Nutrition for Life for violations of Texas law, including misrepresenting and/or omitting material information about Nutrition for Life International, Inc.'s business. In August 1997, the company paid $2 million in cash to common stockholders and holders of warrants during the class period to settle the case. The company also paid the plaintiffs' attorney fees of $600,000.[22]

1998: FTC fine

In 1998, Trudeau was fined $500,000, the funds to be used for consumer redress by the FTC, relating to six infomercials he had produced and in which the FTC determined he had made false or misleading claims. These infomercials included "Hair Farming," "Mega Memory System," "Addiction Breaking System," "Action Reading," "Eden's Secret," and "Mega Reading." The products included a "hair farming system" that was supposed to "finally end baldness in the human race," and "a breakthrough that in 60 seconds can eliminate" addictions, discovered when a certain "Dr. Callahan" was "studying quantum physics."

2004: FTC contempt of court and injunction

In June 2003, the FTC filed a complaint in the U.S. District Court for the Northern District of Illinois against Trudeau and some of his companies (Shop America (USA), LLC; Shop America Marketing Group, LLC; and Trustar Global Media, Limited), alleging that disease-related claims for Coral Calcium Supreme were false and unsubstantiated. In July 2003, Trudeau entered into a stipulated preliminary injunction that prohibited him from continuing to make the challenged claims for Coral Calcium Supreme and Biotape.

In the summer of 2004, the court found Trudeau in contempt of court for violating the preliminary injunction, because he had sent out a direct mail piece and produced an infomercial making prohibited claims. The court ordered Trudeau to cease all marketing for coral calcium products.

In September 2004, Trudeau agreed to pay $2 million ($500,000 in cash plus transfer of residential property located in Ojai, California, and a luxury vehicle) to settle charges that he falsely claimed that a coral calcium product can cure cancer and other serious diseases and that a purported analgesic called Biotape can permanently cure or relieve severe pain. He also agreed to a lifetime ban on promoting products using infomercials, but excluded restrictions to promote his books via infomercials.[23,24,25] Trudeau was the only person ever banned by the FTC from selling a product via television. Lydia Parnes, speaking for the FTC's Bureau of Consumer Protection stated: "This ban is meant to shut down an infomercial empire that has misled American consumers for years."

Trudeau claimed the government was trying to discredit his book because he was "exposing them."

2005: *Trudeau v. FTC*

On February 28, 2005, Trudeau filed a complaint against the FTC in the U.S. District Court for the District of Columbia seeking declaratory and injunctive relief. Trudeau also filed a motion for preliminary injunction, which the court denied.

The complaint charged that the FTC had retaliated against him for his criticism of the agency by issuing a press release that falsely characterized and intentionally and deliberately misrepresented the 2004 Final Order. That conduct, Trudeau asserted, exceeded the FTC's authority under 15 U.S.C. § 46(f) and violated the First Amendment. The FTC responded with a motion to dismiss the complaint for lack of subject-matter jurisdiction under Federal Rule of Civil Procedure 12(b)(1), and for failure to state a claim for which relief can be granted under Rule 12(b)(6).

The district court granted the FTC's motion to dismiss. First, the court concluded that it lacked subject-matter jurisdiction because the press release was not "a 'final agency action'" under "section 704 of the [Administrative Procedure Act]", 5 U.S.C. § 704. Second, the court held, "in the alternative, that Trudeau's claims failed to state a viable cause of action as a matter of law."

Trudeau later filed an appeal which was unsuccessful in reversing the court's ruling.[26]

2005: *Trudeau v. New York Consumer Protection Board*

Trudeau filed a lawsuit on August 11, 2005, accusing the New York State Consumer Protection Board of violating his First Amendment rights by contacting television stations in New York state and urging them to pull Trudeau's infomercials promoting his book *Natural Cures "They" Don't Want You to Know About*.[27] Trudeau won a temporary restraining order on September 6, 2005 prohibiting the Board from sending letters to the television stations. The temporary restraining order was replaced by a preliminary injunction. However, Trudeau lost a motion to have the Board send a "corrective letter" to the television stations and subsequently dropped all claims for monetary damages. The case is still in litigation.Wikipedia:Citation needed

2007: FTC contempt of court action

The FTC filed a contempt of court action against Trudeau and the companies that market *The Weight Loss Cure 'They' Don't Want You to Know About*, alleging that Trudeau was in contempt of a 2004 court order by "deceptively claiming in his infomercials that the book being advertised establishes a weight-loss protocol that is 'easy' to follow." The action was filed in the U.S. District Court for the Northern District of Illinois on September 17, 2007. According to an FTC press release, Trudeau has claimed that the weight loss plan outlined in the book is easy, can be done at home, and readers can eat anything they want. When consumers buy the book, they find it describes a complex plan that requires intense dieting, daily injections of a prescribed drug that is not easily obtainable, and lifelong dietary restrictions.

On November 19, 2007, Trudeau was found in contempt of the 2004 court order for "patently false" claims in his weight loss book. U.S. District Court Judge Robert W. Gettleman ruled that Trudeau "clearly misrepresents in his advertisements the difficulty of the diet described in his book, and by doing so, he has misled thousands of consumers." On August 7, 2008, Gettleman issued an order that Trudeau was not to appear in infomercials for any product in which he has any interest, for three years from the date of the order; and was to pay a penalty of $5,173,000, an estimate of the royalties received from the weight loss book. On November 4, 2008, Gettleman amended the judgment to $37,616,161, the amount consumers paid in response to the deceptive infomercials. The court denied Trudeau's request to reconsider or stay this ruling on December 11 of the same year.

Trudeau appealed the ruling to the United States Court of Appeals for the Seventh Circuit which upheld the contempt finding, but sent the case back to the lower court to explain the basis of the $37,616,161 damage finding and the three-year infomercial ban. After the lower court justified the basis for the damage finding, and set a $2 million performance bond for future infomercial advertising, Trudeau again appealed to the Seventh Circuit, which affirmed the damage award on November 29, 2011.

2010: Arrest on criminal contempt of court charge

On February 11, 2010, Trudeau was arrested and appeared in U.S. District Court before Gettleman for criminal contempt of court after he "asked his supporters to email the federal judge overseeing a pending civil case brought against him by the Federal Trade Commission." He was forced to turn over his passport, pay a $50,000 bond and was warned he could face future prison time for interfering with the direct process of the court.[28] On February 17, Gettleman sentenced Trudeau to 30 days in jail and forfeiture of the $50,000 bond. Well-known critic of Trudeau, Stephen Barrett, the creator of Quackwatch.org, "has for years labeled Trudeau a fraud" and was quoted: "He struck me as somebody who (believes he) is omnipotent. That is, no one can touch him," Barrett said. "That's almost been the case." Trudeau appealed the ruling and on May 20 the Seventh Circuit Court of Appeals granted his motion, dismissing the contempt citation.

2011: Loss of appeal against $37.6m fine

On November 28, 2011, the U.S. Food and Drug Administration and the Federal Trade Commission issued warnings to companies selling human chorionic gonadotropin (HCG) as weight loss products as the claims are unsupported. The HCG diet was popularized by Trudeau's *The Weight-Loss Cure "They" Don't Want You to Know About* book in 2007.

On Nov. 29, 2011, Trudeau lost his 2010 appeal in the Seventh Circuit Court of Appeals. The court found that the $37.6 million fine for violating his 2004 settlement with the Federal Trade Commission was appropriate as Trudeau had aired 32,000 infomercials and described the figure as "conservative." The court considered sales only from the 800 number used to place orders and excluded internet and store sales. Additionally, the court found that requiring Trudeau to make a $2 million performance bond prior to participating in an infomercial was constitutional.

2013–2014: Additional contempt citations, asset concealment, imprisonment

In September 2013 Judge Robert Gettleman held Trudeau in civil contempt for violation of multiple court orders and failure to pay the $37 million fine assessed in 2010. Noting that he continued to maintain a lavish lifestyle, despite insisting that he had been "completely wiped out" financially, Gettleman appointed a receiver to identify and catalog Trudeau's assets and holdings. A month later Trudeau was arrested after refusing to cooperate with the receiver's investigation. In November a jury found him in criminal contempt for repeated violations of his 2004 agreement as well as subsequent orders and plea deals. Pending sentencing he was held without bail as a flight risk, and for continued failure to disclose hidden assets.

In February 2014 the court-appointed receiver announced that a number of Trudeau's known assets, including a home in Ojai, California, would be auctioned, with proceeds to be applied toward unpaid fines and restitutions. The receiver also assumed control of Trudeau's Global Information Network, a "secret club" that had promised extraordinary money-making opportunities and numerous "secrets to success". He informed its members that the club's business model "likely amounted to an illegal pyramid scheme", and that its relentlessly publicized group of 30 billionaire financial advisors known as the "GIN Council" did not exist. The organization's remaining assets were later auctioned as well.[29]

In March 2014 Trudeau was sentenced to 10 years in prison, an "unusually lengthy" term for a contempt conviction. Judge Ronald Guzman, "visibly irritated" by Trudeau's plea for leniency, described him as "deceitful to the core". "[Trudeau] has treated federal court orders as if they were mere suggestions ... or at most, impediments to be sidestepped, outmaneuvered or just ignored," Guzman said. "That type of conduct simply cannot stand." Trudeau has filed an appeal.[30] He is incarcerated at Federal Prison Camp Montgomery, near Montgomery, Alabama.[31]

Guzman ordered that royalties payable to Trudeau from continuing sales of his books—now owned by a California company called Free is My Favorite LLC, which purchased the rights from Trudeau—be forwarded to a government-controlled trust and used for fine and restitution payments. Infomercials for his *Free Money 'They" Don't Want You to Know About* book, produced and marketed by Free is My Favorite LLC, continue to run on television stations throughout the United States. Trudeau maintains an active Facebook page, where he solicits donations for his "defense fund" and compares his imprisonment to that of Nelson Mandela.

Other criticisms

Medical experience

One common criticism by consumer groups is that Trudeau has had no medical training. Trudeau responds that by not having such training, he is not biased toward pharmaceutical companies and the FDA, and that medical doctors "are taught only how to write out prescriptions" for "poisons" and "cut out pieces of a person's anatomy."[32]

Unsubstantiated claims

Trudeau has been criticized for his inability to provide evidence to back up his claims. Although he recites anecdotes, he has never provided evidence evaluated by licensed medical practitioners. In instances where Trudeau has been asked to provide proof, he has misinterpreted medical studies or cited dubious or fictitious studies. For example, Trudeau cited a nonexistent 25-year research study involving a natural cure for diabetes at the University of Calgary.[33] When ABC News correspondent Jake Tapper confronted him on

Nightline, Trudeau insisted that he had a copy of the study and would provide it; he never did. He later claimed in his infomercials that the university destroyed its findings to prevent reprisals from the pharmaceutical industry. In 2006 University of Calgary officials announced in a public statement that none of Trudeau's claims about the university's research were true, and that its attorneys had sent Trudeau a "cease and desist" letter, demanding that he stop associating himself with the school.[34]

False endorsements

In August 2005, the New York Consumer Protection Board warned consumers that Trudeau has used false claims of endorsements to promote his products, noting that the back cover of *Natural Cures* includes false endorsements. Further, the NYCPB states that Trudeau's television ads "give the false impression that Tammy Faye Messner opposes chemotherapy in favor of the 'natural cures' in Trudeau's book." A representative for Messner before her death from cancer said that was not true and that she was starting chemotherapy again.

The back cover includes the following quote from Dr. Herbert Ley, a former commissioner of the U.S. Food and Drug Administration who died three years before the book was written: "The thing that bugs me is that people think the FDA is protecting them. It isn't. What the FDA is doing and what people think it's doing are as different as night and day." The statement, extracted from a 1969 *New York Times* interview, was made in the context of Ley's resignation from his post as a result of numerous policy disputes.[35,36] Trudeau's lawyer, David J. Bradford, says that this quote does not constitute a false endorsement of the book by Ley, but rather is merely a statement that is in line with the purpose of the book.[37]

Footnotes

- Panozzo, Mike (November 2005). "Being Kevin Trudeau"[38]. *Billiards Digest* **28** (12) (Chicago, IL, US: Luby Publishing). ISSN 0164-761X[39].Wikipedia:Please clarify
- Natural scams "he" doesn't want you to know about[40] – Michael Shermer, *Scientific American*, March 2006Wikipedia:Please clarify
- After Jail and More, Salesman Scores Big with Cure-All Book[41] – *New York Times*, August 28, 2005Wikipedia:Please clarify
- Critique of Health Claims re Coral Calcium[42]Wikipedia:Please clarify
- Would You Buy A Used Cure From This Man?[43] – The Smoking Gun, August 26, 2005Wikipedia:Please clarify
- Consumer Affairs article[44]Wikipedia:Please clarify

- "The Curious Case of Kevin Trudeau, King Catch Me If You Can" by Catherine Bryant Bell, Mississippi Law Journal, vol. 79, page 1043 (summer 2010):[45].

External links

- Kevin Trudeau[46] at the Notable Names Database

MegaMemory

MegaMemory is a commercial system sold through infomercials that claimed to boost memory via learning mnemonic techniques, developed by Kevin Trudeau. It was one of a range of products that the Federal Trade Commission prosecuted for fraud. Trudeau claimed that *help anyone achieve a photographic memory, even people with learning disabilities or low IQ's.* The FTC found that *the memory system would not enable users to achieve a photographic memory, and the advertising claims were false.* Trudeau, along with other marketers, settled out of court for $1.1 million.

External links

- FTC Press Release[47]

Natural Cures "They" Don't Want You to Know About

Natural Cures "They" Don't Want You To Know About is a self-published book by convicted American fraud artist Kevin Trudeau, promoting a variety of non-drug and non-surgical purported cures for many diseases, primarily in support of his business selling such products. Trudeau accuses pharmaceutical companies and the United States government of censoring these products and methods on the basis that it would cut into their profit-margin. The book is the subject of widespread allegations of fraud.

Premise

In the book, Trudeau claims that there are all-natural cures for serious illnesses including cancer, herpes, arthritis, AIDS, acid reflux disease, various phobias, depression, obesity, diabetes, multiple sclerosis, lupus, chronic fatigue syndrome, attention deficit disorder, muscular dystrophy, and that these are being deliberately hidden and suppressed from the public by the Food and Drug Administration (FDA), the Federal Trade Commission, and the major food and drug companies, in an effort to protect the profits of these industries and the authority of the governmental agencies. Trudeau claims that the source of illness are toxins from processed food, nutritional deficiencies, and other environmental sources; and that eliminating these factors will facilitate a cure for most diseases. Trudeau claims that his lack of medical training or expertise is what makes him most qualified to investigate alternative medicine, and reports his opinions in his self-published book. The first edition of the book lacked any mention of specific, brand-name products for any illnesses within its pages, as Trudeau claims the FDA and FTC censored this information and prohibited him from publishing it in the book. Instead, the book contained references to Trudeau's subscription-based website where the actual 'cures' were supposedly posted and accessible for a monthly fee.

In May 2006, Trudeau self-published *More Natural "Cures" Revealed: Previously Censored Brand Name Products That Cure Disease*. This book responded to complaints that its earlier version did not actually contain any cures but pointed consumers to his subscription website. In *More Natural "Cures" Revealed*, Trudeau says that workers at the FDA and FTC want to censor him and, figuratively, burn his books.

Versions

The original book contained 271 pages. After he released *More Natural "Cures" Revealed: Previously Censored Brand Name Products That Cure Disease* in response to earlier criticism, an "Updated Edition" of the original *Natural Cures* was sold shortly thereafter, containing 563 pages. This adds a new Introduction, a Frequently Asked Questions chapter and a chapter on website information. It also adds three appendices, containing newsletter articles, "No-Hunger Bread: A True FDA Horror Story," and locations of several health care practitioners. The FDA article, originally a short letter and summary of the case in the original book, is included in its entirety in the updated edition. One omission in the updated edition is a Glossary section containing several New Age techniques.

According to Trudeau, the chapter "The Cures For All Diseases" was completely censored by the FTC in the original book. The chapter is included titled as "Natural Cures for Specific Diseases" in the updated edition.

His website contains a number of references and articles, notably "FDA Horror Stories" such as "No-Hunger Bread," which describe alleged instances of the FDA suppressing natural cures. Another article addresses 714X, a disproven cancer treatment developed in Canada.

Criticism

The book has been the focus of much controversy since its publication, with widespread allegations of fraud. The New York State Consumer Protection Board issued a warning in 2005 that the book "does not contain the 'natural cures' for cancer and other diseases that Trudeau is promising." It asserted that "Trudeau is not only misrepresenting the contents of his self-published book, he is also using false endorsements to encourage consumers to buy *Natural Cures "They" Don't Want You to Know About.*"[48] The Board also alleged that Trudeau was selling the consumer's contact information to other marketers without their consent and hitting purchasers with unauthorized charges.[49]

Skeptical author Michael Shermer writes:

> *As for the "natural cures" themselves, some are not cures at all but just obvious healthy lifestyle suggestions: eat less, exercise more, reduce stress. Some of the natural cures are flat-out wrong, such as oral chelation for heart disease, whereas others are laughably ludicrous, such as a magnetic mattress pad and crocodile protein peptide for fibromyalgia. Worst of all are the natural cures that the book directs the reader to Trudeau's Web page to find. When you go there, however, and click on a disease to get the cure, you first have to become a Web site member at $1000 lifetime or $9.95 a month. It is a classic con man's combo: bait and switch (the book directs them to the Web page) and double-dipping (sell them the book, then sell them the membership).*[50]

Shermer and other critics have argued that Trudeau has used *Natural Cures* to circumvent a Federal Trade Commission ruling that Trudeau is barred "from appearing in, producing, or disseminating future infomercials that advertise any type of product, service, or program to the public." The FTC issued its decision after it found that Trudeau had defrauded consumers by making numerous false claims about his merchandise in infomercials.[51]

Others have criticized the book for making such claims as, "If your body is alkaline, you cannot get cancer [...] and if you have cancer, it goes away."[52]

The book makes extensive unreferenced claims that some drugs cause such conditions as AIDS, headaches, bloating, indigestion, heartburn, nausea, allergies, asthma, fibromyalgia, arthritis, diabetes, constipation, yeast infections, dandruff, acne, halitosis, fatigue, depression, stress, and inability to lose weight.

Further reading

- Trudeau, Kevin, *Natural Cures 'They" Don't Want You To Know About*, Alliance Publishing, 2005. ISBN 0-9755995-1-8
- Candice Choi, Associated Press, *No Sure Cure, The Detroit News, page 3b, 25 Sep 2005*, in court records.[53]

External links

- Analysis of Kevin Trudeau's "Natural Cures" Infomercial (2004)[54] by Stephen Barrett, M.D.
- What Kevin Trudeau doesn't want you to know[55]
- King Con – Selling Questionable Cures?[56] – John Stossel, Glenn Rupel and Frank Mastropolo, January 20, 2006
- Natural scams "he" doesn't want you to know about[57] – Michael Shermer, Scientific American, March 2006
- Is Infomercial King a Helper or Huckster?[58] – Jake Tapper, January 13, 2006
- " Wait, There's More: Kevin Trudeau's 'Natural Cures,' Swallowed by Millions Without A Prescription[59]" Libby Copeland. *Washington Post*, Sunday, October 23, 2005; D01

The Weight-Loss Cure "They" Don't Want You to Know About

The Weight-Loss Cure "They" Don't Want You To Know About

Author	Kevin Trudeau
Language	English
Subject	weight loss
Genre	self-help
Publisher	Alliance Publishing
Publication date	1 April 2007
Pages	256
ISBN	978-0-9787851-0-9
OCLC	122341864[60]
Dewey Decimal	613.25 22
LC Class	RM222.2 .T78 2007

The Weight Loss Cure "They" Don't Want You to Know About is a weight loss book written by controversial author Kevin Trudeau. It was released in April 2007 by Alliance Publishing.

Trudeau was convicted of felonies[61] and fined by the Federal Trade Commission for making fraudulent claims pertaining to the book, in part because it gives medical advice but he has no medical training.[62] The book repeats a refuted claim to change activity in the hypothalamus, linked to the pituitary gland, with the intention to control hunger and regulation of fat cells, by using herbal supplements and repeated use of the hCG hormone; this claim was originally made by Albert T. W. Simeons in the 1950s. Simeons' results were not reproduced by other researchers and in 1976 in response to complaints the FDA required Simeons and others to include the following disclaimer on all advertisements:

> *These weight reduction treatments include the injection of HCG, a drug which has not been approved by the Food and Drug Administration as safe and effective in the treatment of obesity or weight control. There is no substantial evidence that HCG increases weight loss beyond that resulting from caloric restriction, that it causes a more attractive or "normal" distribution of fat, or that it decreases the hunger and discomfort associated with calorie-restrictive diets.*

— 1976 FDA-mandated disclaimer for HCG diet advertisements

The book follows up his two other bestselling but critically panned books, *Natural Cures "They" Don't Want You to Know About* and *More Natural Cures Revealed: Previously Censored Brand Name Products That Cure Disease*. *Weight Loss Cure* has appeared on the bestseller's lists of the *Wall Street Journal*, *USA Today*, *Publishers Weekly*, and *The New York Times*.

Legal issues

The FTC has filed a contempt of court action against Trudeau and the companies that market his book alleging that Trudeau is in contempt of a 2004 court order by "deceptively claiming in his infomercials that the book being advertised establishes a weight-loss protocol that is "easy" to follow. The action was filed in the U.S. District Court for the Northern District of Illinois on September 17, 2007.[63] According to a FTC Press Release, Trudeau claims that the weight loss plan outlined in the book is easy, can be done at home, and readers can eat anything they want. When consumers buy the book, they find it describes a complex plan that requires intense dieting, daily injections of a prescribed drug that is not easily obtainable, and lifelong dietary restrictions.[64]

On November 16, 2007, Trudeau was found in contempt of the 2004 court order for making "patently false" claims in his weight loss book. U.S. District Court Judge Robert W. Gettleman ruled that Trudeau "clearly misrepresents in his advertisements the difficulty of the diet described in his book, and by doing so, he has misled thousands of consumers." A penalty will be determined at a later hearing.[65,66,67] In October 2008, Trudeau was fined more than $5 million and banned from infomercials for three years for continuing to make fraudulent claims pertaining to the book.[68]

Complaints about Trudeau's weight loss system and business practices can be found at the Consumer Affairs[69] website. In summary, the complaints tend to refer to a problem of unsubscribing from the website and its monthly fees as well as the inability to follow the protocol, detailed by Trudeau, in the United States due to product availability and legal reasons.

Book diet plan

The book's diet has been compared to a diet plan by British endocrinologist Albert T. W. Simeons in the 1950s. The book describes a multi-month, 3-phase plan that involves changing to all organic foods,[70,71] with repeated colonic cleansing and liver cleansing, followed by a 2nd-phase period of daily use of human chorionic gonadotropin (hCG), typically injections, under the direction of a healthcare provider or doctor. The use of hCG in men has been found to increase testosterone, which is linked to muscle growth;[72] however, in women, hCG does not produce any consistent or biologically significant increase in testosterone. For men, hCG can have some potential side-effects, including: gynecomastia (growing female breasts), water retention, increase in sex drive, mood alterations, headaches, and high blood pressure. These side effects are known to those who have taken hCG in much larger quantities (5000iu at one time) than what is being recommended in this diet plan (200iu at the most).[73] Due to such side effects, othersWikipedia:Manual of Style/Words to watch#Unsupported attributions warn to limit hCG to 3-week periods (with 4-week breaks) and recommend professional guidance from a physician. Also, herbs, such as tongkat ali ("longjack"), might be used rather than risk hCG.

In Phase 3, use of hCG stops, but food continues to be 100% organic. Other recommended activities include walking an hour a day or more, eating organic grapefruit, and doing breathing exercises. Scheduled doctor visits, buying organic foods and hCG can be very expensive for the average consumer, but wealthy people have paid to follow the plan, and the plan might work for people who can afford it. According to an analysis by Carrie Poppy of Skeptical Inquirer, the weight loss plan would cost the user up to $18,000 if followed to the letter.[74]

As early as 1962, the *Journal of the American Medical Association* warned against the Simeons Diet.[75] The FTC ordered clinics and promoters of the Simeons Diet and hCG to cease making false claims about the effectiveness of hCG and its approval status by the FDA for weight loss.[76] Clinical research trials published by the Journal of the American Medical Association and the American Journal of Clinical Nutrition[77] have shown that hCG is ineffective as a weight-loss aid.

Sales

Although the book is controversial, and is ranked on Amazon.com as 2 stars (out of 5 stars),[78] as of August 12, 2007 (4 months after release), it ranked #16 on the Amazon bestseller list,[79] behind another diet book, *Skinny Bitch*, ranked at #13 of the Amazon bestselling books (ranked by sales volume through Amazon sales). The book *The Weight Loss Cure* has also appeared on the bestseller's lists of the *Wall Street Journal, USA Today, Publishers Weekly*, and *The New York Times*.

References

- "The Rationale for Banning Human Chorionic Gonadotropin and Estrogen Blockers in Sport" (medical analysis), David J. Handelsman, medical report in *The Journal of Clinical Endocrinology & Metabolism*, Vol. 91, No. 5 1646-1653, year 2006, webpage: EJ1646[80].
- Associated Press: Lists of Best Selling Books[81].
- New York Times[82] bestsellers.
- Consumer Affairs page on Kevin Trudeau[69].
- King Con – Selling Questionable Cures?[83] – John Stossel, Glenn Rupel and Frank Mastropolo, January 20, 2006
- Natural scams "he" doesn't want you to know about[84] – Michael Shermer, Scientific American, March 2006
- Is Infomercial King a Helper or Huckster?[85] – Jake Tapper, January 13, 2006
- "The Curious Case of Kevin Trudeau, King Catch Me If You Can" by Catherine Bryant Bell, Mississippi Law Journal, vol. 79, page 1043 (summer 2010):[86].

Quackery

Quackery is the promotion of fraudulent or ignorant medical practices. A "**quack**" is a "fraudulent or ignorant pretender to medical skill" or "a person who pretends, professionally or publicly, to have skill, knowledge, or qualifications he or she does not possess; a charlatan".[87] The word *quack* derives from the archaic word *quacksalver*, of Dutch origin (spelled *kwakzalver* in contemporary Dutch), literally meaning "hawker of salve".[88] In the Middle Ages the word *quack* meant "shouting". The quacksalvers sold their wares on the market shouting in a loud voice.[89]

Common elements of general quackery include questionable diagnoses using questionable diagnostic tests, as well as alternative or refuted treatments, especially for serious diseases such as cancer. "Health fraud" is often used as a synonym for quackery, but quackery's salient characteristic is its more aggressive promotion ("quacks quack!"). "Pseudo-medicine" is a term for treatments known to be ineffective, regardless of whether their advocates themselves believe in their effectiveness.

Figure 2: *WPA poster, 1936–38*

Definition

In determining whether a person is committing quackery, the central question is what is acceptable evidence for the efficacy and safety of whatever treatments, cures, regimens, or procedures the alleged quack advocates.

Since it is difficult to distinguish between those who knowingly promote unproven medical therapies and those who are mistaken as to their effectiveness, U.S. courts have ruled in defamation cases that accusing someone of quackery or calling a practitioner a *quack* is not equivalent to accusing that person of committing medical fraud. To be both quackery and fraud, the quack must know they are misrepresenting the benefits and risks of the medical services offered (instead of, for example, promoting an ineffective product they honestly believe is effective).Wikipedia:Citation needed

In addition to the ethical problems of promising benefits that can not reasonably be expected to occur, quackery also includes the risk that patients may choose to forego treatments that are more likely to help them, in favor of ineffective treatments given by the "quack".Wikipedia:Citation needed

Stephen Barrett's Quackwatch defines the practice this way:

> *To avoid semantic problems, quackery could be broadly defined as "anything involving overpromotion in the field of health." This definition would*

Figure 3: *William Hogarth: Marriage à-la-mode: The Visit to the Quack Doctor*

Figure 4: *Pietro Longhi: The Charlatan, 1757*

include questionable ideas as well as questionable products and services, regardless of the sincerity of their promoters. In line with this definition, the word "fraud" would be reserved only for situations in which deliberate deception is involved.

Paul Offit has proposed four ways in which alternative medicine "becomes quackery":[90]

1. "...by recommending against conventional therapies that are helpful."
2. "...by promoting potentially harmful therapies without adequate warning."
3. "...by draining patients' bank accounts,..."
4. "...by promoting magical thinking,..."

Quacksalver

Unproven, usually ineffective, and sometimes dangerous medicines and treatments have been peddled throughout human history. Theatrical performances were sometimes given to enhance the credibility of purported medicines. Grandiose claims were made for what could be humble materials indeed: for example, in the mid-19th century Revalenta Arabica was advertised as having extraordinary restorative virtues as an empirical diet for invalids; despite its impressive name and many glowing testimonials it was in truth only ordinary lentil flour, sold to the gullible at many times the true cost.

Even where no fraud was intended, quack remedies often contained no effective ingredients whatsoever. Some remedies contained substances such as opium, alcohol and honey, which would have given symptomatic relief but had no curative properties. The few effective remedies sold by quacks included emetics, laxatives and diuretics. Some ingredients did have medicinal effects: mercury, silver and arsenic compounds may have helped some infections and infestations; willow bark contained salicylic acid, chemically closely related to aspirin; and the quinine contained in Jesuit's bark was an effective treatment for malaria and other fevers. However, knowledge of appropriate uses and dosages was limited.

Criticism of quackery in academia

The science based medicine community has criticized the infiltration of alternative medicine into mainstream academic medicine, education, and publications, accusing institutions of "diverting research time, money, and other resources from more fruitful lines of investigation in order to pursue a theory that has no basis in biology." R.W. Donnell coined the phrase "quackademic medicine" to describe this attention given to alternative medicine by academia.

Referring to the Flexner Report, he said that medical education "needs a good Flexnerian housecleaning."

For example, David Gorski criticized Brian M. Berman, founder of the University of Maryland Center for Integrative Medicine, for writing that "There [is] evidence that both real acupuncture and sham acupuncture [are] more effective than no treatment and that acupuncture can be a useful supplement to other forms of conventional therapy for low back pain." He also castigated editors and peer reviewers at the *New England Journal of Medicine* for allowing it to be published, since it effectively recommended deliberately misleading patients in order to achieve a known placebo effect.

History in Europe and the United States

With little understanding of the causes and mechanisms of illnesses, widely marketed "cures" (as opposed to locally produced and locally used remedies), often referred to as patent medicines, first came to prominence during the 17th and 18th centuries in Britain and the British colonies, including those in North America. Daffy's Elixir and Turlington's Balsam were among the first products that used branding (e.g. using highly distinctive containers) and mass marketing to create and maintain markets. A similar process occurred in other countries of Europe around the same time, for example with the marketing of Eau de Cologne as a cure-all medicine by Johann Maria Farina and his imitators. Patent medicines often contained alcohol or opium, which, while presumably not curing the diseases for which they were sold as a remedy, did make the imbibers feel better and confusedly appreciative of the product.

The number of internationally marketed quack medicines increased in the later 18th century; the majority of them originated in Britain[91] and were exported throughout the British Empire. By 1830, British parliamentary records list over 1,300 different "proprietary medicines," the majority of which were "quack" cures by modern standards.

A Dutch organisation that opposes quackery, Vereniging tegen de Kwakzalverij was founded in 1881, making it the oldest organisation of this kind in the world. It has published its magazine *Nederlands Tijdschrift tegen de Kwakzalverij* (NTtdK, "Dutch Magazine against Quackery") ever since. In these early years the *Vereniging tegen de Kwakzalverij* played a part in the professionalisation of medicine. Its efforts in the public debate helped to make the Netherlands one of the first countries with governmental drug regulation.

In 1909, in an attempt to stop the sale of quack medicines, the British Medical Association published *Secret Remedies, What They Cost And What They Contain*. This publication was originally a series of articles published in the

Figure 5: *Dalbys Carminative, Daffy's Elixir and Turlington's Balsam of Life bottles dating to the late 18th and early 19th centuries. These "typical" patent or quack medicines were marketed in very different, and highly distinctive, bottles. Each brand retained the same basic appearance for more than 100 years.*

British Medical Journal between 1904 and 1909. The publication was composed of 20 chapters, organising the work by sections according to the ailments the medicines claimed to treat. Each remedy was tested thoroughly, the preface stated: "Of the accuracy of the analytical data there can be no question; the investigation has been carried out with great care by a skilled analytical chemist." The book did lead to the end of some of the quack cures, but some survived the book by several decades. For example, Beecham's Pills (identified as containing only aloes, ginger and soap, but claiming to cure 31 medical conditions) were still on sale in 1997.[92]

British patent medicines started to lose their dominance in the United States when they were denied access to the American market during the American Revolution, and lost further ground for the same reason during the War of 1812. From the early 19th century "home-grown" American brands started to fill the gap, reaching their peak in the years after the American Civil War.[93] British medicines never regained their previous dominance in North America, and the subsequent era of mass marketing of American patent medicines is usually considered to have been a "golden age" of quackery in the United

Figure 6: *Clark Stanley's Snake Oil*

States. This was mirrored by similar growth in marketing of quack medicines elsewhere in the world.

In the United States, false medicines in this era were often denoted by the slang term snake oil, a reference to sales pitches for the false medicines that claimed exotic ingredients provided the supposed benefits. Those who sold them were called "snake oil salesmen," and usually sold their medicines with a fervent pitch similar to a fire and brimstone religious sermon. They often accompanied other theatrical and entertainment productions that traveled as a road show from town to town, leaving quickly before the falseness of their medicine was discovered. Not all quacks were restricted to such small-time businesses however, and a number, especially in the United States, became enormously wealthy through national and international sales of their products.

One among many examples is that of William Radam, a German immigrant to the USA who, in the 1880s, started to sell his "Microbe Killer" throughout the United States and, soon afterwards, in Britain and throughout the British colonies. His concoction was widely advertised as being able to "Cure All Diseases" (W. Radam, 1890) and this phrase was even embossed on the glass bottles the medicine was sold in. In fact, Radam's medicine was a therapeutically useless (and in large quantities actively poisonous) dilute solution of sulfuric acid, coloured with a little red wine. Radam's publicity material, particularly his books (see for example Radam, 1890), provide an insight into the

Figure 7: *Cartoon depicting a quack doctor using hypnotism (1780, France).*

role that pseudo-science played in the development and marketing of "quack" medicines towards the end of the 19th century.

Similar advertising claims[94] to those of Radam can be found throughout the 18th, 19th, 20th and 21st centuries. "Dr." Sibley, an English patent medicine seller of the late 18th and early 19th centuries, even went so far as to claim that his Reanimating Solar Tincture would, as the name implies, "restore life in the event of sudden death". Another English quack, "Dr. Solomon" claimed that his Cordial Balm of Gilead cured almost anything, but was particularly effective against all venereal complaints, from gonorrhoea to onanism. Although it was basically just brandy flavoured with herbs, it retailed widely at 33 shillings a bottle in the period of the Napoleonic wars, the equivalent of over $100 per bottle today.

Not all patent medicines were without merit. Turlingtons Balsam of Life, first marketed in the mid-18th century, did have genuinely beneficial properties. This medicine continued to be sold under the original name into the early 20th century, and can still be found in the British and American Pharmacopoeias as "Compound tincture of benzoin". It can be argued that for some of these medicines this is an example of the infinite monkey theorem in action.

The end of the road for the quack medicines now considered grossly fraudulent in the nations of North America and Europe came in the early 20th century.

Figure 8: *Electro-metabograph machine on display in the "Quackery Hall of Fame" in the Science Museum of Minnesota, St. Paul, Minnesota, USA.*

February 21, 1906 saw the passage into law of the Pure Food and Drug Act in the United States. This was the result of decades of campaigning by both government departments and the medical establishment, supported by a number of publishers and journalists (one of the most effective of whom was Samuel Hopkins Adams, whose series "The Great American Fraud" was published in Colliers Weekly starting in late 1905). This American Act was followed three years later by similar legislation in Britain, and in other European nations. Between them, these laws began to remove the more outrageously dangerous contents from patent and proprietary medicines, and to force quack medicine proprietors to stop making some of their more blatantly dishonest claims.

Medical quackery and promotion of nostrums and worthless drugs were among the most prominent abuses that led to formal self-regulation in business and, in turn, to the creation of the NBBB.[95]

Contemporary culture

"Quackery is the promotion of false and unproven health schemes for a profit. It is rooted in the traditions of the marketplace", with "commercialism overwhelming professionalism in the marketing of alternative medicine". Considered by many an archaic term, *quackery* is most often used to denote the

Figure 9: *"Tho-radia powder" box, an example of radioactive quackery.*

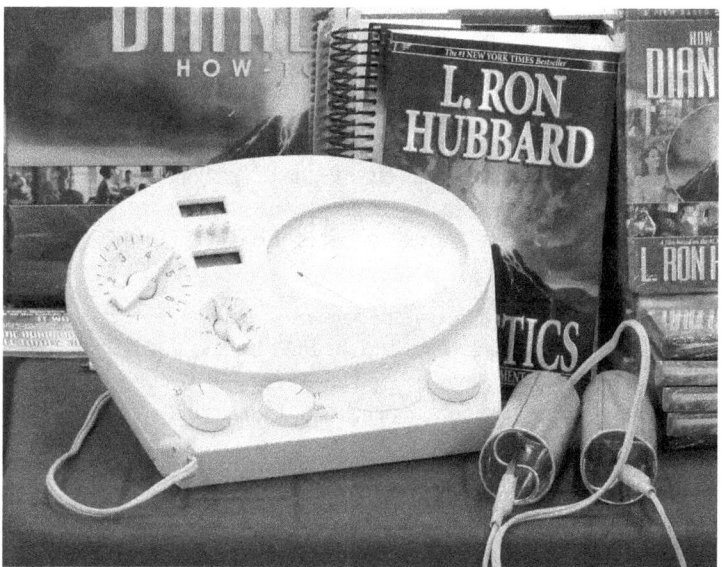

Figure 10: *Scientology's E-Meter, a quack device for measuring 'engrams'*

Figure 11: *The 1929 Revigator (sometimes misspelled Revigorator) was a pottery crock lined with radioactive ore that emitted radon.*

peddling of the "cure-alls" described above. Quackery continues even today; it can be found in any culture and in every medical tradition. Unlike other advertising mediums, rapid advancements in communication through the Internet have opened doors for an unregulated market of quack cures and marketing campaigns rivaling the early 20th century. Most people with an e-mail account have experienced the marketing tactics of spamming—in which modern forms of quackery are touted as miraculous remedies for "weight-loss" and "sexual enhancement", as well as outlets for unprescribed medicines of unknown quality.

While quackery is often aimed at the aged or chronically ill, it can be aimed at all age groups, including teens, and the FDA has mentioned[96] some areas where potential quackery may be a problem: breast developers, weight loss, steroids and growth hormones, tanning and tanning pills, hair removal and growth, and look-alike drugs.

In a 1992 article in the journal *Clinical Chemistry*, then president of The National Council Against Health Fraud, William T. Jarvis, wrote:

> The U.S. Congress determined quackery to be the most harmful consumer fraud against elderly people. Americans waste $27 billion annually on

questionable health care, exceeding the amount spent on biomedical research. Quackery is characterized by the promotion of false and unproven health schemes for profit and does not necessarily involve imposture, fraud, or greed. The real issues in the war against quackery are the principles, including scientific rationale, encoded into consumer protection laws, primarily the U.S. Food, Drug, and Cosmetic Act. More such laws are badly needed. Regulators are failing the public by enforcing laws inadequately, applying double standards, and accrediting pseudomedicine. Non-scientific health care (e.g., acupuncture, ayurvedic medicine, chiropractic, homeopathy, naturopathy) is licensed by individual states. Practitioners use unscientific practices and deception on a public who, lacking complex health-care knowledge, must rely upon the trustworthiness of providers. Quackery not only harms people, it undermines the scientific enterprise and should be actively opposed by every scientist.

For those in the practice of any medicine, to allege quackery is to level a serious objection to a particular form of practice. Most developed countries have a governmental agency, such as the Food and Drug Administration (FDA) in the US, whose purpose is to monitor and regulate the safety of medications as well as the claims made by the manufacturers of new and existing products, including drugs and nutritional supplements or vitamins. The Federal Trade Commission (FTC) participates in some of these efforts. To better address less regulated products, in 2000, US President Clinton signed Executive Order 13147 that created the White House Commission on Complementary and Alternative Medicine. In 2002, the commission's final report made several suggestions regarding education, research, implementation, and reimbursement as ways to evaluate the risks and benefits of each. As a direct result, more public dollars have been allocated for research into some of these methods.

Individuals and non-governmental agencies are active in attempts to expose quackery. According to Norcross et al. (2006) several authors have attempted to identify quack psychotherapies, e.g., Carroll, 2003; Della Sala, 1999; Eisner, 2000; Lilienfeld, Lynn, & Rohr 2003; Singer and Lalich 1996. The evidence-based practice (EBP) movement in mental health emphasizes the consensus in psychology that psychological practice should rely on empirical research. There are also "anti-quackery" websites, such as Quackwatch, that help consumers evaluate claims. Quackwatch's information is relevant to both consumers and medical professionals.

People's Republic of China

Zhang Wuben, a quack who posed as skilled in traditional Chinese medicine in the People's Republic of China, based his operation on representations that raw eggplant and mung beans were a general cure-all. Zhang, who has escaped legal liability as he portrayed himself as a nutritionist, not a doctor, appeared on television in China and authored a best-selling book, *Eat Away the Diseases You Get from Eating*. Zhang, who charged the equivalent of $450 for a 10-minute examination, had a two-year waiting list when he was exposed. Investigations launched after a run on mung beans revealed that contrary to his representations, he did not come from a family of accomplished traditional practitioners (中医世家) and never had the medical degree from Beijing Medical University he claimed to have. His only education was a brief correspondence or night school course, completed after he was laid off from a textile factory. Zhang, despite negative publicity on the national level, continues to practice but has committed himself to finding a cheaper cure-all than mung beans. His clinic, Wuben Hall, adjacent to Beijing National Stadium, was torn down as an illegal structure. Much of Zhang Wuben's success was due to the efforts of Chinese entrepreneurs, including one government-owned company, who promoted him.[97,98,99]

Hu Wanlin, who did hold himself out as a doctor, was exposed in 2000 and sentenced to 15 years in prison. He adulterated his concoctions with sodium sulfate, Glauber's salt, a poison in large doses. That case resulted in creating a system of licensing medical doctors in China.

Presence and acceptance

There have been several suggested reasons why quackery is accepted by patients in spite of its lack of effectiveness:

- Ignorance

    Those who perpetuate quackery may do so to take advantage of ignorance about conventional medical treatments versus alternative treatments, or may themselves be ignorant regarding their own claims. Mainstream medicine has produced many remarkable advances, so people may tend to also believe groundless claims.

- Placebo Effect

    Medicines or treatments known to have no pharmacological effect on a disease can still affect a person's perception of their illness, and this belief in its turn does indeed sometimes have a therapeutic effect, causing the patient's condition to improve. This is *not* to say that no real cure

Figure 12: *Albert Anker "der Qacksalber"(1879)*

Figure 13: *Gerard Dou The Quack (1652)*

Figure 14: *Jan Steen De piskijker*

Figure 15: *Jan Steen, De kwakzalver*

of biological illness is effected—though we might describe a placebo effect as being "all in the mind"", we now know that there is a genuine neurobiological basis to this phenomenon. People report reduced pain, increased well-being, improvement, or even total alleviation of symptoms. For some, the presence of a caring practitioner and the dispensation of medicine is curative in itself.

- Regression Fallacy

Certain "self-limiting conditions", such as warts and the common cold, almost always improve, in the latter case in a rather predictable amount of time. A patient may associate the usage of alternative treatments with recovering, when recovery was inevitable.

- Confirmation Bias

Also called myside bias, is the tendency to search for, interpret, or prioritize information in a way that confirms one's beliefs or hypotheses. It is a type of cognitive bias and a systematic error of inductive reasoning.

- Distrust of Conventional Medicine

Many people, for various reasons, have a distrust of conventional medicine, or of the regulating organizations such as the FDA, or the major drug corporations. For example, "CAM may represent a response to disenfranchisement [discrimination] in conventional medical settings and resulting distrust".[100]

- Conspiracy theories

Anti-quackery activists ("quackbusters") are accused of being part of a huge "conspiracy" to suppress "unconventional" and/or "natural" therapies, as well as those who promote them. It is alleged that this conspiracy is backed and funded by the pharmaceutical industry and the established medical care system – represented by the AMA, FDA, ADA, CDC, WHO, etc. – for the purpose of preserving their power and increasing their profits. In the case of chiropractic, the case for a conspiracy was supported by a court decision in an antitrust lawsuit, *Wilk v. American Medical Association*, ruling that the AMA had engaged in an unlawful conspiracy in restraint of trade "to contain and eliminate the chiropractic profession."

- Fear of side effects

A great variety of pharmaceutical medications can have very distressing side effects, and many people fear surgery and its consequences, so they may opt to shy away from these mainstream treatments.

- Cost

There are some people who simply cannot afford conventional treatment, and seek out a cheaper alternative. Nonconventional practitioners can often dispense treatment at a much lower cost. This is compounded by reduced access to healthcare.

- Desperation

   People with a serious or terminal disease, or who have been told by their practitioner that their condition is "untreatable," may react by seeking out treatment, disregarding the lack of scientific proof for its effectiveness, or even the existence of evidence that the method is ineffective or even dangerous. Despair may be exacerbated by the lack of palliative non-curative end-of-life care.

- Pride

   Once people have endorsed or defended a cure, or invested time and money in it, they may be reluctant to admit its ineffectiveness, and therefore recommend the cure that did not work to others.

- Fraud

   Some practitioners, fully aware of the ineffectiveness of their medicine, may intentionally produce fraudulent scientific studies and medical test results, thereby confusing any potential consumers as to the effectiveness of the medical treatment.

Persons accused of quackery

Deceased

- **Thomas Allinson** (1858–1918), founder of naturopathy. His views often brought him into conflict with the Royal College of Physicians of Edinburgh and the General Medical Council, particularly his opposition to doctors' frequent use of drugs, his opposition to vaccination and his self-promotion in the press. His views and publication of them led to him being labeled a quack and being struck off by the General Medical Council for *infamous conduct in a professional respect*.
- **Lovisa Åhrberg** (1801–1881), the first Swedish female doctor. Åhrberg was met with strong resistance from male doctors and was accused of quackery. During the formal examination she was acquitted of all charges and allowed to practice medicine in Stockholm even though it was forbidden for women in the 1820s. She later received a medal for her work.Wikipedia:Citation needed
- **Johanna Brandt** (1876–1964), a South African naturopath who advocated the "Grape Cure" as a cure for cancer.

- **Hulda Regehr Clark** (1928–2009), was a controversial naturopath, author, and practitioner of alternative medicine who claimed to be able to cure all diseases and advocated methods that have no scientific validity.
- **Samuel Hahnemann** (1755–1843), founder of homeopathy. Hahnemann believed that all diseases were caused by "miasms," which he defined as irregularities in the patient's vital force. He also said that illnesses could be treated by substances that in a healthy person produced similar symptoms to the illness, in extremely low concentrations, with the therapeutic effect increasing with dilution and repeated shaking.[101]
- **Lawrence B. Hamlin** (in 1916), was fined under the 1906 Pure Food and Drug Act for advertising that his Wizard Oil could kill cancer.
- **L. Ron Hubbard** (1911–1986), was the founder of the Church of Scientology. He was an American science fiction writer, former United States Navy officer, and creator of Dianetics. He has been commonly called a quack and a conman by both critics of Scientology and by many Psychiatric organizations in part for his often extreme anti-psychiatric beliefs.
- **John Harvey Kellogg** (1852–1943), was a medical doctor in Battle Creek, Michigan, USA who ran a sanitarium using holistic methods, with a particular focus on nutrition, enemas and exercise. Kellogg was an advocate of vegetarianism and invented the corn flake breakfast cereal with his brother, Will Keith Kellogg.
- **Franz Anton Mesmer** (1734–1815), born **Friedrich Anton Mesmer**, was a German physician and astrologist, who invented what he called *magnétisme animal*.
- **D.D. Palmer** (1845–1913), was a grocery store owner that claimed to have healed a janitor of deafness after adjusting the alignment of his back. He founded the field of chiropractic based on the principle that all disease and ailments could be fixed by adjusting the alignment of someone's back. His hypothesis was disregarded by medical professionals at the time and despite a considerable following has yet to be scientifically proven.Wikipedia:Verifiability D.D. Palmer established a magnetic healing facility in Davenport, Iowa, styling himself 'doctor'. Not everyone was convinced, as a local paper in 1894 wrote about him: "A crank on magnetism has a crazy notion that he can cure the sick and crippled with his magnetic hands. His victims are the weak-minded, ignorant and superstitious, those foolish people who have been sick for years and have become tired of the regular physician and want health by the short-cut method...he has certainly profited by the ignorance of his victims...His increase in business shows what can be done in Davenport, even by a quack."
- **Louis Pasteur** (1822–1895), was a French chemist best known for his remarkable breakthroughs in microbiology. His experiments confirmed

the germ theory of disease, also reducing mortality from puerperal fever (childbed), and he created the first vaccine for rabies. He is best known to the general public for showing how to stop milk and wine from going sour – this process came to be called *pasteurization*. His hypotheses initially met with much hostility, and he was accused of quackery on multiple occasions. However, he is now regarded as one of the three main founders of microbiology, together with Ferdinand Cohn and Robert Koch.

- **Linus Pauling** (1901–1994), a Nobel Prize winner in chemistry, Pauling spent much of his later career arguing for the treatment of somatic and psychological diseases with orthomolecular medicine. Among his claims were that the common cold could be cured with massive doses of vitamin C. Together with Ewan Cameron he wrote the 1979 book "Cancer and Vitamin C", which was again more popular with the public than the medical profession, which continued to regard claims about the effectiveness of vitamin C in treating or preventing cancer as quackery. A biographer has discussed how controversial his views on megadoses of Vitamin C have been and that he was "still being called a 'fraud' and a 'quack' by opponents of his 'orthomolecular medicine'".[102]

- **Wilhelm Reich** (1897–1957), Austrian-American Psychoanalyst. Claimed that he had discovered a primordial cosmic energy called Orgone. He developed several devices, including the Cloudbuster and the Orgone Accumulator, that he believed could use orgone to manipulate the weather, battle space aliens and cure diseases, including cancer. After an investigation, the FDA concluded that they were dealing with a "fraud of the first magnitude". On February 10, 1954, the U.S. Attorney for Maine filed a complaint seeking a permanent injunction under Sections 301 and 302 of the Federal Food, Drug, and Cosmetic Act, to prevent interstate shipment of orgone accumulators and to ban some of Reich's writing promoting and advertising the devices. Reich refused to appear in court, arguing that no court was in a position to evaluate his work. Reich was arrested for contempt of court, and convicted to 2 years in jail, a $10,000 fine, and his Orgone Accumulators and work on Orgone were ordered destroyed. On August 23, 1956, six tons of his books, journals, and papers were burned in the 25th Street public incinerator in New York. On March 12, 1957 he was sent to Danbury Federal Prison, where Richard C. Hubbard, a psychiatrist who admired Reich, examined him, recording paranoia manifested by delusions of grandiosity, persecution, and ideas of reference. On November 18, 1957 Reich died of a heart attack 9 months later while he was in the federal penitentiary in Lewisburg, Pennsylvania.

- **William Herbert Sheldon** (1898–1977), who created the theory of somatotypes corresponding to intelligence.

Living

- **Mehmet Oz** (born 1960), as host of *The Dr. Oz Show*, has been accused of promoting pseudoscientific health treatments and supplements, and faced a hearing at the United States Senate for his role in helping companies sell fraudulent medicine.

- **Kevin Trudeau** (born 1963) published several books about cures relating to maladies, weight loss, and debt. He is currently in an Alabama jail for failing to pay a $37.6 million fine that he incurred as a result of claims he made in his book about weight loss cures.

- **Andrew Wakefield** (born 1957) published a fraudulent study in *The Lancet* in 1998 claiming that the MMR vaccine increases the chance of autism. His research has been described as "an elaborate fraud". None of his results could be reproduced by other researchers. The study claimed the combined MMR vaccine increased the risk of autism, while Wakefield had just applied for patent on separate vaccines for the three diseases, and therefore the study, if accepted, would have generated a large profit for Wakefield.[103]

- **Ty Bollinger** and **Webster Kehr** are modern promoters of ineffective cancer remedies through fraudulent and deceptive websites like cancertutor.com and new-cancer-treatments.org. People who follow the advice of these modern quacks are apt to forgo essential medical treatments such as surgery, chemotherapy and radiation therapy.

References

- Carroll, 2003. The Skeptics Dictionary[104]. New York: Wiley.
- Della Sala, 1999. Mind Myths: Exploring Popular Assumptions about the Mind and Brain. New York: Wiley.
- Eisner, 2000. The Death of Psychotherapy; From Freud to Alien Abductions. Westport; CT: Praegner.
- Lilienfeld, SO., Lynn, SJ., Lohr, JM. 2003; Science and Pseudoscience in Clinical Psychology. New York. Guildford
- Norcross, JC, Garofalo.A, Koocher.G. (2006) Discredited Psychological Treatments and Tests; A Delphi Poll. Professional Psychology; Research and Practice. vol37. No 5. 515–522
- Radam, W. (1890) Microbes and the microbe killer. New York: The Knickerbocker Press. 369pp.

External links

> Wikiquote has quotations related to: *Quackery*

> Wikimedia Commons has media related to *Quackery*.

> Look up *quackery* in Wiktionary, the free dictionary.

- Chisholm, Hugh, ed. (1911). "Quack". *Encyclopædia Britannica* (11th ed.). Cambridge University Press.
- Quackery[105] at DMOZ
- Medline Plus – entry on Health Fraud[106]
- How to Spot Health Fraud[107] Article from the Food and Drug Administration
- 'Miracle' Health Claims: Add a Dose of Skepticism[108] Article at the Federal Trade Comiision
- Museum of Questionable Medical Devices[109] – Science Museum of Minnesota
- " Quackery[110]." *Handbook of Texas.*

International Pool Tour

The **International Pool Tour** was a professional sports tour created in 2005 by Kevin Trudeau and hosted by Rebecca Grant.[111] It aimed to elevate pool (pocket billiards) to the level of other modern sports. Closely modeled on the PGA Tour, the IPT offered the largest prize funds in pool history in its first year. The tour attracted the top pool players in the world. It differed from the many nine-ball tournaments, as all IPT events were eight-ball matches.[112] The company was based in Hinsdale, Illinois.

Many pool enthusiasts were initially skeptical, but the first event was successful, and at the time was the biggest tournament in billiards history.[113] However by the end of 2006, the tour was in serious financial trouble, and was forced to stop staging major tournaments.

Figure 16: *IPT Tour Members Colin Colenso, Keith McCready, Bernie Friend, and Stefan Santl at the IPT King of the Hill Shootout in Orlando, Florida, December 2005 adhering to Trudeau's mandatory dress code*

Events

- The first IPT event, the "World 8-Ball Championship" was held at Mandalay Bay in Las Vegas, Nevada. It was an exhibition match between Mike Sigel and Loree Jon Jones in 2005. For their participation, Sigel (winner) won $150,000 and Jones (loser) won $75,000. The prize money drew attention due to the fact that these payouts for an exhibition match were bigger than winning prizes from major championships.[114]

- IPT King of the Hill 8-Ball Shootout- December 2005: an invitational event at the Orlando Convention Center in Orlando, Florida, consisting of 42 players who competed in a round-robin format. BCA Hall of Famers in attendance received $30,000 just for showing up. Efren Reyes defeated Sigel in the finals and pocketed $200,000.[115] All of the 165 matches were filmed and were later available for sale as DVDs.[116] The total prize money paid out was $1,125,000, which made it the biggest pool event in history. Select matches from the tournament were turned into a weekly TV series that had a dedicated time slot, in prime time, on Versus (then OLN).

Figure 17: *IPT Starship Stage at North American Open held in Las Vegas, July 2006, for TV rounds and Finals*

- IPT North American Open- 2006: the first full field IPT tournament consisting of 200 players from more than 40 countries. The North American Open paid out $2,000,000 in prize money, and was held at the Venetian, Las Vegas. The tournament was broadcast live in Europe for one week straight in prime time, a first for the billiards industry. Select matches from this event were turned into the second weekly TV series, in a dedicated time slot in prime time, on Versus (then OLN).

- IPT World Open- 2006: the second full field IPT tournament consisting of 200 players from more than 40 countries. The World Open advertised a $3,000,000 prize fund. The IPT offered live coverage of the tournament daily through streaming video. At the conclusion of the tournament, players were told that the prize checks were not on site and that they would be sent in the mail shortly. However, the IPT had run into major financial problems due to the lack of sponsorship and other failed financing options. Players and fans were outraged, but tour management insisted that players would be paid in full. Ultimately, the players were paid in full, but it took nine installments of 11% each to finally pay the players. The nine installments were paid over a 14-month period.Wikipedia:Citation needed

The IPT was not in a financial position to continue hosting large world-class events, so they shifted their strategy to live streaming matches that pitted the best players against each other. These professionally produced events started around the same time as the final payment installment was sent to the players from the World Open. The IPT cited these matches as promotional and their intent was to promote the sport and build up web traffic once again in order to deploy a new strategy.

- IPT Ultimate 8-Ball- Earl Strickland vs. Johnny Archer, December 19, 2007: two of the biggest names in professional pool played in a race to 15 of 8-ball. The event streamed for free and it was reported that it drew a large live audience. The winner (Archer) received a $5,000 cash prize, and Strickland received $1,000 for his efforts. IPT paid each player's expenses.

- IPT Ultimate 8-Ball- Corey Deuel vs. Francisco Bustamante, January 23, 2008: the second of the challenge matches was also streamed free and drew a large audience. The winner (Bustamante) was paid $5,000 plus expenses and the loser (Deuel) received $1,000 plus expenses for his performance.

- IPT Ultimate 8-Ball- Marlon Manalo vs. Rodney Morris, March 4, 2008: the third of the live challenge matches was streamed free and drew a very large audience. Manalo won $5,000 plus expenses for winning the match. Morris won $1,000 plus expenses for his performance. This match also marked the approximate launch of Rodney Morris's new energy drink "Extreme Focus," which is now being promoted globally.

- IPT Ultimate 14.1 Straight Pool, April 29, 2008: the IPT decided to feature an undercard match of 14.1 straight pool, which marked the first time the IPT ever played anything other than 8-ball. The match featured reigning World Champion Oliver Ortmann and John Schmidt who was arguably one of the best straight pool players in the world. Schmidt won the match and $3,000 plus expenses. Ortmann received $1,000 plus expenses for his performance.

- IPT Ultimate 8-Ball, April 29, 2008: the IPT chose to allow fan voting to determine the contestants of this 8-ball match. The crowd favorite was Efren Reyes. His opponent was a shock to the world as the fans responded to the call for help from teenager Austin Murphy, a gifted young player from California. Reyes easily won the match and $5,000 plus expenses. Murphy won $1,000 plus expenses for his performance.

- IPT Ultimate 14.1 Straight Pool, June 2008: John Schmidt won in his last victory the chance to defend his win against Hall of Fame legend Mike Sigel. Most fans agreed that Sigel was past his prime and posed no threat to Schmidt's mastery. Much to the surprise of the world, Sigel played nearly perfect pool and handled Schmidt, who was visibly impressed by

Sigel's game. Sigel won $3,000 plus expenses, and Schmidt won $1,000 plus expenses for his performance.

- IPT Ultimate 8-Ball, June 2008: In this eight ball match, English player Karl Boyes was originally supposed to play Alex Pagulayan. At the last moment, Pagulayan's manager contacted the IPT to inform them that he had lost his passport and that he would not be able to attend. IPT management called Tony Robles and asked him to fill in for Pagulayan. Robles accepted and flew from New York to L.A. in the middle of the night in order to make it to the match on time. Robles played well and beat Boyes in a close match. Robles won $5,000 plus expenses, and Boyes won $1,000 plus expenses for his performance. The match was attended by celebrity Joe Rogan.

Other information

In the era of pool champions Willie Mosconi and Irving Crane, the standard dress code for professional pool saw players dressed in tuxedos when competing, but beginning in the 1970s, the dress code had relaxed in competition with contenders wearing sneakers, baseball caps, T-shirts, and blue jeans. Trudeau re-established a dress code for the IPT members and required all IPT members and competitors to adhere to it, to project a better image for pool. All male pool players were required to wear suits, long-sleeved shirts, and leather shoes.

In the events Trudeau refused to follow some of the rules normally required by pool's governing bodies, in particular the policy that all prize money be held in escrow. Despite this, both the Women's Professional Billiards Association and the U.S. Professional Pool Players Association allowed their players to join the IPT.

In September 2006, just prior to the IPT World Open Eight-ball Championship in Reno, Nevada, Kevin Trudeau announced that the IPT had entered into an agreement to be acquired by Ho Interactive,[117,118] a new company started by casino owner billionaire Stanley Ho, a deal which failed. Two new sponsors were also announced offsetting the bad news that the IPT championship scheduled for October 2006 in London, England, had been cancelled.Wikipedia:Citation needed

Tournaments

Tournament	Date	Location	Winner	Nationality	Prize	Runner-up	Nationality
King of the Hill Eight-ball Shootout	2005, November 30 to December 4	Orlando, Florida	Efren Reyes (1)	Philippines	$200,000	Mike Sigel	USA
North American Open Eight-ball Championship	2006, July 22 to July 30	Las Vegas, Nevada	Thorsten Hohmann (1)	Germany	$350,000	Marlon Manalo	Philippines
World Open Eight-ball Championship	2006, September 3 to September 9	Reno, Nevada	Efren Reyes (2)	Philippines	$500,000	Rodney Morris	USA

Ed Foreman

Edgar Franklin "Ed" Foreman, Jr.	

Member of the U.S. House of Representatives from Texas's 16th district	
In office January 3, 1963 – January 3, 1965	
Preceded by	J.T. Rutherford
Succeeded by	Richard C. White
Member of the U.S. House of Representatives from New Mexico's 2nd district	
In office January 3, 1969 – January 3, 1971	
Preceded by	At-large: E.S. "Johnny" Walker Thomas G. Morris
Succeeded by	Harold Runnels
Personal details	
Born	December 22, 1933 Portales, Roosevelt County New Mexico, USA
Political party	Republican
Spouse(s)	Barbara Lynn Southard Foreman (married 1955)
Children	Preston Kirk Foreman Rebecca Lynn Foreman
Residence	Odessa, Ector County, Texas Las Cruces, New Mexico Dallas, Texas
Alma mater	Eastern New Mexico University New Mexico State University

Occupation	Civil engineer Businessman Motivational speaker
Religion	United Methodist

Edgar Franklin "Ed" Foreman, Jr. (born December 22, 1933), is a motivational speaker in Dallas who served one term in the United States House of Representatives from Texas's 16th congressional district from 1963 to 1965 and again from 1969 to 1971 in New Mexico's 2nd district, then newly established.[119]

Early years

Foreman was born on a sweet potato and peanut farm near Portales in Roosevelt County in southeastern New Mexico to Edgar Foreman Sr., and the former Lillian Childress.[120]

From 1952 to 1953, Foreman attended in Portales Eastern New Mexico University, then Eastern New Mexico College. He transferred to New Mexico State University in Las Cruces, where in 1955 he obtained a Bachelor of Science degree in civil engineering. From 1953 to 1956, Foreman was employed by Phillips Petroleum Company. From 1956 to 1957, he served in the United States Navy. He headed Foreman Brine Sales and Service in Odessa, Texas, from 1956 to 1962. He was formerly the president of Valley Transit Mix, Atlas Land Company, and Foreman Oil, Inc.

Political career

Represented West Texas, 1963–1965

In 1962, while he resided in Odessa, Foreman was elected to Congress from the 16th District in West Texas, which stretched from El Paso to the Permian Basin. His victory is attributed to the incumbent Democratic Representative J.T. Rutherford having been linked with the Billy Sol Estes scandal. In that same election, the Democrat, later Republican, John B. Connally, Jr., was elected governor over the Republican oilfield equipment executive Jack Cox.

Foreman was defeated when he sought re-election in 1964, a year in which President Lyndon B. Johnson, a Texan, was romping to reelection over Republican U.S. Senator Barry M. Goldwater of Arizona, and the Republicans suffered massive losses throughout the nation.

Represented southern New Mexico, 1969–1971

In 1968 while residing in Las Cruces, Foreman ran for Congress in the southern district of New Mexico and upset the two-term Democrat E.S. "Johnny" Walker of Albuquerque. Richard Nixon won New Mexico's electoral votes that year over Hubert H. Humphrey, and that Republican momentum helped Foreman to get elected. Foreman was unseated after a single term in 1970 by Democrat Harold Runnels.

Appointment to two federal jobs

After losing a House seat for the second time in six years, Foreman in 1971 was appointed assistant secretary of the interior in the Nixon administration and the following year, 1972, he was appointed to a position at the United States Department of Transportation where he stayed until 1976.

Motivational speaking

Foreman's motivational speaking is in the genre of Dr. Norman Vincent Peale, his personal mentor.Wikipedia:Citation needed Among his topics are "How to Make Every Day a Terrific Day!", "Making Quality Performance a Lifestyle" and "Acquiring The Basic Habit Patterns Of Winners."

Foreman's message as a motivational speaker is one of health, wealth, and happiness. He caters primarily to business leaders. He is credited to the phrase, "I'm alive, I'm alert, and I feel great!"

Philanthropy and personal life

On August 26, 1955, Foreman married the former Barbara Lynn Southard, and the couple has two children, Preston Kirk Foreman and Rebecca Lynn Foreman. In 1960, he was named the "Outstanding Young Man of Odessa." In 1962, he was named one of five "Outstanding Young Men of Texas." He was active in the Midcontinent Oil and Gas Association. Foreman is United Methodist. He is also affiliated with the Masonic lodge, Shriners, and Rotary International.

Foreman enjoys motorcycles, hot-air balloons, and international travel.Wikipedia:Citation needed

Early in 2006, Foreman and his brother, Harold "Chub" Foreman, also an NMSU graduate in engineering, donated $1.5 million to the School of Engineering at their *alma mater*.Wikipedia:Citation needed

Support of Kevin Trudeau

Foreman is an associate of Kevin Trudeau, a businessman notorious for his fraudulent infomercials and his disregard for the law. During Trudeau's sentencing to ten years in prison for fraud, Foreman repeatedly interrupted the court proceedings to announce to the judge that he's a former U.S. Congressman. After being told to stop interrupting Foreman went limp when he was finally physically removed from the courtroom and arrested.[121]

References

http://www.barberusa.com/motive/foreman_ed.html http://www.edforeman.com/front.cfm http://www.nmsu.edu/~ucomm/Releases/2006/january/foreman_gift.htm http://bioguide.congress.gov/scripts/biodisplay.pl?index=F000272 http://bioguide.congress.gov/scripts/biodisplay.pl?index=R000510 http://bioguide.congress.gov/scripts/biodisplay.pl?index=S000463 http://www.albertsons.com

Congressional Quarterly's Guide to U.S. Elections, U.S. House edition

External links

- http://www.edforeman.com/

United States House of Representatives		
Preceded by **J.T. Rutherford**	**U.S. Representative from Texas' 16th congressional district** Edgar Franklin "Ed" Foreman, Jr.**1963–1965**	Succeeded by **Richard C. White**
Preceded by **At-large: E. S. "Johnny" Walker Thomas G. Morris**	**U.S. Representative from New Mexico's 2nd congressional district** Edgar Franklin "Ed" Foreman, Jr.**1969–1971**	Succeeded by **Harold Runnels**

Greg Caton

Gregory James Caton	
Born	April 6, 1956
Nationality	American
Other names	James Carr
Citizenship	American
Education	AA (1975), Los Angeles Valley College
Alma mater	Los Angeles Valley College
Known for	Herbalist, Alternative Medicine Promoter
Home town	Glendale, California
Call-sign	N5OY
Website	Gregcaton.com[122]

Gregory James Caton (born April 6, 1956) is an American businessman, inventor, manufacturer and promoter of various herbal products, the main one being Cansema which is claimed to cure skin cancer,[123] although the U.S. Food and Drug Administration (FDA) banned it in 2003 as worthless.[124] Caton is the founder of Alpha Omega Labs, a manufacturer of natural health care products, that currently distributes internationally from Guayaquil, Ecuador.[125]

Early life and education

Caton attended Los Angeles Valley College, a community college in the San Fernando Valley, and then served in the US Navy as a cryptologist from 1975 through 1978Wikipedia:Citation needed. Caton has been an avid amateur and short wave radio operator.[126]

First businesses

Caton founded Consumer Express in 1984.[127] which later became Nutrition for Life,[128] a multi-level marketing (MLM) company. The firm traded briefly on the NASDAQ stock exchange.[129]

Nutrition for Life[130] entered into a business agreement with Kevin Trudeau[131] After the change of ownership of Consumer Express, Caton authored a book (which was since withdrawn) on his version of the alleged fraud surrounding this transaction. Down-Line News reviewed this work in February 1993 on their website.[132] Caton filed a suit against Kevin Trudeau in the US Fifth District Court of Appeals, in response to a libel suit by Trudeau in 1996 over Caton's aforementioned book.

In January 1996, Kevin Trudeau filed a libel suit against Caton in Illinois state court based on statements Caton made in a book and on an Internet website. Caton removed the action to federal court, but on Trudeau's motion, the action was remanded. Thereafter, Caton failed to respond to Trudeau's claims and the court entered a default and noticed an evidential hearing. On June 5, 1996, after a hearing, the court rendered a default judgment against Caton, awarding Trudeau $5 million in compensatory damages and $5 million in punitive damages.

In November 1996, Caton filed for Chapter 7 bankruptcy in response to the judgment. Shortly afterward, the company was subject to a class action lawsuit filed in Harris County, Texas.[133] Nutrition for Life filed for Chapter 7 bankruptcy on July 8, 2003.

Caton then took up a project to detail the issues associated with multi-level marketing on a site entitled *MLM Credit Bureau*. He was featured in an online article by Ami Mills on the Metroactive website in 1996 regarding his work.[134]

Lumen Foods, Alpha Omega Labs and Herbologics

Caton started Alpha Omega Labs in 1995 using the pseudonym "James Carr".[135] Alpha Omega Labs became a provider of over 300 alternative health products with 14 distributors around the world, before its closure by the U.S. Food and Drug Administration (FDA) in 2003. Caton pled guilty to charges that he defrauded consumers.[136]

Lumen Foods was featured in an article by the online newspaper World Net Daily, alleging that the firm was under seizure of its accounts due to fraudulent activity.[137] Caton vigorously refuted the claim, which he alleged was related to issues surrounding the Y2K panic.[138]

In early 2000, Lumen Foods reportedly "broke ranks" with the health food industry when it was reported that it would actively include Genetically modified organism (GMO) products in its offerings.[139]

"They have it all wrong", said Lumen Foods' President, Greg Caton. "FDA, USDA, and EPA have all done exhaustive research into their safety and have found nothing that remotely suggests that either the consumer or the environment are at risk from GM seed", he said.[140]

This earned significant attention from non-GMO advocates. Caton spoke at Cornell University's sponsored symposium, Informing the Dialogue about

Agricultural Biotechnology, in November 1999. His topic was GMO Controversy & the Whole Foods Industry: Why Wholesale Condemnation of Agricultural Biotechnology Hurts our Most Ingredient-Sensitive Markets[141] Lumen Foods reversed their position later in the year, supposedly from pressure by their customers.[142]

Alpha Omega was the topic of an exposé by *Business Week* in their review of the book *Natural Causes*.[143] The review in *Business Week* references the case of Sue Gilliatt, a nurse from Indianapolis who claimed she used Cansema, as well as a product named "H3O" (also sold by Caton) for skin cancer on her nose and that they burned off her nose (in the lawsuit, H3O was primarily blamed).[144,145,146,147] Caton contested Gilliatt's assertions, claiming that due to the individual's use of additional alternative medicine, exclusive attribution of damages from H3O could not be determined. Furthermore, according to Caton, Gilliatt contradicted herself several times in her various court testimonies.[148] Caton even claims that Gilliatt's nose appears to have been surgically removed, citing photographs.[149] The use of escharotics (caustic pastes) such as Cansema to treat skin cancer is "unproven" and can have "serious consequences", according to dermatologists.[150]

Federal conviction

In 2003, United States Federal agents from the joint task force (including U.S. FDA, Bureau of Alcohol, Tobacco and Firearms and local law enforcement) raided Caton's offices, factory and home.[151] As a result of the raid, Caton pled guilty in 2004 and was sentenced to 33 months in prison for weapons possession by a felon and for defrauding customers and violating FDA regulations.[152,153] Caton had received a previous felony conviction for counterfeiting in 1990.[154]

Caton filed for a writ of habeas corpus based upon ineffective counsel in 2005. This was denied with prejudice by the courts.[155]

Probation violation and extradition from Ecuador

On 5 June 2006, after serving his sentence,[156] Greg Caton was released on three years probation with specific restrictions against possession of firearms or manufacture of non-FDA approved materials.[157] Caton and his family relocated to Ecuador in the summer of 2007.[158] Alpha Omega Labs were reopened in June 2008.

On 27 October 2007, Caton was found in violation of the terms of his probation.[159] In September 2008, a filing was made with the U.S. patent office in which Caton expressed a fear of arrest for violation of his probation, if he returned to the US.[160]

Caton's probation violation was reported to Interpol, and was placed in their database; it was reported on Interpol website on 30 September 2008. In February 2009, Caton was featured in *Parade Magazine*'s "On the Run In America" as an Interpol international fugitive.

On 3 December 2009, Caton was arrested at a checkpoint in Ecuador and held in prison. What followed was a complex set of legal manoeuvres involving multiple parties. According to vague reports by Cathryn Caton, his wife, these maneuvers included various members of the Ecuadorian judiciary and Police officials. A judicial hearing on the case was scheduled in Guayaquil, Ecuador on 14 December 2009.[161]

Caton was sentenced in a Louisiana court in May 2010 to serve the remainder of his probation (24 months) in prison. He filed a motion of appeal on June 23, 2011, under the provision that the court failed to consider sentencing guidelines. This appeal was denied[162,163]

Authored works

- Caton, G.J.; *Lumen: Food For A New Age*, Calcasieu Graphics & Pressworks, 1986. ISBN 0-939955-00-8
- Caton, Greg; *MLM Fraud: A Practical Handbook for the Network Marketing Professional*, (self-published), 1990. ISBN 0-939955-03-2

Additional reading

- Hurley, Dan, *Natural Causes: Death, Lies, and Politics in America's Vitamin and Herbal Supplement Industry*. Broadway Publishers (2007) ISBN 0-7679-2042-2

External links

- Alpha Omega Lab Site[164]

Reno R. Rollé

Reno Richard Rollé[165] (born September 24, 1961) is the CEO of Rollé Wiseman, LLC a direct consumer marketing and management firm co-founded with entertainment industry expert and respectedWikipedia:Manual of Style/Words to watch#Unsupported attributions Attorney, Todd R. Wiseman.

In 2007, Reno Rollé co-founded BōKU International,[166] an award winning, USDA certified Organic, Kosher and Vegan super food company which now serves thousands of customers in 65 countries throughout the world.

That same year, Reno Rollé co-authored and published "The Ultimate Guide To Natural Health Quick Reference" with Nevada medical oncologist and world renowned anti-aging physician, James W. Forsythe M.D., H.M.D.

Reno Rollé previously held the position of CEO for Shop America USA. Based in Bradford, England and operating in the U.S., Shop America specialized in long- and short-form direct response television (infomercial) marketing. During this time Reno Rollé co-created the book and marketing campaign for "Natural Cures 'They' Don't Want You to Know About" (written by Kevin Trudeau). This book held the #1 spot on the The New York Times Best Seller list for several weeks from 2005 to 2006 and has sold an estimated 10 million plus copies. In an article written by Christopher Dreher and published on Salon.com in 2005, ("What Kevin Trudeau doesn't want you to know"), Rolle weighs in on the controversy from an industry point of view.

Reno Rollé was a founding principle of the National Lampoon Acquisition Group,[167] LLC an investment group that orchestrated the acquisition of J2 Communications, Inc. (NASDAQ:JTWO) a small cap public company that owned the widely recognized comedic brand, National Lampoon, Inc. Mr. Rollé founded National Lampoon Home Entertainment in 2002<reg name="nl"/> to produce and distribute National Lampoon branded DVDs and has Produced or Executive Produced several feature films under this institutional moniker.

Between 1997 and 2001 Reno Rollé was the co-founder, Chairman and CEO of Synergy Worldwide, Inc., a product engineering, design and marketing company. In 1999, Synergy produced "Mastering the Flow", a blackjack card counting program that became a long running and very successful gaming infomercial. In September 2000, Synergy was honored with the distinguished R&D 100 Award for Mr. Rollé's invention, The Spin Fryer. This award, referred to as the "Oscars of Inventions," by the Chicago Tribune recognizes the most technologically significant inventions in history. Past winners include: anti-lock brakes, the fax machine, the ATM (automated teller machine), and polarized film. The Spin Fryer was subsequently licensed to Salton, Inc.

(NYSE:SFP) for marketing and distribution under the George Foreman line of kitchen products.

From 1994 to 1997 Reno Rollé was a co-founder of HSN Direct, a direct response television joint venture with Home Shopping Network, Inc. (NASDAQ: IACI)[168] Mr. Rollé's primary responsibility was to negotiate and manage the majority of HSND's contracts, including marketing and distribution, production, talent and joint venture agreements. In addition, Reno Rollé oversaw all aspects of new business development including: media, production, regulatory compliance and operations. While successful in multiple consumer categories, highlighting Mr. Rollé's tenure with HSND was his role in the development and launch of the Ab Isolator and EZ Crunch abdominal exercise products, both easily achieving sales north of $100 million. In 1986, Reno Rollé and his wife Lynn founded Rollé Ltd.[169] in Long Beach Island, New Jersey. The company pioneered the concept of a patented, weighted beach blanket (Patent # 4,703,528) and achieved success in the manufacture and sale of its flagship product, the Rollé Blanket which still to this day is considered the finest product of its type in the world.

Reno Rollé lives in Ojai, CA with his Wife Lynn and two children. He is a current member of the Ojai Valley Youth Foundation Partnership council.

Ronald Hoffman

Ronald Hoffman, M.D. is an American physician, author, and broadcaster in the United States who hosts *Intelligent Medicine*, a syndicated radio talk show, and the *Intelligent Medicine Podcast*[170]. He is the founder and director of the Hoffman Center in New York City, and is a practitioner of holistic medicine.

Biography

Born in southern California, Hoffman studied Medicine at the Albert Einstein College of Medicine and was trained in Internal Medicine at the Manhattan V.A. In 1985 he founded the Hoffman Center, which is a unique, first of its kind, medical practice that pioneered alternative and complementary medical care.

In 1987 Dr. Hoffman started *Intelligent Medicine* (originally called *Health Talk*), a nationally syndicated medical radio talk show. And in June 2013 Dr. Hoffman debuted the *Intelligent Medicine Podcast*. Both shows promote the healthy benefits of nutritional therapy (not just by eating the right meals, but by nutritional supplements); he personally consumes around 15 different supplements per day. The supplements Dr. Hoffman appears to be most interested in are Vitamin D, Magnesium (particularly Magnesium Taurate), Olive Leaf Extract, EGCG from green tea, and Fish oil. On almost every show of his he mentions a new medical study that backs his arguments about the risks involved with mineral and/or vitamin deficiency. Deficiency, Hoffman argues, can cause symptoms of diminishing health such as scurvy, disorders of cell metabolism, tuberculosis, poor psychological health (such as depression), osteoporosis, tinnitus, various forms of cancer, senescence (premature), cardiovascular diseases, and much more.

Although Dr. Hoffman maintains a friendly atmosphere on his show, he occasionally uses his radio time to voice criticisms of certain medical "experts." He is a vehement critic of author and convicted felon Kevin Trudeau, who wrote the famous controversial book *Natural Cures "They" Don't Want You To Know About*. He considers him to be a swindler that is an embarrassment to the field of complementary medicine.

Dr. Hoffman moved to New York for college and has remained. He owns homes in Manhattan and Hampton Bays.

Bibliography

Books

Books authored by Dr. Ronald Hoffman include:

- 1997: *Natural Therapies for Mitral Valve Prolapse* Keats Pub (ISBN 978-0879837655)
- 1999: *The Natural Approach to Attention Deficit Disorder (ADD)*, McGraw-Hill (ISBN 978-0879837792)
- 1999: *Lyme Disease (Good Health Guides)*, McGraw-Hill (ISBN 978-0879836177)
- 2006: *How to Talk With Your Doctor: The Guide for Patients And Their Physicians Who Want to Reconcile And Use the Best of Conventional And Alternative Medicine* (with Sidney Stevens) (ISBN 978-1591201120)

External links

- Hoffman Center[171].
- Dr. Ronald Hoffman - Audio Archive[172].
- The Intelligent Medicine Podcast[170]

Robert Barefoot

Robert R. Barefoot (born 1944) is a controversial proponent of alternative medicine and a self claimed expert of Calcium. He has been cited by both the United Kingdom's Independent Television Commission and the FTC in the United States for making misleading ads and making unsubstantiated claims, including medical claims.

Background

Born in Edmonton, Alberta, Canada, Robert Barefoot graduated with Honors from Northern Alberta Institute of Technology with a certificate in chemical research technology. Even though he is sometimes referred to as "Dr. Robert Barefoot", he does not possess any doctoral degree. He now lives in Wickenburg, Arizona.

According to unverifiable information on his website, Barefoot has researched enhanced hydrocarbon and metal extraction in the mining industry for which he obtained several international patents. He has also published six research papers on mineral diagenesis and analytical chemistry. Barefoot's research with Dr. Carl Reich on terminal cancer patients led Barefoot to write one of his best-selling books, "The Calcium Factor."[173] The book has been ranked in Amazon's top 500 sales listings.[174]

Until 2004, he presented his products in an infomercial hosted by Kevin Trudeau.

Litigation

When the Attorney General of Maryland brought a case against the marketers of T-Up, an unproven cancer and AIDS treatment,[175] Barefoot was called upon to be an expert witness on the use of caesium chloride on humans in conjunction with high pH therapy but was dismissed based on his lack of professional training and research in this particular area.[176]

Criticism

According to a critical *Time* magazine article by Leon Jaroff, "The monthly cost of the recommended dose of Barefoot's calcium tablets is some 15 times greater than that of the ordinary drug store variety." Jaroff called Barefoot's marketing of coral calcium "one of the more successful scams of our age" and "sheer nonsense," and labeled him a "huckster". He ended his article with a call for intervention by the U.S. Food and Drug Administration (FDA):

> When are the chickens ever going to come home to roost? Barefoot has been getting away with this scam for years, conning his naive audience, and presumably enriching himself along the way. Isn't it well past time for the Federal Trade Commission to step in?

Upon further analysis, it is apparent that Coral Calcium is nothing more than calcium carbonate and magnesium (there are other elements and minerals present in trace amounts) which can be bought at the local home improvement store as limestone and costs about $1.00 per bag. Wikipedia:Citation needed

External links

- Official website[177]
- A Critical Look at Robert Barefoot and Coral Calcium[178]

Donald Barrett

For the drummer, see Donald Barrett (musician).

Donald Barrett is the founder and president of ITV Direct, a company which produces infomercials for broadcast in the United States. Almost all are related to health and nutrition, or in the company's words, "products that positively impact people."Wikipedia:Citation needed He has also promoted Lorraine Day, and other alternative medical practitioners.Wikipedia:Citation needed Recently he founded ITV Ventures, an affiliate company which offers the public network marketing opportunities connected to its infomercial business.[179] ITV closed on October 3, 2008.[180]

On September 24, 2013, Donald Barrett became the Co Host of Unspoken Cures Radio, along with Matt Ryncarz. Unspoken Cures radio is formerly known as Fusion Power Hour, and it is broadcast on The Arena Sports Network.[181][182]

Controversy

On April 19, 2004, Barrett in his capacity as President of ITV Direct, Inc./ Direct Marketing Concepts, Inc. received a Warning Letter from the Food and Drug Administration notifying him that the product Supreme Greens was being marketed as an unlicensed drug with false or misleading claims. The letter requested that ITV Direct correct the deceptive practices.[183]

In June 2004, the FTC filed a lawsuit in the United States District Court for the District of Massachusetts alleging that Direct Marketing Concepts, Inc., ITV Direct, Inc., and their president, Donald W. Barrett had deceptively marketed Supreme Greens and Coral Calcium Daily by claiming that it could prevent, treat, and cure cancer, heart disease, arthritis, and diabetes. They also claimed it caused substantial weight loss, and was safe for use by pregnant women, children – including those as young as one year old, and persons taking any form of medication.[184] In July 2004, ITV Direct was enjoined from marketing Supreme Greens.[185]

On October 5, 2007, the FTC sued ITV Direct, Inc. and Donald Barrett for misrepresenting Kevin Trudeau's "Weight-Loss Cure" book in the infomercial they produced to market it.[186] In response to the FTC's suit, ITV Direct sued the FTC for alleged harassment and violation of free speech rights.Wikipedia:Citation needed Subsequently, on November 19, 2007, in a separate FTC action, Trudeau was found in contempt of a 2004 court order for making "patently false" claims in the weight loss book.[187]

On July 19, 2008, a federal judge ruled that two infomercials produced by Beverly-based ITV Direct for "Coral Calcium" and "Supreme Greens" were deceptive and that the firm's owners are liable for restitution being sought by the Federal Trade Commission, which is seeking nearly $55 million. The judge also dismissed a countersuit filed by Donald Barrett, ITV's president, who claimed the FTC was violating his First Amendment rights by taking him to court to force him to pull the ads.[188]

On May 2, 2011, Barrett pleaded guilty to failing to report income and to selling a product touted as a disease preventative without approval from the FDA.[189] On September 29, 2011, Barrett was sentenced to one year of probation, including three months in a community correction center and another three months of house arrest.

Leigh Valentine

Leigh Valentine is an entrepreneur in the beauty industry, author, and Christian ministry leader. She is the CEO of Leigh Valentine Beauty and creator of the Non-Surgical Face-Lift Kit. She is founder of *Mothers Supporting Israel*, a leader with CUFI (Christians United for Israel)[190] under the leadership of Pastor John Hagee of Cornerstone Church in San Antonio, Texas; an active supporter of the traveling Holocaust Museum[191], and is involved in several children's charitable outreaches. Valentine has appeared on *The 700 Club*, *Paula White Today*, *Living the Life*, *100 Huntley Street*, *LeSea's Harvest Show* and Trinity Broadcasting Network.

Early years

Leigh Valentine was born Leigh Ann Middleton in Des Moines, Iowa to Dr. Robert Middleton and Mary Shuman Middleton. Robert Middleton was a surgeon and family physician and Mary was a manager with Stanley Home Products. Mary's position with Stanley Home Products brought about the family's move to St. Louis, Missouri when Leigh was 5 years old.

Education

Valentine graduated from the private all-girls school Incarnate Word Academy High School in 1973. Valentine went on to graduate from Stephens College in Columbia, Missouri in 1978 with a double major in Fashion Merchandising and Business Administration. She later graduated from RHEMA Bible Training Center in Tulsa Oklahoma.

Modeling/acting career

According to her book, *Successfully You*, while working at Bloomingdale's department store, she was discovered by a talent scout who offered her the opportunity to audition for the role of the new Slim-Fast girl, which she landed, and which launched her also into a modeling and acting career. A member of the Screen Actors Guild (S.A.G.), Valentine starred in national commercials and made numerous television appearances. Valentine became Miss Missouri USA in 1977. Shortly after winning the title, she was involved in a horrific car crash which involved a lengthy recuperation period; the doctors were not certain if she would even walk again. Valentine fully recovered.

Business

Leigh is the CEO of Leigh Valentine Beauty. After working in the beauty industry for Estee Lauder, Revlon and Lancôme, Valentine started her own anti-aging skin care company. She began by mixing samples in her own sink[192] and, in 1998, she launched her own Health and Beauty Line. Valentine is the creator and formulator of the "Non-Surgical Face Lift Kit". For over ten years, Valentine made hundreds of live appearances on QVC, selling over $250 million of product on QVC and through her infomercials, including one with Kevin Trudeau. Her Non-Surgical Face Lift Kit infomercial is purported to be the longest running infomercial for a beauty product in history. Web page: http://www.valentinespa.com/

Early ministry work

Leigh Valentine is also an international Christian ministry speaker. Shortly after graduating RHEMA Bible Training Center in Oklahoma, she and her first husband, Robert Valentine led/pastored an outreach church in Manhattan, New York. They also planted a church in Connecticut, and formed "Heart to Heart Ministries." Later, Valentine joined Norvel Hayes, founder of New Life Bible College in Cleveland, Tennessee, as an international evangelist and speaker.[5]

Marriage to Robert Tilton

In 1994, Valentine married Evangelist Robert Tilton three months after he divorced his first wife, Marte Tilton.[193] The marriage lasted three years. During the divorce, Valentine asked the court to include the church and all its property as community property in the proceedings.[194]

Infomercial

"Paid Programming" redirects here. For the Adult Swim television pilot of same name, see Paid Programming (TV pilot).

An **infomercial** is a form of television commercial, which generally includes a phone number or website. Most often used as a form of direct response television (DRTV), long-form infomercials are typically 28:30 or 58:30 minutes in length.[195,196,197] Infomercials are also known as **paid programming** (or **teleshopping** in Europe). This phenomenon started in the United States, where infomercials were typically shown overnight (usually 2:00 a.m. to 6:00 a.m.), outside of peak prime time hours for commercial broadcasters. Some television stations chose to air infomercials as an alternative to the former practice of signing off. By 2009, most infomercial spending in the U.S. occurs during the early morning, daytime and evening hours. Stations in most countries around the world have instituted similar media structures. The infomercial industry is worth over $200 billion.

While the term "infomercial" was originally applied only to television advertising, it is now sometimes used to refer to any presentation (often on video) which presents a significant amount of information in an actual, or perceived, attempt to promote a point of view. When used this way, the term may be meant to carry an implication that the party making the communication is exaggerating truths or hiding important facts. Often, it is unclear whether the actual presentation fits this definition because the term is used in an attempt to discredit the presentation. Hence, political speeches or conventions may be derogatorily referred to as "infomercials" for a specific point of view.[198]

Format

The word "infomercial" is a portmanteau of the words "information" and "commercial". As in any other form of advertisement, the content is a commercial message designed to represent the viewpoints and to serve the interest of the sponsor. Infomercials are often made to closely resemble standard television programs. Some imitate talk shows and try to downplay the fact that the program is actually a commercial message. A few are developed around storylines and have been called "storymercials". However, most do not have specific television formats but craft different elements to create what they hope is a compelling story about the product offered.

Infomercials are designed to solicit a direct response which is specific and at once quantifiable and are, therefore, a form of direct response marketing (not to be confused with direct marketing). For this reason, infomercials generally feature between two and four internal commercials of 30 to 120 seconds, which invite the consumer to call or take other direct action. Despite the overt request for direct action, many consumers respond to the messages in an infomercial with purchases at retail outlets. For many infomercials, the largest portion of positive response is for consumers to take action by purchasing at a retail store. For others, the advertiser will instead promote the item as "not sold in stores." Some advertisers who make this choice dislike sharing profit with retailers while many simply lack the immense resources necessary to get their products into the retail industry channels prior to achieving on-air success. In the latter case, many hope to use profit from direct sales to build their business/company in order to achieve later retail distribution. Stand-alone shorter commercials, 30 to 120 seconds in length with a call-to-action, are erroneously called infomercials; when used as an independently-produced commercial, they are generally known as **DRTV Spots** or **Short Form DRTV**. Many products and services that advertise using infomercials often also used these shorter spots to advertise during regular programming.

Many traditional infomercial producers make use of flashy catchphrases, repeat basic ideas, or employ scientist-like characters or celebrities as guests or hosts in their ad. The book *As Seen on TV* (Quirk Books) by Lou Harry and Sam Stall highlights the history of products as the Flowbee, the Chia Pet, and Ginsu knives. Sometimes, traditional infomercials use limited time offers or claim one can only purchase the wares from television to add pressure for viewers to buy their products.

Products using infomercial marketing

The products frequently marketed through infomercials at the national level include cleaning products, appliances, food preparation devices, dietary supplements, alternative health aids, memory improvement courses, books, compilation albums, videos of numerous genera, real estate investment strategies, beauty supplies, baldness remedies, sexual enhancement supplements, weight loss products, personal fitness devices, home exercise machines, and adult chat lines. Automobile dealerships, attorneys, and jewelers are among the types of businesses that air infomercials on a local level.

Major brands (such as Apple, Microsoft and Thermos-Grill2Go[199]) have used infomercials for their ability to communicate more complicated and in-depth product stories. This practice started in the early 1990s and has increased since. Brands generally eschew the "cheesy" trappings of the traditional infomercial business in order to create communication they believe creates a better image of their products, brands and consumers. Apple's use of the infomercial medium was immediately discontinued with Steve Jobs' 1997 return to the helm of the company.

History

Early infomercials

During the early days of television, many television shows were specifically created by sponsors with the main goal of selling their product, the entertainment angle being a hook to hold audience attention (this is how soap operas got their name). A good example of this is the early children's show *The Magic Clown* on NBC, which was created by Tico Bonomo essentially as an advertisement for Bonomo's Turkish Taffy.[200] It is claimed that the first infomercial for a commercial product appeared in 1949 or 1950, for a blender. Accounts vary on whether this was for a VitaMix blender as claimed by Vitamix or from Waring Blenders as claimed in various online sources. Eventually, limits imposed by the Federal Communications Commission (FCC) on the amount of advertising that could appear during an hour of television did away with these programs, forcing sponsors into the background; however, few infomercials, mainly those for greatest hits record sets and Shop Smith power tools, did exist during the period when commercial time was restricted.Wikipedia:Citation needed

It is quite possible that the first modern infomercial series which ran in North America was on San Diego-area television station XETV, which during the 1970s ran a one-hour television program every Sunday consisting of advertisements for local homes for sale. As the station was actually licensed by the Mexican government to the city of Tijuana, but broadcasts all of its programs in English for the U.S. market, the FCC limit at that time of a maximum of 18 minutes of commercials in an hour did not apply to the station.

Credited for coining the word "infomercial" was hospitality/entertainment impresario Paul Ruffino, whose CineStar company was a pioneer in purchasing program-length commercial time. The first infomercial as it is well known today aired in 1982. Entrepreneur Robert E. Murphy, Jr., looking to market "New Generation", a hair growth treatment, reached out to a Chicago ad agency where he met Frank Cannella, who convinced broadcast stations and cable networks to sell time for this format. The show was such a hit, that other companies quickly began purchasing program-length commercial time as well, and the "infomercial" was born.

After 1984

Infomercials proliferated in the United States after 1984 when the Federal Communications Commission eliminated regulations that were established in the 1950s and 1960s to govern the commercial content of television.Wikipedia:Citation needed Infomercials particularly exploded in the mid-1990s with motivational and personal development products, and infamous "get-rich-quick scheme"s based on the premise that one could quickly become wealthy by either selling anything through classified ads or through real estate flipping. These were hawked by personalities such as Don Lapre and Carleton H. Sheets, among others.

When they first appeared, infomercials were most often scheduled in the United States and Canada during late-night/early morning hours. As stations have found value in airing them at other times, by 2008 a large portion of infomercial spending occurs in the early morning, daytime, early prime and even prime time periods. There are also entire networks (such as cable channels Corner Store TV, Access Television Network and GRTV) that specialise in an all-infomercial format for the sole purpose of cable and satellite providers receiving revenue from the channel operator from any sales for their area, or to fill empty time on local programming channels. In the past these channels were allowed in carriage contracts to overlay the paid programming of national cable networks such as Versus until around 2006, when a Stanley Cup playoffs game on Versus was interrupted in many areas during a quadruple-overtime National Hockey League game for cable operator-programmed infomercials which caused vehement fan reaction against the interruption; within weeks Versus had removed this allotment from their carriage agreement to prevent a repeat occurrence quietly, along with most other networks.Wikipedia:Citation needed CNBC, which airs only one hour of infomercials nightly during the business week, airs up to 28 hours of infomercials on Saturdays and Sundays during the time where the network's business news coverage otherwise airs on Monday through Fridays; since the September–October 2008 financial crisis, CNBC has inserted a *paid programming* bug on the top right corner of the screen during all airings of infomercials.

A comparison of television listings from 2007 with 1987 verifies that many North American broadcasters now air infomercials in lieu of syndicated television series reruns and movies, which were formerly staples during the more common hours infomercials are broadcast (like the overnight hours). Infomercials are a near-permanent staple of Ion Television's daytime and overnight schedules (although their presence has lessened since 2008, due to expansions of entertainment programming on the network's schedule; as of 2014, Ion only airs infomercials from overnights to mid-mornings); multichannel providers such as DirecTV have objected in the past to carrying Ion feeds which consist largely of paid programming, though in comparison the satellite service does carry several infomercial-only channels.[201]

United Kingdom

As with other advertising, content is supervised by the Advertising Standards Authority (ASA) and regulated by Ofcom. Advertising rules are written and maintained by the Committees of Advertising Practice (CAP), working closely with the ASA and Ofcom.

In the UK, "admags" (advertisement magazines) were originally a feature of the regional commercial ITV stations from launch in 1955, but were banned in 1963. The word 'teleshopping' was coined in 1979 by Michael Aldrich, who invented real-time transaction processing from a domestic television and subsequently installed many systems throughout the UK in the 1980s. This would now be referred to as online shopping. In the 1989, the *Satellite Shop* was the launched as the first UK shopping channel. Shortly afterwards, infomercials began on satellite television and they became known as *teleshopping*. Until 2009, the UK permitted neither paid infomercials nor teleshopping on broadcast television. However in 2009, Ofcom allowed up to three hours of infomercials a day on any channel.

Airtime for political messages, known as Party Political Broadcasts, is allocated free of charge to political parties according to a formula approved by Parliament and is available only on broadcast television and radio channels. The Communications Act 2003 prohibits political advertising. Television advertising of pharmacy-only and prescription drugs is also prohibited.

Televangelists

Some U.S. televangelists such as Robert Tilton and Peter Popoff buy television time from infomercial brokers representing television stations around the U.S. and even some widely distributed cable networks that are not averse to carrying religious programming. A block of such programming appears weekdays on BET under the umbrella title *BET Inspiration* (which fully replaced the direct response variety of infomercials on the channel in 1997). The vast majority of religious programming in the United States is distributed through paid infomercial time; the fees that televangelists pay for coverage on most religious stations are a major revenue stream for those stations, in addition to programming the networks produce themselves (the money to pay for this air time comes mainly through listener donations, with less scrupulous televangelists using hard sell tactics to coerce faithful viewers to send money, sometimes by using a variant of the prosperity gospel).

TiVo

TiVo uses paid programming time weekly on the Discovery Channel on early Thursday mornings and Ion Television on early Wednesday mornings in order to record interactive and video content to be presented to subscribers of their service in a form of linear datacasting without the need to interfere with a subscriber's Internet bandwidth (or lack thereof if they solely use the machine's dial-up connection for updating). The program is listed as *Teleworld Paid Program*, named for TiVo's corporate name at its founding.

The 2007–2010 financial crisis

During the financial crisis that lasted from 2007 to 2010, many struggling individual television stations began to devote more of their programming schedules to infomercials, thereby reducing syndication contracts for regular programming. There have been stations that have found that the revenue from infomercial time sales were higher than the revenues possible through the traditional television advertising and syndication sales options. However, the reduced ratings from airing infomercials can have a domino effect and harm ratings for other programming on the station.[202]

A feature-length documentary that chronicles the history of the infomercial is *Pitch People*.

In 2008Wikipedia:Citation needed, Tribune Media Services and Gemstar-TV Guide/Rovi began to relax the guidelines for listing infomercials within their electronic program guide listings. Previously all infomercials were listed under the title "Paid Programming" (except for exceptions listed below), but now infomercial producers are allowed to submit a title and limited synopsis (phone numbers/websites to order a product/service seem to be disallowed) of the program's content to the listings providers.

Fox's Saturday morning programming

In November 2008, Fox announced that it would discontinue its Saturday morning children's programming block 4Kids TV dispute with 4Kids Entertainment over compensation and issues with distribution on Fox stations; the network opted to replace part of 4Kids TV with a two-hour block of infomercials under title of *Weekend Marketplace* in January 2009 (two additional hours were given back to Fox's stations). This made Fox the first major network (excluding a borderline example with Ion Television) to carry a schedule of paid programming. However, many local stations already utilize Saturday morning slots to air locally programmed paid programming or programs such as *Video Car Lot*, which features one dealer presenting their current selection of pre-owned vehicles to encourage customers to visit their lot, or "home tour" programming where a home builder records a tour of a model home to entice homebuyers to purchase a plot in their subdivisions. Though it was hoped by Fox that it would result in unique and exclusive paid programming made exclusively for them, the five-year block was generally disdained by both viewers and Fox affiliates alike (revenue for the advertising was not shared with affiliates, and no local time for commercials between programs were offered) and never featured an infomercial exclusive to Fox; some stations opted to use the extra time on Saturday morning for E/I programming, with infomercials relegated to before or after the block, or even limited to afternoons, if local newscasts are shown earlier. Other stations refused *Weekend Marketplace* outright and it went unaired in several markets, or buried in other time slots as being listed as generic paid programming to give viewers full clarity as to what the programming was. In September 2014, *Weekend Marketplace* was replaced in some markets for the E/I-focused *Xploration Nation* programming block, but continues under the same format as it did at the start.

Criticism and legal issues

In the United States, the Federal Trade Commission (FTC) requires that any infomercial 15 minutes or longer must disclose to viewers that it is a paid advertisement. An infomercial is required to be "clearly and conspicuously" marked as a "paid advertisement for [particular product or service], sponsored by [sponsor]" at the beginning and end of the advertisement and before ordering instructions are displayed.

Because infomercials may sometimes take a sensational tone, and because some of the products and services sold may be of a questionable nature, consumer advocates recommend careful investigation of the infomercial's sponsor,[203] the product being advertised, and the claims being made before making a purchase. To that end, some television stations and networks normally run their own disclaimers prior to, (sometimes) during, or after the infomercial, stating that in addition to the program being a paid advertisement, the broadcaster bears no responsibility or liability for the infomercial's content (the legality of a station or network attempting to absolve itself of liability for a program they air, while profiting from the same program, has never been tested in court). A few stations also encourage viewers to contact their local Better Business Bureau or state or local consumer protection agency to report any questionable products or claims that air on such infomercials. Some channels, such as CNBC and Fox Business Network, include a "paid programming" bug in a corner of the screen during the duration of each infomercial on that channel, which is especially important for any financial products to avoid an exploitation of an 'as seen on (network)' claim of endorsement by the network; other channels, particularly smaller networks such as RFD-TV, have publicly disavowed infomercials and have refused to air them (RFD-TV has since lifted its ban on infomercials but still only airs them in graveyard slots). Considerable FTC scrutiny is also given to results claims like those in diet/ weight loss advertisements. They especially focus on the gray areas surrounding claims stated by "testimonials" because the producer's choice to include a specific testimonial is an action as intentional as writing a scripted claim. The rules controlling endorsements are modified from time to time to increase consumer protection and fill loopholes.[204] Industry organizations like the Electronic Retailing Association, who represents infomercial marketers, often try to minimize the impact of these rule changes. Additionally, the FTC has been enforcing laws regarding testimonials and have filed suits against several companies for publishing "non-typical" and "completely fabricated" customer testimonials to support their claims within the infomercials. In 2006, the first third-party testimonial verification company[205] was launched, and now independently validates the consumer testimonials used in many infomercials.

Since the 1990s, federal and state consumer protection agencies have either successfully sued or been critical of several prominent infomercial pitchmen, including Kevin Trudeau, Donald Barrett and Matthew Lesko. Don Lapre, a salesman notorious for his get-rich-quick schemes, committed an apparent suicide while in federal custody awaiting a trial for several dozen counts of fraud.[206]

Parodies

The Infomercial format has been widely parodied:

- In a sort of self-parody, the movie *Santo Gold's Blood Circus* features a musical number in which mail-order jewelry salesman "Santo Gold" Rigatuso (who financed the film) advertises his wares. Santo Gold promoted the film heavily in its infomercials.
- A skit in the cartoon series *Tiny Toon Adventures* has an infomercial hostess trying to sell a clothesline for $39.95, but has to include additional offers to try to justify the high price.
- In the *Garfield and Friends* episode "Dread Giveaway", Garfield dreams of attempting to give away Nermal in an infomercial, but no one wants to take him.
- In the 2003 live-action film *The Cat in the Hat*, the cat performs an entire talkshow-style infomercial spoof for a magical (but disastrous) cupcake maker. In the spoof, the Cat plays the roles of host *and* guest/expert.
- In the direct-to-video movie *The Lion King 1½*, Pumbaa sits on the remote in mid-movie and the screen switches to a jewelry infomercial from QVC.

- Quebec-based Têtes à Claques has produced several infomercial parodies in French.
- The comedy duo Tim Heidecker and Eric Wareheim have produced several infomercial parody segments that are showcased on their oddball comedy show *Tim and Eric Awesome Show, Great Job!*, notably one for a CD-ROM-based version of the internet called the "Innernette". It employs many of the cliched infomercial hallmarks and phrases such as enthusiastic demonstrations, and outlandish claims of user satisfaction.
- "Weird Al" Yankovic parodied infomercials in the song *Mr. Popeil*, a homage to inventor and infomercial spokesperson Ron Popeil, on his 1984 album *"Weird Al" Yankovic in 3-D* (Popeil himself had used the song in some of his infomercials). Well known pitchmen like Popeil and Billy Mays have been the inspiration for many of these parodies.
- *Saturday Night Live*'s "Bassomatic" skit featuring Dan Aykroyd in the 1970s may have presaged the genre.
- In the "Home-Cooked Eds" episode of the Cartoon Network series *Ed, Edd & Eddy*, the Kanker Sisters decide to watch infomercials after taking over Eddy's house in yet another misguided attempt at affectation.
- Robot Chicken has parodied numerous infomercials, along with their hosts. Popular examples include Mick Hastie, Cathy Mitchell and Billy Mays. Shortly following Mays' demise, he was parodied posthumously on *South Park*.
- Adult Swim aired a highly elaborate parody of an infomercial, *Paid Programming*, several times in November 2009. The clearest evidence that the parody, which advertised various fictional "Icelandic Ultra Blue" products, was not real was the use of profanity and the fact that Adult Swim (or as a whole, the parent network it shares channel space with, Cartoon Network) does not air infomercials. In late 2014, their infomercials block aired *Too Many Cooks*, which became a highly popular viral video shortly thereafter.
- The ABC improvisation-comedy show *Whose Line Is It Anyway?* regularly satires infomercials in two of its segments. One is "Greatest Hits", where the infomercial hosts (usually including show regulars Colin Mochrie and Ryan Stiles) attempt to sell an album of "greatest hits" about unlikely subjects, with songs mentioned usually sung by the other show regular Wayne Brady. The other one concerns them trying to make useless junk seem desirable.
- Some of the most outstanding sketches from the Australian television sketch show "SkitHOUSE" feature a fictional telemarketing company called "Nothing Suss".
- UK children's sketch show *Horrible Histories* features an infomercial host character called the Shouty Man, who enthusiastically pitches unusual

past-time products.
- A significant part of the plot of *Requiem for a Dream* revolves around a sinister infomercial parody and one of the characters' strong desire to appear in it.

Other uses and definitions

Political infomercials

In the United States, the strategy of buying prime-time programming slots on major networks has been utilized by political candidates for both presidential and state office to present infomercial-like programs to sell a candidate's merits to the public. Fringe presidential candidate Lyndon LaRouche regularly bought time on CBS and local stations in the 1980s. In the 1990s, Ross Perot also bought network time in 1992 and 1996 to present his presidential policies to the public. The National Rifle Association has also aired programs via paid programming time to present their views on issues such as gun control and other issues while appealing to the public to join their organization.

Use during the 2008 Presidential campaign

Hillary Clinton bought an hour of primetime programming on the Hallmark Channel in 2008 before the Super Tuesday primary elections, and on Texas-based regional sports network FSN Southwest before that state's primary to present a town hall-like program. Fellow presidential candidate Barack Obama's 2008 presidential campaign used infomercials extensively. including running a 24-hour channel on Dish Network.[207] One week before the 2008 general election, Obama purchased a 30-minute slot at 8 p.m. Eastern and Pacific Time during primetime on seven major networks (NBC, CBS, MSNBC, Fox, BET, TV One and Univision (with Spanish subtitles)) to present a "closing argument" to his campaign. The combination of these networks reportedly drew a peak audience of over 33 million viewers of the half-hour program, making it the single most watched infomercial broadcast in the history of U.S. television.[208]

Children's programming

Although not meeting the definition of an infomercial *per se*, animated children's programming in the 1980s and early 1990s, which included half-hour animated series for franchises such as *Transformers*, *My Little Pony*, *Go-Bots* and *Bravestarr* were often described by media experts and parents derisive of these types of series as essentially program-length commercials, as they also sold the tie-in toy lines and food products for the shows within commercials.

The Children's Television Act of 1990 was instrumental in ending this practice and setting commercial limits. Currently, any advertisement for a tie-in product within the show is considered a violation of the FCC rules and is considered a "program length commercial" by their standards, putting the station at risk of paying large fines for violations.

These regulations do not apply to cable networks; for instance, Disney Channel currently features tie-ins for virtually all of its shows (in addition to standard program promotions and promotions for other Disney products) instead of commercials, while only going as far as promoting DVD and CD versions of those programs, while competitor Discovery Family (the former Hub Network) is a consortium between Discovery Communications and toymaker Hasbro, which airs many shows based on their properties on the network, an arrangement that would be impossible on broadcast television. Nickelodeon often brokers time to Mattel on Sunday mornings for their series of children's films promoting their line of Barbie dolls, which promote the release on DVD of those films.

However, as seen in the aftermath a case where the characters for shoe company Skechers's children's shoe commercials were adapted into a full-length series, *Zevo-3* for Nicktoons,[209,210] effectively cable networks usually use FCC rules as a basic guideline and rarely stray away from the basic tenets of the CTA to avoid risking their reputations with parents, consumer advocates and other groups which would argue for equivalent FCC controls for cable networks as broadcast networks for children's content.

Daytime programming

A new genre of locally produced television rose in the mid-2000s as television stations (especially those affiliated with NBC and Fox, where NBC gave up the most programming time; Fox has no daytime programming *per se*) saw network time on weekday mornings after 9 a.m. returned to local control and saw new national talk shows either fail or not attract the right demographic to a timeslot. Beginning with *Daytime* on Media General-owned station WFLA-TV in Tampa, Florida in the early 2000s, a new format came into use; these programs used the structure of a traditional locally produced daytime show with its usual format of light talk, health features, beauty tips and recipe segments (which were popular from the early 1970s up to the early 1990s, when expanding local newscasts became a much less expensive, more dependable form of revenue). Some of these shows, such as ABC affiliate WKBW-TV's long-running *AM Buffalo* in Buffalo, New York, seamlessly made the transition from a traditional local talk show to a paid program with little notice.

This type of program usually features light talk, designed to draw in mainly a stay-at-home female audience, followed by presentations of various products, services, and packages by local businesses; for example, a basement waterproofing system might be discussed by the representative of a company in that business with the hosts, along with perhaps a special offer for viewers; a chiropractor (or other medical professional) might discuss back pain or other health-related issues, and provide contact information for his/her practice. These segments, though carefully disclaimed after concerns were brought up about the original program model of *Daytime*, are designed to give a business a detailed presentation of their service that might not be possible in a traditional 30-second pre-recorded commercial, or the minute-long slots which have a short demonstration of the product and an offer prevalent during early evening programming.

Although locally produced, the programs are also presented by hosts which are not associated in any way with the station's newsroom, or by a host who formerly anchored a station's newscasts and (while still familiar with the station's viewers) may be looking for an easier and less harried work schedule. Under most guidelines, hosts cannot appear in newscasts and in productions run by the sales department at the same time, due to ethical concerns about sponsorships influencing newscasts. Thus, news anchors and reporters cannot host these shows, nor can hosts of these shows appear in newscasts as reporters; for instance, in the case of the aforementioned *AM Buffalo*, host Linda Pellegrino was forced to resign her post as a weather anchor on WKBW when *AM Buffalo* began adding sponsored segments. In fact, if a breaking news event takes place during the program, it is usually cut off with only a quick pause and no mention by the host that they are sending viewers to the news desk for details on the story. In definition, these programs can be considered infomercials, albeit not exactly meeting the letter of the definition.

Other broadcasters as have adopted the model are:

- Meredith Corporation, which uses a modified form for their national/local hybrid program *Better*; the nationally-produced program was canceled in May 2015.
- Belo, which used a modified form on many of its stations, branded *Great Day (city)* in several markets; WFAA-TV in Dallas, Texas uses the name *Good Morning Texas* to have some similarity to *Good Morning America* as WFAA is an ABC affiliate, while NBC affiliate KGW in Portland, Oregon brands its program *Greater Portland Today* to have similarity with the *Today* show. These programs remain in production following Belo's merger with the broadcasting unit of the Gannett Company in 2013.
- LIN Media, which features the same format with localized titles on many of its stations (on WLUK-TV in Green Bay, Wisconsin, it is known as *Living with Amy*, while WNAC-TV in Providence, Rhode Island brands their program *The Rhode Show*, and Norfolk, Virginia station WVBT

titles their program *The Hampton Roads Show*). These two programs remain in production following LIN's merger with the broadcast unit of Media General in 2014, while *Living with Amy* remain in production following WLUK-TV sold to Sinclair Broadcast Group in 2014.
- Journal Broadcast Group stations acquired by the E.W. Scripps Company in April 2015 also feature a format called *The Morning Blend* on many of their stations, which is much closer to the *Daytime* format.

Infomercial companies

Traditional infomercial marketers (for example, Guthy-Renker and Telebrands) source the products, pay to develop the infomercials, pay for the media, and are responsible for all sales of the product. Sometimes, they sell products they source from inventors. Telebrands's process of bringing a product to the air and to market was seen in the 2009 Discovery Channel series *PitchMen*, which featured Billy Mays and Anthony Sullivan, along with the top executives of Telebrands.

There is also a well-developed network of suppliers to the infomercial industry. These suppliers generally choose to focus on either traditional infomercials (hard sell approaches) or on using infomercials as advertising/sales channels for brand companies (branded approaches). In the traditional business, services are usually supplied by infomercial producers or by media buying companies. In the brand infomercial business, services are often provided by full service agencies who deliver strategy, creative, production, media, and campaign services.

Use around the world

The infomercial industry was started in the United States and that has led to the specific definitions of infomercials as direct response television commercials of specific lengths (30, 60 or 120 seconds; five minutes; or 28 minutes and 30 seconds). Infomercials have spread to other countries from the U.S. However, the term "infomercial" needs to be defined more universally to discuss use in all countries. In general, worldwide use of the term refers to a television commercial (paid programming) that offers product for direct sale to consumer via response through the web, by phone, or by mail.

There are few structures that apply everywhere in the international infomercial business. The regulatory environment in each country as well as that country's television traditions have led to variations in format, lengths, and rules for long form commercials and television commercials selling direct to consumer. For example, in the early 1990s long form paid programming in Canada was required to consist only of photographs without moving video (this restriction no longer exists).

Many products which started in the United States have been taken into international distribution on television. In addition, each country has local entrepreneurs and marketers using the medium for local businesses. What may be called infomercials are most commonly found in North and South America, Europe, Japan and Southeast Asia.

In many countries, the infrastructure of direct response television distributors, telemarketing companies and product fulfillment companies (shipping, customer service) are more difficult and these missing pieces have limited the spread of the infomercial.

Research on effectiveness

Research has been conducted on consumer perceptions of infomercials. Agee and Martin (2001) found that infomercial purchases involved some degree of planning rather than being purely impulse purchases. Aspects of advertising content also influenced whether the purchase decision was impulsive or planned.[211] Martin, Bhimy and Agee (2002) studied the use of advertising content such as the use of testimonials and consumer characteristics. Based on a survey of 878 people who had bought products after viewing infomercials, they found that infomercials were more effective if they used expert comments, testimonials, product demonstrations, and other approaches. Consumer age and product type also influenced perceived effectiveness.[212]

References

Further reading

- Nathanson, Jon (November 14, 2013). "The Economics of Infomercials"[213]. *Priceonomics*. Retrieved November 15, 2013.

Big Pharma conspiracy theory

This article is about a conspiracy theory. For the pharmaceutical industry in general, see Pharmaceutical industry.

According to the **Big Pharma conspiracy theory** the medical establishment in general, and pharmaceutical companies in particular, operate for sinister purposes and against the public good.

History and definition

The term *Big Pharma* is used to refer collectively to global pharmaceutical industry. According to Steve Novella the term has come to connote a demonized form of the pharmaceutical industry. Professor of writing Robert Blaskiewicz has written that conspiracy theorists use the term *Big Pharma* as "shorthand for an abstract entity comprised of corporations, regulators, NGOs, politicians, and often physicians, all with a finger in the trillion-dollar prescription pharmaceutical pie".

According to Blaskiewicz, the Big Pharma conspiracy theory has four classic traits: first, the assumption that the conspiracy is perpetrated by a small malevolent cadre; secondly, belief that the public at large is ignorant of the truth; thirdly, that its believers treat lack of evidence as evidence; and finally, that the arguments deployed in support of the theory are irrational, misconceived or otherwise mistaken.

Manifestations

The conspiracy theory has a variety of different specific manifestations. Each has different narratives, but they always cast "Big Pharma" as the villain of the piece.

Alternative treatments

In *Natural Cures 'They" Don't Want You to Know About*, Kevin Trudeau proposes that there are all-natural cures for serious illnesses including cancer, herpes, arthritis, AIDS, acid reflux disease, various phobias, depression, obesity, diabetes, multiple sclerosis, lupus, chronic fatigue syndrome, attention deficit disorder, muscular dystrophy, and that these are all being deliberately hidden and suppressed from the public by the Food and Drug Administration, the Federal Trade Commission, and the major food and drug companies.[214]

HIV/AIDS

In a 2006 column for *Harpers* magazine, journalist Celia Farber claimed that the antiretroval drug nevirapine was part of a conspiracy by the "scientific-medical complex" to spread toxic drugs. Farber said that AIDS is not caused by HIV and that nevirapine had been unethically administered to pregnant women in clinical trials, leading to a fatality. Farber's theories and claims were refuted by scientists, but, according to Seth Kalichman, the resulting publicity represented a breakthrough moment for AIDS denialism.

Reception

Steven Novella writes that while the pharmaceutical industry has a number of aspects which justly deserve criticism, the "demonization" of it is both cynical and intellectually lazy. Novella considers that overblown attacks on *Big Pharma* actually let the pharmaceutical industry "off the hook" since they distract from and tarnish more considered criticisms.

Tammy Faye Messner

Tammy Faye Messner	
	Tammy Faye Messner in April 2004
Born	Tamara Faye LaValley March 7, 1942 International Falls, Minnesota
Died	July 20, 2007 (aged 65) Loch Lloyd, Missouri
Occupation	Christian singer, evangelist, entrepreneur, author, actress, television personality, co-founder of Heritage USA and PTL-The Inspirational Network
Years active	1962–2007
Spouse(s)	• Jim Bakker (1961–1992) • Roe Messner (1993–2007)
Children	Tammy Sue Bakker Chapman, Jamie Charles Bakker
Parent(s)	Carl LaValley and Rachel Fairchild
Website	tammyfaye.com[215]

Tamara Faye LaValley Bakker Messner (March 7, 1942 – July 20, 2007) was an American Christian singer, evangelist, entrepreneur, author, talk show host, and television personality. She was married from 1961 to 1992 to televangelist, and later convicted felon, Jim Bakker. She co-hosted with him on *The PTL Club* (1976–1987). She was a participant in the 2004 season of the reality show *The Surreal Life*.[216]

Early life

The eldest of eight children, Tammy Faye was born Tamara Faye LaValley in International Falls, Minnesota, to Pentecostal preachers Rachel Minnie (née Fairchild) and Carl Oliver LaValley. Her parents were married in 1941, one year before Tammy Faye was born. Shortly after she was born, a painful divorce soured her mother against other ministers,[217] alienating her from the church. After the divorce, Tammy Faye continued living in a strict atmosphere with her mother and brother. In 1948, when she was six, her mother married Fred Grover, who worked in paper mills. His salary increased their income, and the marriage also added six children to the household.Wikipedia:Citation needed

As a child in the 1950s, she helped her mother with household chores and babysat her younger siblings;Wikipedia:Citation needed but she was often spoiled by her favorite aunt, Virginia Fairchild, who was a retired department store manager.Wikipedia:Citation needed She attended her aunt's church in 1952.

When she was accompanied by a friend to the Assemblies of God church, at age 10, she said she "felt the glow of God's love and wanted to call herself upon the Lord."Wikipedia:Citation needed Her entire family gathered around her for celebrations, particularly Christmas, which was her favorite holiday. In 1956, she started spending summers at Bible camp and was voted "Queen". Also in 1956, she attended Falls High School, where she sang in the choir, and got an after-school job at Woolworth's. She didn't attend school dances, baseball games, or even movies, as her church did not allow it.Wikipedia:Citation needed Before she graduated in 1960, her mother suggested that Tammy Faye would become a minister.Wikipedia:Citation needed

Marriage to Jim Bakker

In 1960, she met Jim Bakker when they were students at North Central Bible College in Minneapolis, Minnesota.[218] Tammy Faye worked in a boutique for a time while Jim found work in a restaurant inside a department store in Minneapolis. They were married on April 1, 1961. The following year, they moved to South Carolina, where they began their ministry.

Their marriage produced two children, Tammy Sue (Sissy) Bakker Chapman (born 1970) and Jamie Charles (Jay) Bakker (born 1975).

PTL Club

Jim and Tammy Bakker had been involved with television from the time of their departure from Minneapolis until they moved to the Charlotte area via Portsmouth, Virginia, where they were founding members of the 700 Club. While in Portsmouth, they were hosts of the popular children's show "Jim and Tammy". They then created a puppet ministry for children on Pat Robertson's Christian Broadcasting Network (CBN) from 1964 to 1973 and co-founded the Trinity Broadcasting Network with personal friends Paul and Jan Crouch in California. Jim and Tammy founded the PTL Club (Praise The Lord) in the mid-1970s.

During the PTL shows, she provided a sentimental touch to stories and loved to sing. In a move that sharply distinguished her from other televangelists, she showed a more tolerant attitude regarding homosexuality, and she featured people suffering from AIDS on PTL, urging her viewers to follow Christ and show sympathy and pray for the sick. Wikipedia:Citation needed

PTL collapse

The Bakkers' control of PTL collapsed in 1987 after revelations that $287,000 had been paid from the organization to buy the silence of Jessica Hahn, who claims a forced sexual encounter with Jim Bakker.Wikipedia:Citation needed

The revelations invited scrutiny of the Bakkers, and charges made about their opulent lives, including media reports of an air-conditioned doghouse at their Tega Cay, South Carolina, lakefront parsonage as well as gold-plated bathroom fixtures, dominated newscasts in the 1980s. The Bakkers' home, owned by the ministry, was actually an older home built in the early 1970s, and it was a few miles away from Heritage USA.Wikipedia:Citation needed Jim Bakker stated that the much-talked-about dog house was heated with an old heater to keep the dogs warm in the winter and the reported gold-plated fixtures were actually brass.Wikipedia:Citation needed The home was later sold by the ministry and burned to the ground not long thereafter.Wikipedia:Citation needed Jim Bakker wrote in his book *I Was Wrong* that he watched the home burn on live television while incarcerated.

The epilogue from the publishers of this book contains the following:

> On July 22, 1996, shortly after Jim Bakker had completed the writing of this book, a federal jury ruled that PTL was not selling securities by offering Lifetime Partnerships at Heritage USA. The jury's ruling thus affirms what Jim Bakker has contended from the first day he was indicted and throughout this volume.

Wikipedia:Citation needed

The *Charlotte Observer* ran exposés of PTL's finances and management practices. PTL went bankrupt after being taken over by controversial Lynchburg, Virginia-based Baptist televangelist Jerry Falwell, who offered to step in following the scandals in 1988. Charges surfaced that Falwell's interest in PTL and Heritage USA was solely an attempt to gain control of its profitable cable television network, something which Falwell failed to establish for his own ministry despite numerous requests to the Federal

Communications Commission (FCC) for permission to obtain a satellite license.Wikipedia:Citation needed Tammy Faye later forgave Falwell regarding these tactics before Falwell's death in 2007, two months before Tammy Faye's own death.Wikipedia:Citation needed

After PTL

Marriage to Roe Messner

Tammy stood by Bakker through the scandal, including several instances when she cried on camera. In 1989 Bakker was sentenced to 45 years in prison on 24 fraud and conspiracy counts.

In 1992, while Bakker was still in prison she filed for divorce, saying in a letter to the New Covenant Church in Orlando, Florida:

> *For years I have been pretending that everything is all right, when in fact I hurt all the time...I cannot pretend anymore.*[219]

On October 3, 1993, she married Roe Messner in Rancho Mirage, California,[220] after Messner divorced his own wife. They moved to the Charlotte suburb of Matthews, North Carolina. Tammy and Roe were neighbors to Christian recording star and friend David L Cook.

Messner, who had a contracting business, Messner Enterprises, in the Andover, Kansas, suburb of Wichita, Kansas, had built much of Heritage USA as well as numerous other large churches and had been a family friend to the Bakkers throughout the PTL years.

Messner was the one who produced the money for the $265,000 payment to Hahn, later billing PTL for work never completed on the Jerusalem Amphitheater at Heritage USA.[221]

In the Bakkers' fraud trial, Messner testified for Bakker's defense saying that Falwell had sent Messner to the Bakker home in Palm Springs, California, to make an offer to "keep quiet."

According to Messner's testimony, Tammy wrote the offer on her stationery, listing a $300,000-a-year lifetime salary for Jim, $100,000 a year for Tammy, a house, and a year's worth of free phone calls and health insurance. However, Messner said that Bakker wrote on it: "I'm not making any demands on PTL. I'm not asking for anything.".[222,223] Falwell denied making any offer.

In the messy bankruptcy of PTL, Messner was listed as the single biggest creditor of PTL with an outstanding claim of $14 million. In court papers, the new operators accused Messner of $5.3 million in inflated or phony billings to PTL.[224]

Messner filed for personal and corporate bankruptcy in 1990, saying he owed nearly $30 million to more than 300 creditors. He wound up being convicted of bankruptcy fraud. As he faced sentencing in 1996, he said that he could not afford to treat his prostate cancer because he lacked health insurance.[225]

In July 2007, on more solid financial footing, the Messners relocated to a suburb of Kansas City, Missouri, the Village of Loch Lloyd, Missouri. Coincidentally, Jim Bakker had also moved to Missouri (in 2003), 200 miles southeast of Loch Lloyd in Branson, Missouri. Tammy Faye told *Entertainment Tonight* they had moved to the "dream house" to be closer to Roe's children and grandchildren from his first marriage. The children still live in the Wichita area.[226]

Back in the public eye

As her second husband was jailed and she was first diagnosed with colon cancer, she re-entered the public eye in a series of books, movies and television appearances.

In 1996 she wrote her autobiography, *Tammy: Telling It My Way* (ISBN 0679445153), and she co-hosted a TV talk show titled *The Jim J. and Tammy Faye Show* with Jim J. Bullock.

She was the subject of a documentary titled *The Eyes of Tammy Faye* (1999) and a follow-up film titled *Tammy Faye: Death Defying* (2004) from Lions Gate Entertainment.

She appeared twice on *The Drew Carey Show* in 1996 and 1999, playing the mother of character Mimi Bobeck (Kathy Kinney), who was also known for wearing excessive amounts of makeup.

On September 11, 2003, she published a new autobiography, *I Will Survive... and You Will, Too!* (ISBN 1585422428), in which she described her battles with cancer and her life with Messner.

In 2005, she appeared in an infomercial for alternative medicine promoter Kevin Trudeau. On her site, Tammyfaye.com she credits green supplements as a helpful part of her initial colon cancer remission.

Despite her background in Christian fundamentalism, Tammy Faye became a gay icon after her parting from PTL, appearing in Gay Pride marches with such figures as Lady Bunny and Bruce Vilanch. She supported the LGBT rights movement, including same-sex marriage.[227] She was benevolently referred to as "the ultimate drag queen," and said in her last interview with Larry King that, "When I went — when we lost everything, it was the gay people that came to my rescue, and I will always love them for that."

The Surreal Life

In early 2004, she appeared on the second season of the VH1 reality television series *The Surreal Life*. The show chronicled a twelve-day period wherein she, Ron Jeremy, Vanilla Ice, Traci Bingham, Erik Estrada and Trishelle Cannatella lived together in a Los Angeles house and were assigned various tasks and activities.

Together, the six put on a children's play and managed a restaurant for a day. She also attended a book signing for her best-seller, *I Will Survive... And You Will Too*.

At the end of the show, Messner said she thought of Vanilla Ice and Trishelle Cannatella as children and could relate to them deeply because she had similar feelings and problems when she was their age. She described porn star Jeremy as "a nice man."

Cancer

Tammy Faye's 11 years with cancer was highly publicized. She was first diagnosed with colon cancer in March 1996, and the disease went into remission by the end of that year.[228]

On March 19, 2004, Tammy Faye made an appearance on *Larry King Live* and announced that she had inoperable lung cancer and would soon begin chemotherapy.[229] She continued receiving chemotherapy throughout mid-2004. On November 30, 2004, also on *Larry King Live*, she announced that she was cancer free once again. She described the details of her chemotherapy and continued to appear regularly on King's show. A 2004 television documentary of her struggle with cancer was produced in 2004.[230] It was on King's program again that she announced, on July 20, 2005, that her cancer had returned.

On March 13, 2006, she appeared again on *Larry King Live* and stated that she was continuing to suffer from lung cancer, which had reached stage 4, and that she was continuing to receive treatment for it. She also mentioned having difficulty swallowing food, suffering from panic attacks, and enduring substantial weight loss. As her health continued to worsen, a "Talk of the Town" article in the October 2, 2006, issue of *The New Yorker* stated that she was dying in hospice care, and a December 10, 2006, article in Walter Scott's column in *Parade* reported that her son Jay was "at a North Carolina hospice with his mom, [who is] gravely ill with colon cancer".

Tammy Faye was a guest by phone on CNN's *Larry King Live* on December 15, 2006, and stated that she was receiving hospice care in her home. Tammy Faye appeared in her son Jay's documentary series *One Punk Under*

God, wherein she and Jay talked about her cancer treatments. In one episode, Tammy Faye required the use of oxygen in order to talk.

On May 8, 2007, she issued a statement on her website saying that chemotherapy had stopped, but urging her fans to continue to pray for her. The story was reported on NBC's *The Today Show* on May 11, and a feature in which fans and well-wishers could post get-well messages to Tammy was added to her website. As of July 2007, over 228 pages of wishes had been received.

On July 19, 2007, Tammy Faye made another appearance on CNN's *Larry King Live* in what turned out to be her final interview (she died the following day, just hours after the broadcast). At the time, she said she weighed 65 pounds and was unable to eat solid food. Messner's husband would later say that he believed that she chose to do the interview to say a final goodbye to her fans.

Death

On July 20, 2007, Messner died after 11 years with cancer.[231] What had started as colon cancer had spread to her lungs. She died in her home, said her publicist, Joe Spotts. A family service was held on the morning of July 21, 2007, in the Messner family plot in Waldron, Kansas.[232] The ceremony was officiated by the Rev. Randy McCain, the pastor of Open Door Community Church[233] in Sherwood, Arkansas. She had frequently spoken about her medical problems, saying she hoped to be an inspiration to others. "Don't let fear rule your life," she said. "Live one day at a time, and never be afraid." She had written on her website in May that the doctors had stopped trying to treat the cancer. She died the day after the airing of her interview on *Larry King Live* on CNN. According to CNN.com, the family requested that King officially report the news of her death on July 21, 2007. Her remains were cremated, and her ashes were returned to Waldron Cemetery where they were subsequently buried.

Legacy

In June 2006, a stage musical titled *The Gospel According to Tammy Faye* opened at the Cincinnati Fringe Festival and is currently being developed for a larger professional production.[234] The show features songs by J. T. Buck and a book by Fernando Dovalina. The musical is described as a fantasia which takes a balanced and fair look at its subject. The impetus for the show was provided by a lengthy interview that Messner gave the authors in March 2005.[235,236] The musical aired on August 2006 in Portland, Oregon, and Hood River, Oregon, it was presented on stage at Houston's Alley Theatre at the end of July 2007 under the direction of Les R. Wood. Industry readings presented by the Columbia Gorge Repertory Company were held at the Manhattan Theatre Club in December 2007 the cast including Tony nominee Sally Mayes and veteran Broadway performers William Youmans, Ken Land, Julie Foldesi, James T. Lane and Heather Parcells. The readings were directed by Mindy Cooper. Seth Farber provided musical direction.

Another musical following the life of Tammy Faye, titled *Big Tent*, debuted May 23, 2007 at Off-Broadway's New World Stages, in New York City. The show features music and lyrics by Ben Cohn, Sean McDaniel, a book by Jeffery Self, and direction by Ryan J. Davis.[237] A star-studded concert of songs from the show opened February 18, 2008 at New York's Metropolitan Room.[238]

Discography

Year	Album	Record Label
1970	Tammy Tammy Tammy	Hymntone Records
1977	Tammy Bakker Sings PTL Club Favorites	New Pax Records
1978	Love Never Gives Up	PAX Musical Productions
1979	We're Blest	PTL Club Records & Tapes
1980	Run Toward the Roar	PTL Club Records & Tapes
1980	The Lord's On My Side	PTL Club Records & Tapes
1982	Tammy Sings... You Can Make It!	PTL Club Records & Tapes
1982	Old Hymns	PTL Club Records & Tapes
1984	In the Upper Room	PTL Club Records & Tapes
1984	Movin' on to Victory	PTL Club Records & Tapes
1985	Don't Give Up!	PTL Club Records & Tapes
1986	Enough is Enough	PTL Club Records & Tapes
1987	The Ballad of Jim & Tammy	Sutra Records
19??	Peace in the Midst of the Storm	???
19??	Love, Tammy	???

External links

- Tammy Faye's Official Website and blog[239]
- National Public Radio *All Things Considered* The Re-Invention of Tammy Faye: Former Christian Broadcasting Queen Has New Gay Following[240] June 20, 2002 (Online article with audio of ATC story and video clip of film, *The Eyes of Tammy Faye*)

- Tammy Faye Messner Interview[241] at Archive of American Television
- Tammy Faye Messner (January 15, 2004). *Tammy Faye Messner : NPR*[242] (Audio). Interview with Terry Gross. Fresh Air. NPR. Retrieved July 25, 2007.
- Tammy Faye Bakker[243] at the Internet Movie Database

Nancy Valen

Nancy Valen	
Born	December 16, 1965 Brooklyn, New York, U.S.
Other names	Nancy Valin Nancy Van Patten
Occupation	Actress, producer
Years active	1985–present
Spouse(s)	Nels Van Patten (m. 1994)

Nancy Valen (born December 16, 1965) is an American actress and television producer. She is best known for portraying Captain Samantha Thomas on *Baywatch*.

Early life

Nancy Valen was born in Brooklyn, New York and raised in Hallandale, Florida. By the time she was 12 years old, she was spending summers modeling in New York City and studied acting at Uta Hagen's HB Studios. After graduating from a performing arts high school in Ft. Lauderdale, Florida, Valen won a theatrical scholarship to the University of Florida. She ultimately declined the scholarship in favor of continuing her professional career in Miami. Meanwhile, she attended Broward Community College, where she studied theatre and paid for her tuition by modeling and acting, appearing in two episodes of *Miami Vice*.

After one year of college, Valen went to New York to pursue a theatrical career. Within one month of being in New York, she landed a series regular role on the daytime drama *Ryan's Hope*. Valen stayed with *Ryan's Hope* for two years before moving to Los Angeles to pursue other interests.

Career

Acting

Valen made her film debut in *Porky's Revenge* (1985), followed by a role in *The Heavenly Kid* with Richard Mulligan and Jane Kaczmarek. In 1989, Valen co-starred alongside Patrick Dempsey in the film, *Loverboy*. She also had a small role opposite Kirk Cameron in the film *Listen to Me*. Her other film appearances include *Seven Sundays* alongside Molly Ringwald; directed by Academy Award-winning director, Jean-Charles Tacchella.

In addition to films, Valen has also appeared in various television series. In 1990, she guest starred in an episode of *Saved by the Bell* as the brand new school nurse at Bayside High, Jennifer. That same year, she co-starred in NBC's short-lived musical series *Hull High* under the direction of Kenny Ortega. After the series premiere, *TV Guide* proclaimed her "the most agreeably watchable new star on TV". Valen has also guest starred on 23 series including *Hardball*, *CSI: Crime Scene Investigation*, *Friends*, *Spin City*, *Boy Meets World*, *Miami Vice*, and *Murder She Wrote*.

Valen has also hosted several infomercials for the Bun and Thigh Roller, Slam man, Thin 'n Sexy Body Wrap, Kevin Trudeau's Debt Cures "They" Don't Want You To Know About, Time Life The Heart of Classic Rock, and the Instyler.

Valen has appeared as a guest on *Leno*, *The Oprah Winfrey Show*, *Good Day L.A.* and on the covers and pages of magazines and newspapers including *American Women*, *FHM*, *Cosmopolitan*, *Entertainment Weekly*, and The *Los Angeles Times* Calendar.

Producing

Valen, alongside Craig J. Nevius, formed Windmill Entertainment. Among the television programs she has produced include *Living in TV Land*, *Chasing Farrah*, *William Shatner in Concert*, and *Let's Kill Scott Baio*.

As an Executive Producer/reality series creator, Valen has partnered with a wide variety of companies including Whoop Inc., Renegade83, 44 Blue, Target, and Intuitive Entertainment. Currently Nancy is partnered with Authentic Entertainment on the series *WHEN STAMIE MET TRACY*. The series follows two former *L Word* stars as they raise their three children with their extended modern family. In addition, Valen works with Jarrett Creative Group in partnership with the Biography Channel for the networks' highest rated series, *Celebrity Ghost Stories* and the hit series, *Celebrity Close Calls*.

In the scripted world, Valen has partnered with VH1, ABC, FOX Television and Emmy award winning producer, Tony To. Valen is in development and is a Co-Executive Producer on *ACTION HEROES INC.* for ABC/Fox Studios. The action-comedy movie franchise stars William Shatner, Robert Wagner and Lee Majors as three former TV heroes turned real life detectives.

Personal life

Since October 1994, Valen has been married to Nels Van Patten (son of actor Dick Van Patten).Wikipedia:Citation needed

Filmography

Film

Year	Title	Role	Notes
1985	*Porky's Revenge!*	Ginger	
1985	*Heavenly Kid, TheThe Heavenly Kid*	Melissa	
1989	*Big Picture, TheThe Big Picture*	Young Sharon	
1989	*Loverboy*	Jenny Gordon	
1989	*Listen to Me*	Mia	
1992	*Final Embrace*	Candy Vale / Laurel Parrish	
1993	*Little Devils: The Birth*	Lynn	
1994	*Seven Sundays*	Nicky	
1998	*Black Thunder*	Mela	
2003	*Written in Blood*	Mary Ramson	
2007	*Wager, TheThe Wager*	Tanya Steele	

Television

Year	Title	Role	Notes
1985	*Miami Vice*	Lana	Episode: "The Home Invaders"
1986	*Ryan's Hope*	Melinda Weaver	1 episode
1988	*Charles in Charge*	Tammy	Episode: "Barbelles"
1989	*Murder, She Wrote*	Selina Williams Waverly	Episode: "Night of the Tarantula"

1989	Baywatch	Hallie	Episode: "Panic at Malibu Pier"
1990	Hull High	Donna Breedlove	Main role (8 episodes)
1990	Saved by the Bell	Jennifer	Episode: "From Nurse to Worse"
1991	Young Riders, TheThe Young Riders	Samantha Edgars	Episode: "Color Blind"
1991	Full House	Lisa Green	Episode: "Take My Sister, Please"
1992	Murder, She Wrote	Lily Roland	Episode: "Danse Diabolique"
1992	Perry Mason: The Case of the Fatal Framing	Mala Sikorski	TV film
1993	Silk Stalkings	Sylvia DeCastro	Episode: "Team Spirit"
1994	Silk Stalkings	Dr. Jillian Dupree	Episodes: "Natural Selection: Parts 1 & 2"
1994	Fortune Hunter	Madison Reynolds	Episode: "The Cursed Dagger"
1994	Walker, Texas Ranger	Laura	Episodes: "Something in the Shadows: Parts 1 & 2"
1994	Hardball	Jennifer	Episode: "Pilot"
1994	Boy Meets World	Ms. Kelly	Episode: "Pairing Off"
1995	Friends	Lorraine	Episode: "The One with the Candy Hearts"
1996-1997	Baywatch	Samantha Thomas	Main role (22 episodes)
1997	Viper	Bianca Carson	Episode: "Whistle Blower"
1998	Dune 2000	Fremen Kari (voice)	Video game
1999	Love Boat: The Next Wave, TheThe Love Boat: The Next Wave	Leslie	Episode: "Other People's Business"
2001	Black Scorpion	Det. Angela Archer / Angel of Death	Episode: "Kiss of Death"
2002	Spin City	Ashley	Episode: "Sex, Lies and Video Date"

External links

- Nancy Valen[244] at the Internet Movie Database
- Official website[245]
- Nancy Valen[246] on Twitter

Federal Trade Commission

Federal Trade Commission

Seal of the Federal Trade Commission

Flag of the Federal Trade Commission

Agency overview	
Formed	September 26, 1914
Preceding Agency	• Bureau of Corporations
Jurisdiction	Federal government of the United States
Headquarters	Washington, D.C.
Employees	1,131 (December 2011)
Agency executive	• Edith Ramirez, Chairman
Website	www.ftc.gov[247]
Footnotes	

The **Federal Trade Commission (FTC)** is an independent agency of the United States government, established in 1914 by the Federal Trade Commission Act. Its principal mission is the promotion of consumer protection and the elimination and prevention of anticompetitive business practices, such as coercive monopoly. The Federal Trade Commission Act was one of President Woodrow Wilson's major acts against trusts. Trusts and trust-busting were significant political concerns during the Progressive Era. Since its inception, the FTC has enforced the provisions of the Clayton Act, a key antitrust statute, as well as the provisions of the FTC Act, 15 U.S.C. § 41[248] et seq. Over time,

Figure 18: *Apex Building, built in 1938 (FTC headquarters) in Washington, D.C.*

the FTC has been delegated with the enforcement of additional business regulation statutes and has promulgated a number of regulations (codified in Title 16 of the Code of Federal Regulations).

Legislative development

Following the Supreme Court decisions against Standard Oil and American Tobacco in May 1911, the first version of a bill to establish a commission to regulate interstate trade was introduced on January 25, 1912, by Oklahoma congressman Dick Thompson Morgan. He would make the first speech on the House floor advocating its creation on February 21, 1912. Though the initial bill did not pass, the questions of trusts and antitrust dominated the 1912 election.[249] Most political party platforms in 1912 endorsed the establishment of a federal trade commission with its regulatory powers placed in the hands of an administrative board, as an alternative to functions previously and necessarily exercised so slowly through the courts.[250]

With the election decided in favor of the Democrats and Wilson, Morgan reintroduced a slightly amended version of his bill during the April 1913 special session. The national debate culminated in Wilson's signing of the FTC Act on September 26, with additional tightening of regulations in the Clayton Antitrust Act three weeks later. The new Federal Trade Commission would absorb the staff and duties of Bureau of Corporations, previously established under the Department of Commerce and Labor in 1903. The FTC could additionally challenge "unfair methods of competition" and enforce the Clayton Act's more specific prohibitions against certain price discrimination, vertical arrangements, interlocking directorships, and stock acquisitions.

Current membership

The following table lists commissioners as of June 2013.

Member	Political party	Sworn in	Term expiration
Edith Ramirez (Chair)	Democratic	April 5, 2010	September 25, 2015
Julie Brill	Democratic	April 6, 2010	September 25, 2016
Maureen K. Ohlhausen	Republican	April 4, 2012	September 25, 2018
Joshua D. Wright	Republican	January 11, 2013	September 25, 2019
Terrell McSweeny	Democratic	April 28, 2014	September 25, 2017

List of former Commissioners

Recent former commissioners were:

Commissioner	Years
Caspar Weinberger	December 31, 1969 – August 6, 1970
Philip Elman	April 21, 1961 – October 18, 1970
Miles W. Kirkpatrick	September 14, 1970 – February 20, 1973
Everette MacIntyre	September 26, 1961 – August 30, 1973
Mary Gardner Jones	October 29, 1964 – November 2, 1973
David J. Dennison, Jr.	October 18, 1970 – December 31, 1973
Mayo J. Thompson	July 8, 1973 – September 26, 1975
Lewis A. Engman	February 20, 1973 – December 31, 1975
Calvin J. Collier	March 24, 1976 – December 31, 1977
Stephen A. Nye	May 5, 1974 – May 5, 1978
Elizabeth Hanford Dole	December 4, 1973 – March 9, 1979
Paul Rand Dixon	March 21, 1961 – September 25, 1981
David Clanton	August 26, 1975 - October 14, 1983

Michael Pertschuk	April 21, 1977 – October 15, 1984
George W. Douglas	December 27, 1982 – September 18, 1985
James C. Miller III	September 25, 1982 – October 5, 1985
Patricia P. Bailey	October 29, 1979 – May 15, 1988
Margo E. Machol	November 29, 1988 – October 24, 1989 [recess appointment]
Daniel Oliver	April 21, 1986 – August 10, 1989
Terry Calvani	November 18, 1983 – September 25, 1990
Andrew Strenio	March 17, 1986 – July 15, 1991
Deborah K. Owen	October 25, 1989 – August 26, 1994
Dennis A. Yao	July 16, 1991 – August 31, 1994
Christine A. Varney	October 17, 1994 – August 5, 1997
Janet D. Steiger	August 11, 1989 – September 28, 1997
Roscoe B. Starek, III	November 19, 1990 – December 18, 1997
Mary L. Azcuenaga	November 27, 1984 – June 3, 1998
Robert Pitofsky	June 29, 1978 – April 30, 1981 & April 11, 1995 – May 31, 2001
Sheila F. Anthony	September 30, 1997 – August 1, 2003
Timothy Muris	June 4, 2001 – August 15, 2004
Mozelle W. Thompson	December 17, 1997 – August 31, 2004
Orson Swindle	December 18, 1997 – June 30, 2005
Thomas B. Leary	November 17, 1999 – December 31, 2005
Deborah Platt Majoras	August 16, 2004 – March 29, 2008
Pamela Jones Harbour	August 4, 2003 – April 6, 2010
William Kovacic	January 4, 2006 – October 3, 2011
J. Thomas Rosch	January 5, 2006 - Sept 2012
Jon Leibowitz	March 2, 2009 – March 7, 2013

Bureaus

Bureau of Consumer Protection

The Bureau of Consumer Protection's mandate is to protect consumers against unfair or deceptive acts or practices in commerce. With the written consent of the Commission, Bureau attorneys enforce federal laws related to consumer affairs and rules promulgated by the FTC. Its functions include investigations, enforcement actions, and consumer and business education. Areas of principal concern for this bureau are: advertising and marketing, financial products and practices, telemarketing fraud, privacy and identity protection, etc. The bureau also is responsible for the United States National Do Not Call Registry.

Under the FTC Act, the Commission has the authority, in most cases, to bring its actions in federal court through its own attorneys. In some consumer protection matters, the FTC appears with, or supports, the U.S. Department of Justice.

Bureau of Competition

The Bureau of Competition is the division of the FTC charged with elimination and prevention of "anticompetitive" business practices. It accomplishes this through the enforcement of antitrust laws, review of proposed mergers, and investigation into other non-merger business practices that may impair competition. Such non-merger practices include horizontal restraints, involving agreements between direct competitors, and vertical restraints, involving agreements among businesses at different levels in the same industry (such as suppliers and commercial buyers).

The FTC shares enforcement of antitrust laws with the Department of Justice. However, while the FTC is responsible for civil enforcement of antitrust laws, the Antitrust Division of the Department of Justice has the power to bring both civil and criminal action in antitrust matters.

Bureau of Economics

The Bureau of Economics was established to support the Bureau of Competition and Consumer Protection by providing expert knowledge related to the economic impacts of the FTC's legislation and operation.

Activities of the FTC

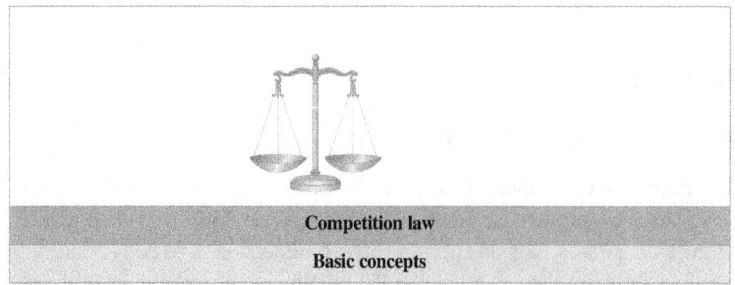

- History of competition law
- Monopoly
  - Coercive monopoly
  - Natural monopoly
- Barriers to entry
- Herfindahl–Hirschman Index
- Market concentration
- Market power
- SSNIP test
- Relevant market
- Merger control

Anti-competitive practices

- Monopolization
- Collusion
  - Formation of cartels
  - Price fixing
  - Bid rigging
- Product bundling and tying
- Refusal to deal
  - Group boycott
  - Essential facilities
- Exclusive dealing
- Dividing territories
- Conscious parallelism
- Predatory pricing
- Misuse of patents and copyrights

Enforcement authorities and organizations

- International Competition Network
- List of competition regulators

- Template:Competition law
- Template talk:Competition law
- 251

The FTC puts out its mission by investigating issues raised by reports from consumers and businesses, pre-merger notification filings, congressional inquiries, or reports in the media. These issues include, for instance, false advertising and other forms of fraud. FTC investigations may pertain to a single company or an entire industry. If the results of the investigation reveal unlawful conduct, the FTC may seek voluntary compliance by the offending business through a consent order, file an administrative complaint, or initiate federal litigation.

Traditionally an administrative complaint is heard in front of an independent administrative law judge (ALJ) with FTC staff acting as prosecutors. The case is reviewed *de novo* by the full FTC commission which then may be appealed to the U.S. Court of Appeals and finally to the Supreme Court.

Under the FTC Act, the federal courts retain their traditional authority to issue equitable relief, including the appointment of receivers, monitors, the imposition of asset freezes to guard against the spoliation of funds, immediate access to business premises to preserve evidence, and other relief including financial disclosures and expedited discovery. In numerous cases, the FTC employs this authority to combat serious consumer deception or fraud. Additionally, the FTC has rulemaking power to address concerns regarding industry-wide practices. Rules promulgated under this authority are known as *Trade Rules*.

In the mid-1990s, the FTC launched the fraud sweeps concept where the agency and its federal, state, and local partners filed simultaneous legal actions against multiple telemarketing fraud targets. The first sweeps operation was *Project Telesweep* in July 1995 which cracked down on 100 business opportunity scams.

In 1984,[252] the FTC began to regulate the funeral home industry in order to protect consumers from deceptive practices. The FTC Funeral Rule requires funeral homes to provide all customers (and potential customers) with a General Price List (GPL), specifically outlining goods and services in the funeral industry, as defined by the FTC, and a listing of their prices. By law, the GPL must be presented to all individuals that ask, no one is to be denied a written, retainable copy of the GPL. In 1996, the FTC instituted the Funeral Rule Offenders Program (FROP), under which "funeral homes make a voluntary payment to the U.S. Treasury or appropriate state fund for an amount less than what would likely be sought if the Commission authorized filing a lawsuit for civil penalties. In addition, the funeral homes participate in the NFDA compliance program, which includes a review of the price lists, on-site training of the staff, and follow-up testing and certification on compliance with the Funeral Rule."

One of the Federal Trade Commission's other major focuses is identity theft. The FTC serves as a federal repository for individual consumer complaints regarding identity theft. Even though the FTC does not resolve individual complaints, it does use the aggregated information to determine where federal action might be taken. The complaint form is available online or by phone (1-877-ID-THEFT).

The FTC has been involved in the oversight of the online advertising industry and its practice of behavioral targeting for some time. In 2011 the FTC proposed a "Do Not Track" mechanism to allow Internet users to opt-out of behavioral targeting.

In 2013, the FTC issued a comprehensive revision of its Green guides, which set forth standards for environmental marketing.

Figure 19: *Endorsement Guides from the FTC*

The FTC imposes civil penalties against companies that breach filing requirements, whether intentionally or not. Warren Buffett's Berkshire Hathaway agreed to a $856,000 civil penalty in August 2014 after failing to report in advance a December 2013 conversion of convertible notes. The FTC, in a statement referred to the matter as an "inadvertent error."

Unfair or deceptive practices affecting consumers

Section 5 of the Federal Trade Commission Act, 15 U.S.C. § 45[253] grants the FTC power to investigate and prevent deceptive trade practices. The statute declares that "unfair methods of competition in or affecting commerce, and unfair or deceptive acts or practices in or affecting commerce, are hereby declared unlawful." Unfairness and deception towards consumers represent two distinct areas of FTC enforcement and authority. The FTC also has authority over unfair methods of competition between businesses.

Deception practices

In a letter to the Chairman of the House Committee on Energy and Commerce, the FTC defined the elements of deception cases. First, "there must be a representation, omission or practice that is likely to mislead the consumer." In the case of omissions, the Commission considers the implied representations understood by the consumer. A misleading omission occurs when information is not disclosed to correct reasonable consumer expectations. Second, the Commission examines the practice from the perspective of a reasonable consumer being targeted by the practice. Finally the representation or omission must be a material one—that is one that would have changed consumer behavior.

In its 2000 Dot Com Disclosures guide, the FTC said that "[d]isclosures that are required to prevent deception or to provide consumers material information about a transaction must be presented clearly and conspicuously." The FTC suggested a number of different factors that would help determine whether the information was "clear and conspicuous" including:

- the **placement** of the disclosure in an advertisement and its **proximity** to the claim it is qualifying,
- the **prominence** of the disclosure,
- whether items in other parts of the advertisement **distract attention** from the disclosure,
- whether the advertisement is so lengthy that the disclosure needs to be **repeated**,
- whether disclosures in audio messages are presented in an adequate **volume and cadence** and visual disclosures appear for a sufficient **duration**, and
- whether the language of the disclosure is **understandable** to the intended audience.[254]

However, the "key is the overall net impression.

In *F.T.C. v. Cyberspace.com* the FTC found that sending consumers mail that appeared to be a check for $3.50 to the consumer attached to an invoice was deceptive when cashing the check constituted an agreement to pay a monthly fee for internet access. The back of the check, in fine print, disclosed the existence of this agreement to the consumer. The FTC concluded that the practice was misleading to reasonable consumers, especially since there was evidence that less than one percent of the 225,000 individuals and businesses billed for the internet service actually logged on.

In *In re Gateway Learning Corp.* the FTC alleged that Gateway committed unfair and deceptive trade practices by making retroactive changes to its privacy policy without informing customers and by violating its own privacy policy by selling customer information when it had said it would not. Gateway settled the complaint by entering into a consent decree with the FTC that required it to surrender some profits and placed restrictions upon Gateway for the following 20 years.

In *In the Matter of Sears Holdings Management Corp.*, the FTC alleged that a research software program provided by Sears was deceptive because it collected information about nearly all online behavior, a fact that was only disclosed in legalese, buried within the end user license agreement.

Unfair practices

Courts have identified three main factors that must be considered in consumer unfairness cases: (1) whether the practice injures consumers; (2) whether the practice violates established public policy; and (3) whether it is unethical or unscrupulous.[255]

FTC activities in the healthcare industry

In addition to prospective analysis of the effects of mergers and acquisitions, the FTC has recently resorted to retrospective analysis and monitoring of consolidated hospitals.[256] Thus, it also uses retroactive data to demonstrate that some hospital mergers and acquisitions are hurting consumers, particularly in terms of higher prices. Here are some recent examples of the FTC's success in blocking or unwinding of hospital consolidations or affiliations:

1. Phoebe Putney Memorial Hospital and Palmyra Medical Center in Georgia. In 2011, the FTC successfully challenged in court the $195 million acquisition of Palmyra Medical Center by Phoebe Putney Memorial Hospital.[257] The FTC alleged that the transaction would create a monopoly as it would "reduce competition significantly and allow the combined Phoebe/Palmyra to raise prices for general acute-care hospital services charged to commercial health plans, substantially harming patients and local employers and employees". The Supreme Court on February 19, 2013 ruled in favor of the FTC.
2. ProMedica health system and St. Luke's hospital in Ohio. Similarly, court attempts by ProMedica health system in Ohio to overturn an order by the FTC to the company to unwind its 2010 acquisition of St. Luke's hospital were unsuccessful.[258] The FTC claimed that the acquisition would hurt consumers through higher premiums because insurance companies would be required to pay more. In December 2011, an administrative judge upheld the FTC's decision noting that the behavior of ProMedica health system and St. Luke's was indeed anticompetitive and ordered ProMedica to divest St. Luke's to a buyer that would be approved by the FTC within 180 days of the date of the order.
3. OSF healthcare system and Rockford Health System in Illinois. In November 2011, the FTC filed a lawsuit alleging that the proposed acquisition of Rockford by OSF would drive up prices for general acute-care inpatient services as OSF would face only one competitor (SwedishAmerican health system) in the Rockford area and would have a market share of 64%.[259] Later in 2012, OSF announced that it had abandoned its plans to acquire Rockford Health System.

Further reading

- Davis, G. Cullom. "The Transformation of the Federal Trade Commission, 1914–1929," *The Mississippi Valley Historical Review*, (1962), 49#3 pp. 437–455 in JSTOR[260]
- MacLean, Elizabeth Kimball. "Joseph E. Davies: The Wisconsin Idea and the Origins of the Federal Trade Commission," *Journal of the Gilded Age and Progressive Era* (2007) 6#3 pp 248–284.

External links

Wikisource has the text of the 1922 Encyclopædia Britannica article *Federal Trade Commission*.

Wikimedia Commons has media related to *Federal Trade Commission*.

- Official website[247]
- Federal Trade Commission[261] in the Federal Register
- Consumer Complaint Assistant, Federal Trade Commission[262]
- Federal Trade Commission Decisions (July 1949 - December 2005)[263]
  This is a compendium of agency decisions in administrative cases brought under 16 C.F.R. parts II and III. Federal court decisions may be found elsewhere, in published federal case reports. The site's search engine can limit its results from the archive.
- Federal Trade Commission Identity Theft Complaint Form[264]

Food and Drug Administration

This article is about the United States Food and Drug Administration. For agencies with the same name in other countries, see Food and Drug Administration (disambiguation).

"FDA" redirects here. For other uses, see FDA (disambiguation).

Food and Drug Administration

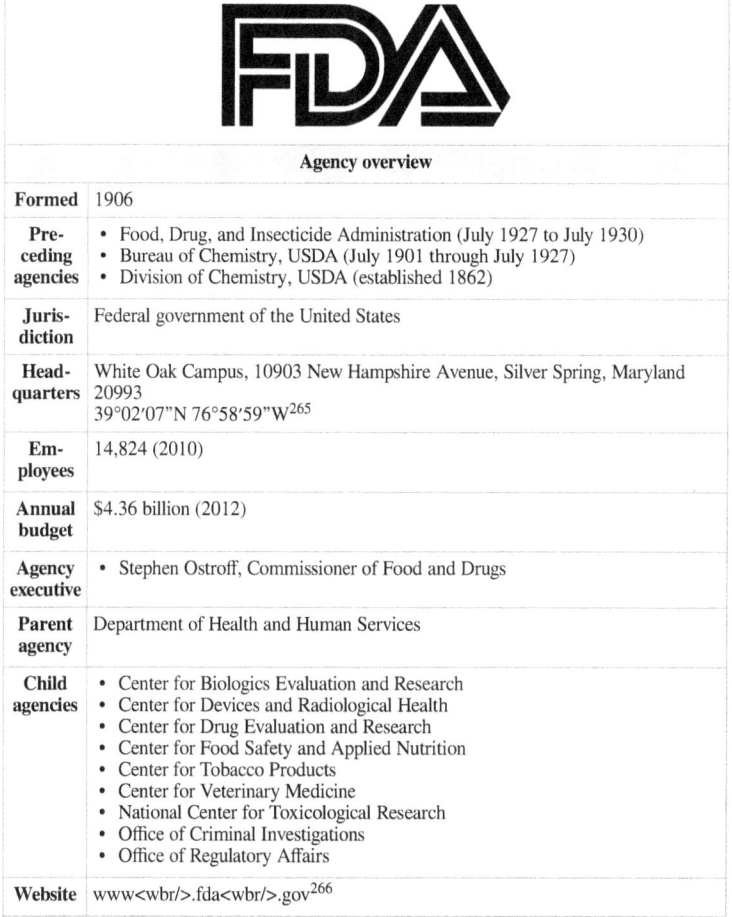

Agency overview	
Formed	1906
Preceding agencies	• Food, Drug, and Insecticide Administration (July 1927 to July 1930) • Bureau of Chemistry, USDA (July 1901 through July 1927) • Division of Chemistry, USDA (established 1862)
Jurisdiction	Federal government of the United States
Headquarters	White Oak Campus, 10903 New Hampshire Avenue, Silver Spring, Maryland 20993 39°02′07″N 76°58′59″W[265]
Employees	14,824 (2010)
Annual budget	$4.36 billion (2012)
Agency executive	• Stephen Ostroff, Commissioner of Food and Drugs
Parent agency	Department of Health and Human Services
Child agencies	• Center for Biologics Evaluation and Research • Center for Devices and Radiological Health • Center for Drug Evaluation and Research • Center for Food Safety and Applied Nutrition • Center for Tobacco Products • Center for Veterinary Medicine • National Center for Toxicological Research • Office of Criminal Investigations • Office of Regulatory Affairs
Website	www<wbr/>.fda<wbr/>.gov[266]

The **Food and Drug Administration** (**FDA** or **USFDA**) is a federal agency of the United States Department of Health and Human Services, one of the United States federal executive departments. The FDA is responsible for protecting and promoting public health through the regulation and supervision of food safety, tobacco products, dietary supplements, prescription and over-the-counter pharmaceutical drugs (medications), vaccines, biopharmaceuticals, blood transfusions, medical devices, electromagnetic radiation emitting devices (ERED), cosmetics, animal foods & feed and veterinary products.

The FDA was empowered by the United States Congress to enforce the Federal Food, Drug, and Cosmetic Act, which serves as the primary focus for the

Figure 20: *FDA Building 31 houses the Office of the Commissioner and the Office of Regulatory Affairs.*

Agency; the FDA also enforces other laws, notably Section 361 of the Public Health Service Act and associated regulations, many of which are not directly related to food or drugs. These include regulating lasers, cellular phones, condoms and control of disease on products ranging from certain household pets to sperm donation for assisted reproduction.

The FDA is led by the Commissioner of Food and Drugs, appointed by the President with the advice and consent of the Senate. The Commissioner reports to the Secretary of Health and Human Services. The Dr. Stephen Ostroff is the current acting commissioner, who took over for Dr. Margaret Hamburg who resigned in March 2015.

The FDA has its headquarters in unincorporated White Oak, Maryland. The agency also has 223 field offices and 13 laboratories located throughout the 50 states, the United States Virgin Islands, and Puerto Rico. In 2008, the FDA began to post employees to foreign countries, including China, India, Costa Rica, Chile, Belgium, and the United Kingdom.

Organization

The FDA is an agency within the Department of Health and Human Services. The agency consists of fourteen Centers and Offices:[267]

- Department of Health and Human Services
  - **Food and Drug Administration**
  - Office of the Commissioner
  - Office of Operations
    - Office of Equal Employment Opportunity
    - Office of Human Resources
    - Office of Finance, Budget and Acquisition
    - Office of Information Management and Technology
      - Office of Informatics & Technology Innovation
        - Director: Taha A. Kass-Hout (also holds post of Chief Health Informatics Officer for the FDA)
      -
      - Office of Information Management
    - Office of Security Operations
      - Office of Facilities Engineering and Mission Support Services
  - Office of Policy, Planning, Legislation, and Analysis
  - Office of Medical Products and Tobacco
  - Center for Biologics Evaluation and Research (CBER)
  - Center for Devices and Radiological Health (CDRH)
  - Center for Drug Evaluation and Research (CDER)
  - Center for Tobacco Products (CTP)
  - Office of Foods and Veterinary Medicine
  - Center for Veterinary Medicine (CVM)
  - Center for Food Safety and Applied Nutrition (CFSAN)
  - Office of Global Regulatory Operations and Policy (GO)
  - National Center for Toxicological Research (NCTR)
    - Office of Regulatory Affairs

Location

In recent years, the agency began undertaking a large-scale effort to consolidate its operations in the Washington Metropolitan Area, moving from its main headquarters in Rockville and several fragmented office buildings to the former site of the Naval Ordnance Laboratory in the White Oak area of Silver Spring, Maryland.[268] The site was renamed from the White Oak Naval Surface Warfare Center to the Federal Research Center at White Oak. The first building, the Life Sciences Laboratory, was dedicated and opened with 104 employees on the campus in December 2003. Only one original building from the naval facility was kept. All other buildings are new construction. The project is slated to be completed by 2014.

Regional facilities

While most of the Centers are located in the Washington, D.C. area as part of the Headquarters divisions, two offices – the Office of Regulatory Affairs (ORA) and the Office of Criminal Investigations (OCI) – are primarily field offices with a workforce spread across the country.

The Office of Regulatory Affairs is considered the "eyes and ears" of the agency, conducting the vast majority of the FDA's work in the field. Consumer Safety Officers, more commonly called Investigators, are the individuals who inspect production and warehousing facilities, investigate complaints, illnesses, or outbreaks, and review documentation in the case of medical devices, drugs, biological products, and other items where it may be difficult to conduct a physical examination or take a physical sample of the product.

The Office of Regulatory Affairs is divided into five regions, which are further divided into 20 districts. Districts are based roughly on the geographic divisions of the federal court system. Each district comprises a main district office and a number of Resident Posts, which are FDA remote offices that serve a particular geographic area. ORA also includes the Agency's network of regulatory laboratories, which analyze any physical samples taken. Though samples are usually food-related, some laboratories are equipped to analyze drugs, cosmetics, and radiation-emitting devices.

The Office of Criminal Investigations was established in 1991 to investigate criminal cases. Unlike ORA Investigators, OCI Special Agents are armed, and don't focus on technical aspects of the regulated industries. OCI agents pursue and develop cases where individuals and companies have committed criminal actions, such as fraudulent claims, or knowingly and willfully shipping known adulterated goods in interstate commerce. In many cases, OCI pursues cases involving Title 18 violations (e.g., conspiracy, false statements, wire fraud, mail fraud), in addition to prohibited acts as defined in Chapter III of the FD&C Act. OCI Special Agents often come from other criminal investigations backgrounds, and work closely with the Federal Bureau of Investigation, Assistant Attorney General, and even Interpol. OCI receives cases from a variety of sources—including ORA, local agencies, and the FBI—and works with ORA Investigators to help develop the technical and science-based aspects of a case. OCI is a smaller branch, comprising about 200 agents nationwide.

The FDA frequently works with other federal agencies, including the Department of Agriculture, Drug Enforcement Administration, Customs and Border Protection, and Consumer Product Safety Commission. Often local and state government agencies also work with the FDA to provide regulatory inspections and enforcement action.

Scope and funding

The FDA regulates more than US$1 trillion worth of consumer goods, about 25% of consumer expenditures in the United States. This includes $466 billion in food sales, $275 billion in drugs, $60 billion in cosmetics and $18 billion in vitamin supplements. Much of these expenditures are for goods imported into the United States; the FDA is responsible for monitoring imports.

The FDA's federal budget request for fiscal year (FY) 2012 totaled $4.36 billion, while the proposed 2014 budget is $4.7 billion. About $2 billion of this budget is generated by user fees. Pharmaceutical firms pay the majority of these fees, which are used to expedite drug reviews. The FDA's federal budget request for fiscal year (FY) 2008 (October 2007 through September 2008) totaled $2.1 billion, a $105.8 million increase from what it received for fiscal year 2007.

In February 2008, the FDA announced that the Bush Administration's FY 2009 budget request for the agency was just under $2.4 billion: $1.77 billion in budget authority (federal funding) and $628 million in user fees. The requested budget authority was an increase of $50.7 million more than the FY 2008 funding – about a three percent increase. In June 2008, Congress gave the agency an emergency appropriation of $150 million for FY 2008 and another $150 million.

Most federal laws concerning the FDA are part of the Food, Drug and Cosmetic Act, (first passed in 1938 and extensively amended since) and are codified in Title 21, Chapter 9 of the United States Code. Other significant laws enforced by the FDA include the Public Health Service Act, parts of the Controlled Substances Act, the Federal Anti-Tampering Act, as well as many others. In many cases these responsibilities are shared with other federal agencies.

Regulatory programs

> Regulation of therapeutic goods in the United States

Prescription drugs
Over-the-counter drugs

- v
- t
- e[269]

The programs for safety regulation vary widely by the type of product, its potential risks, and the regulatory powers granted to the agency. For example, the FDA regulates almost every facet of prescription drugs, including testing, manufacturing, labeling, advertising, marketing, efficacy, and safety—yet FDA regulation of cosmetics focuses primarily on labeling and safety. The FDA regulates most products with a set of published standards enforced by a modest number of facility inspections. Inspection observations are documented on Form 483.

Canada-United States Regulatory Cooperation Council

On February 4, 2011, Canadian Prime Minister Stephen Harper and United States President Barack Obama issued a "Declaration on a Shared Vision for Perimeter Security and Economic Competitiveness" and announced the creation of the Canada-United States Regulatory Cooperation Council (RCC) "to increase regulatory transparency and coordination between the two countries."

Health Canada and the United States Food and Drug Administration (FDA) under the RCC mandate, undertook the "first of its kind" initiative by selecting "as its first area of alignment common cold indications for certain over-the-counter antihistamine ingredients (GC 2013-01-10)."

Figure 21: *FDA Building 51 houses the Center for Drug Evaluation and Research.*

Regulation of food and dietary supplements

Main article: Regulation of food and dietary supplements by the U.S. Food and Drug Administration

The regulation of food and dietary supplements by the U.S. Food and Drug Administration is governed by various statutes enacted by the United States Congress and interpreted by the FDA. Pursuant to the Federal Food, Drug, and Cosmetic Act ("the Act") and accompanying legislation, the FDA has authority to oversee the quality of substances sold as food in the United States, and to monitor claims made in the labeling about both the composition and the health benefits of foods.

The FDA subdivides substances that it regulates as food into various categories—including foods, food additives, added substances (man-made substances that are not intentionally introduced into food, but nevertheless end up in it), and dietary supplements. Specific standards the FDA exercises differ from one category to the next. Furthermore, legislation had granted the FDA a variety of means to address violations of standards for a given substance category.

Drugs

The Center for Drug Evaluation and Research uses different requirements for the three main drug product types: new drugs, generic drugs, and over-the-counter drugs. A drug is considered "new" if it is made by a different manufacturer, uses different excipients or inactive ingredients, is used for a different purpose, or undergoes any substantial change. The most rigorous requirements apply to *new molecular entities*: drugs that are not based on existing medications.

New drugs

New drugs receive extensive scrutiny before FDA approval in a process called a New Drug Application (NDA). New drugs are available only by prescription by default. A change to over-the-counter (OTC) status is a separate process, and the drug must be approved through an NDA first. A drug that is approved is said to be "safe and effective when used as directed."

Some very rare limited exceptions to this multi-step process involving animal testing and controlled clinical trials can be granted out of compassionate use protocols, as was the case during the 2015 Ebola epidemic with the use, by prescription and authorization, of ZMapp and other experimental treatments, and for new drugs that can be used to treat debilitating and/or very rare conditions for which no existing remedies or drugs are satisfactory, or where there has not been an advance in a long period of time. The studies are progressively longer, gradually adding more individuals as they progress from stage I to stage III, normally over a period of years, and normally involve drug companies, the government and its laboratories, and often medical schools and hospitals and clinics. However, any exceptions to the aforementioned process are subject to strict review and scrutiny and conditions, and are only given if a substantial amount of research and at least some preliminary human testing has shown that they are believed to be somewhat safe and possibly effective. The results of these exceptions to the process, and also data during normal clinical trials, provide information for future experiments and eventual treatments, whether there are promising results or not in any given trial, which may or may not be statistically and clinically relevant.

Advertising and promotion

The FDA's Office of Prescription Drug Promotion reviews and regulates prescription drug advertising and promotion through surveillance activities and issuance of enforcement letters to pharmaceutical manufacturers. Advertising and promotion for over-the-counter drugs is regulated by the Federal Trade Commission.

The drug advertising regulation[270] contains two broad requirements: (1) a company may advertise or promote a drug only for the specific indication or medical use for which it was approved by FDA. Also, an advertisement must contain a "fair balance" between the benefits and the risks (side effects) of a drug.

The term off-label refers to drug usage for indications other than those approved by the FDA.

Postmarket safety surveillance

After NDA approval, the sponsor must review and report to the FDA every patient adverse drug experience it learns of. They must report unexpected serious and fatal adverse drug events within 15 days, and other events on a quarterly basis.[271] The FDA also receives directly adverse drug event reports through its MedWatch program.[272] These reports are called "spontaneous reports" because reporting by consumers and health professionals is voluntary.

While this remains the primary tool of postmarket safety surveillance, FDA requirements for postmarketing risk management are increasing. As a condition of approval, a sponsor may be required to conduct additional clinical trials, called Phase IV trials. In some cases, the FDA requires risk management plans for some drugs that may provide for other kinds of studies, restrictions, or safety surveillance activities.

Generic drugs

Generic drugs are chemical equivalents of name-brand drugs whose patents have expired. In general, they are less expensive than their name brand counterparts, are manufactured and marketed by other companies and, in the 1990s, accounted for about a third of all prescriptions written in the United States. For approval of a generic drug, the U.S. Food and Drug Administration (FDA) requires scientific evidence that the generic drug is interchangeable with or therapeutically equivalent to the originally approved drug. This is called an "ANDA" (Abbreviated New Drug Application). As of 2012 80% of all FDA approved drugs are available in generic form.

Generic drug scandal

In 1989, a major scandal erupted involving the procedures used by the FDA to approve generic drugs for sale to the public.[273] Charges of corruption in generic drug approval first emerged in 1988, in the course of an extensive congressional investigation into the FDA. The oversight subcommitee of the United States House Energy and Commerce Committee resulted from a complaint brought against the FDA by Mylan Laboratories Inc. of Pittsburgh.

When its application to manufacture generics were subjected to repeated delays by the FDA, Mylan, convinced that it was being discriminated against, soon began its own private investigation of the agency in 1987. Mylan eventually filed suit against two former FDA employees and four drug-manufacturing companies, charging that corruption within the federal agency resulted in racketeering and in violations of antitrust law. "The order in which new generic drugs were approved was set by the FDA employees even before drug manufacturers submitted applications" and, according to Mylan, this illegal procedure was followed to give preferential treatment to certain companies. During the summer of 1989, three FDA officials (Charles Y. Chang, David J. Brancato, Walter Kletch) pleaded guilty to criminal charges of accepting bribes from generic drugs makers, and two companies (Par Pharmaceutical and its subsidiary Quad Pharmaceuticals) pleaded guilty to giving bribes.

Furthermore, it was discovered that several manufacturers had falsified data submitted in seeking FDA authorization to market certain generic drugs. Vitarine Pharmaceuticals of New York, which sought approval of a generic version of the drug Dyazide, a medication for high blood pressure, submitted Dyazide, rather than its generic version, for the FDA tests. In April 1989, the FDA investigated 11 manufacturers for irregularities; and later brought that number up to 13. Dozens of drugs were eventually suspended or recalled by manufacturers. In the early 1990s, the U.S. Securities and Exchange Commission filed securities fraud charges against the Bolar Pharmaceutical Company, a major generic manufacturer based in Long Island, New York.

Over-the-counter drugs

Over-the-counter (OTC) drugs like aspirin are drugs and combinations that do not require a doctor's prescription.[274] The FDA has a list of approximately 800 approved ingredients that are combined in various ways to create more than 100,000 OTC drug products. Many OTC drug ingredients had been previously approved prescription drugs now deemed safe enough for use without a medical practitioner's supervision like ibuprofen.

Ebola Treatment

In 2014, the FDA added an Ebola treatment being developed by Canadian pharmaceutical company Tekmira to the Fast Track program, but halted the phase 1 trials in July pending the receipt of more information about how the drug works. This is seen as increasingly important in the face of a major outbreak of the disease in West Africa that began in late March 2014 and continued as of August 2014[275].

Figure 22: *The Center for Devices and Radiological Health*

Vaccines, blood and tissue products, and biotechnology

The Center for Biologics Evaluation and Research is the branch of the FDA responsible for ensuring the safety and efficacy of biological therapeutic agents.[276] These include blood and blood products, vaccines, allergenics, cell and tissue-based products, and gene therapy products. New biologics are required to go through a premarket approval process called a Biologics License Application (BLA), similar to that for drugs.

The original authority for government regulation of biological products was established by the 1902 Biologics Control Act, with additional authority established by the 1944 Public Health Service Act. Along with these Acts, the Federal Food, Drug, and Cosmetic Act applies to all biologic products, as well. Originally, the entity responsible for regulation of biological products resided under the National Institutes of Health; this authority was transferred to the FDA in 1972.

Medical and radiation-emitting devices

The Center for Devices and Radiological Health (CDRH) is the branch of the FDA responsible for the premarket approval of all medical devices, as well as overseeing the manufacturing, performance and safety of these devices.[277] The definition of a medical device is given in the FD&C Act, and it includes products from the simple toothbrush to complex devices such as implantable brain pacemakers. CDRH also oversees the safety performance of non-medical devices that emit certain types of electromagnetic radiation. Examples of CDRH-regulated devices include cellular phones, airport baggage screening equipment, television receivers, microwave ovens, tanning booths, and laser products.

CDRH regulatory powers include the authority to require certain technical reports from the manufacturers or importers of regulated products, to require that radiation-emitting products meet mandatory safety performance standards, to declare regulated products defective, and to order the recall of defective or noncompliant products. CDRH also conducts limited amounts of direct product testing.

"FDA-Cleared" vs "FDA-Approved"

Clearance requests are for medical devices that prove they are "substantially equivalent" to the predicate devices already on the market. Approved requests are for items that are new or substantially different and need to demonstrate "safety and efficacy", for example it may be inspected for safety in case of new toxic hazards. Both aspects need to be proved or provided by the submitter to ensure proper procedures are followed.

"FDA-Approved" vs. "FDA-Accepted in Food Processing"

The FDA does not approve applied coatings used in the food processing industry.[278] There is no review process to approve the composition of nonstick coatings, nor does the FDA inspect or test these materials. Through their governing of processes, however, the FDA does have a set of regulations that cover the formulation, manufacturing, and use of nonstick coatings. Hence, materials like Polytetrafluoroethylene (Teflon) are not, and cannot be, considered as FDA Approved, rather, they are "FDA Compliant" or "FDA Acceptable."

Cosmetics

Cosmetics are regulated by the Center for Food Safety and Applied Nutrition, the same branch of the FDA that regulates food. Cosmetic products are not, in general, subject to premarket approval by the FDA unless they make "structure or function claims" that make them into drugs (see Cosmeceutical). However, all color additives must be specifically FDA approved before manufacturers can include them in cosmetic products sold in the U.S. The FDA regulates cosmetics labeling, and cosmetics that have not been safety tested must bear a warning to that effect.

Cosmetic products

Though the cosmetic industry is predominantly responsible in ensuring the safety of its products, the FDA also has the power to intervene when necessary to protect the public but in general does not require pre-market approval or testing. Companies are required to place a warning note on their products if they have not been tested. Experts in cosmetic ingredient reviews also play a role in monitoring safety through influence on the use of ingredients, but also lack legal authority. Overall the organization has reviewed about 1,200 ingredients and has suggested that several hundred be restricted, but there is no standard or systemic method for reviewing chemicals for safety and a clear definition of what is meant by 'safety' so that all chemicals are tested on the same basis.

Veterinary products

The Center for Veterinary Medicine (CVM) is the branch of the FDA that regulates food, food additives, and drugs that are given to animals, including food animals and pets. CVM does not regulate vaccines for animals; these are handled by the United States Department of Agriculture. Wikipedia:Citation needed

CVM's primary focus is on medications that are used in food animals and ensuring that they do not affect the human food supply. The FDA's requirements to prevent the spread of bovine spongiform encephalopathy are also administered by CVM through inspections of feed manufacturers. Wikipedia:Citation needed

Tobacco products

Since the Family Smoking Prevention and Tobacco Control Act became law in 2009, the FDA also has had the authority to regulate tobacco products.[279]

In 2009, Congress passed a law requiring color warnings on cigarette packages and on printed advertising, in addition to text warnings from the U.S. Surgeon General.

The nine new graphic warning labels were announced by the FDA in June 2011 and were scheduled to be required to appear on packaging by September 2012. The implementation date is uncertain, due to ongoing proceedings in the case of R.J. Reynolds Tobacco Co. v. U.S. Food and Drug Administration. R.J. Reynolds, Lorillard, Commonwealth Brands Inc., Liggett Group LLC and Santa Fe Natural Tobacco Company Inc. have filed suit in Washington, D.C. federal court claiming that the graphic labels are an unconstitutional way of forcing tobacco companies to engage in anti-smoking advocacy on the government's behalf.

A First Amendment lawyer, Floyd Abrams, is representing the tobacco companies in the case, contending requiring graphic warning labels on a lawful product cannot withstand constitutional scrutiny. The Association of National Advertisers and the American Advertising Federation have also filed a brief in the suit, arguing that the labels infringe on commercial free speech and could lead to further government intrusion if left unchallenged. In November 2011, Federal judge Richard Leon of the U.S. District Court for the District of Columbia temporarily halted the new labels, likely delaying the requirement that tobacco companies display the labels. The U.S. Supreme Court ultimately could decide the matter.

Regulation of living organisms

With acceptance of premarket notification 510(k) k033391 in January 2004, the FDA granted Dr. Ronald Sherman permission to produce and market medical maggots for use in humans or other animals as a prescription medical device. Medical maggots represent the first living organism allowed by the Food and Drug Administration for production and marketing as a prescription medical device.

In June 2004, the FDA cleared *Hirudo medicinalis* (medicinal leeches) as the second living organism to be used as a medical devices.

The FDA also requires milk to be pasteurized to remove bacteria.

Science and research programs

In addition to its regulatory functions, the FDA carries out research and development activities to develop technology and standards that support its regulatory role, with the objective of resolving scientific and technical challenges before they become impediments. The FDA's research efforts include the areas of biologics, medical devices, drugs, women's health, toxicology, food safety and applied nutrition, and veterinary medicine.

Figure 23: *Harvey W. Wiley, chief advocate of the Food and Drug Act*

History

Main article: History of the Food and Drug Administration

Up until the 20th century, there were few federal laws regulating the contents and sale of domestically produced food and pharmaceuticals, with one exception being the short-lived Vaccine Act of 1813. The history of the FDA can be traced to the latter part of the 19th century and the U.S. Department of Agriculture's Division of Chemistry (later **Bureau of Chemistry**). Under Harvey Washington Wiley, appointed chief chemist in 1883, the Division began conducting research into the adulteration and misbranding of food and drugs on the American market. Wiley's advocacy came at a time when the public had become aroused to hazards in the marketplace by muckraking journalists like Upton Sinclair, and became part of a general trend for increased federal regulations in matters pertinent to public safety during the Progressive Era. The 1902 Biologics Control Act was put in place after a diphtheria antitoxin -derived from tetanus-contaminated serum- was used to produce a vaccine that caused the deaths of thirteen children in St. Louis, Missouri. The serum was originally collected from a horse named Jim who had contracted tetanus.

In June 1906, President Theodore Roosevelt signed into law the Food and Drug Act, also known as the "Wiley Act" after its chief advocate. The Act prohibited, under penalty of seizure of goods, the interstate transport of food that had been "adulterated". The act applied similar penalties to the interstate marketing of "adulterated" drugs, in which the "standard of strength, quality, or purity" of the active ingredient was not either stated clearly on the label or listed in the *United States Pharmacopoeia* or the *National Formulary*.[280]

The responsibility for examining food and drugs for such "adulteration" or "misbranding" was given to Wiley's USDA Bureau of Chemistry. Wiley used these new regulatory powers to pursue an aggressive campaign against the manufacturers of foods with chemical additives, but the Chemistry Bureau's authority was soon checked by judicial decisions, which narrowly defined the bureau's powers and set high standards for proof of fraudulent intent. In 1927, the Bureau of Chemistry's regulatory powers were reorganized under a new USDA body, the Food, Drug, and Insecticide organization. This name was shortened to the Food and Drug Administration (FDA) three years later.[281]

By the 1930s, muckraking journalists, consumer protection organizations, and federal regulators began mounting a campaign for stronger regulatory authority by publicizing a list of injurious products that had been ruled permissible under the 1906 law, including radioactive beverages, the mascara Lash lure, which caused blindness, and worthless "cures" for diabetes and tuberculosis. The resulting proposed law was unable to get through the Congress of the United States for five years, but was rapidly enacted into law following the public outcry over the 1937 Elixir Sulfanilamide tragedy, in which over 100 people died after using a drug formulated with a toxic, untested solvent.

President Franklin Delano Roosevelt signed the new Food, Drug, and Cosmetic Act (FD&C Act) into law on June 24, 1938. The new law significantly increased federal regulatory authority over drugs by mandating a pre-market review of the safety of all new drugs, as well as banning false therapeutic claims in drug labeling without requiring that the FDA prove fraudulent intent. Soon after passage of the 1938 Act, the FDA began to designate certain drugs as safe for use only under the supervision of a medical professional, and the category of "prescription-only" drugs was securely codified into law by the 1951 Durham-Humphrey Amendment. These developments confirmed extensive powers for the FDA to enforce post-marketing recalls of ineffective drugs.

In 1959, the thalidomide tragedy, in which thousands of European babies were born deformed after their mothers took that drug – marketed for treatment of nausea – during their pregnancies,[282] Considering the US was largely spared that tragedy because Dr. Frances Oldham Kelsey of the FDA refused to authorize the medication for market, the 1962 Kefauver-Harris Amendment to the FD&C Act was passed, which represented a "revolution" in FDA regulatory authority. The most important change was the requirement that all new drug applications demonstrate "substantial evidence" of the drug's efficacy for a marketed indication, in addition to the existing requirement for pre-marketing

Figure 24: *Medical Officer Alexander Fleming, M. D., examines a portion of a 240-volume new drug application around the late 1980s. Applications grew considerably after the efficacy mandate under the 1962 Drug Amendments.*

demonstration of safety. This marked the start of the FDA approval process in its modern form.

These reforms had the effect of increasing the time required to bring a drug to market. One of the most important statutes in establishing the modern American pharmaceutical market was the 1984 Drug Price Competition and Patent Term Restoration Act, more commonly known as the "Hatch-Waxman Act" after its chief sponsors. The act extended the patent exclusivity terms of new drugs, and tied those extensions, in part, to the length of the FDA approval process for each individual drug. For generic manufacturers, the Act created a new approval mechanism, the Abbreviated New Drug Application (ANDA), in which the generic drug manufacturer need only demonstrate that their generic formulation has the same active ingredient, route of administration, dosage form, strength, and pharmacokinetic properties ("bioequivalence") as the corresponding brand-name drug. This act has been credited with in essence creating the modern generic drug industry.

Concerns about the length of the drug approval process were brought to the fore early in the AIDS epidemic. In the mid- and late 1980s, ACT-UP and other HIV activist organizations accused the FDA of unnecessarily delaying the approval of medications to fight HIV and opportunistic infections. Partly in response to these criticisms, the FDA issued new rules to expedite approval of drugs for life-threatening diseases, and expanded pre-approval access to drugs for patients with limited treatment options. All of the initial drugs approved for the treatment of HIV/AIDS were approved through these accelerated approval mechanisms.

In two instances, state governments have sought to legalize drugs that have not been approved by the FDA. Under the theory that federal law passed pursuant to Constitutional authority overrules conflicting state laws, federal authorities still claim the authority to seize, arrest, and prosecute for possession and sales of these substancesWikipedia:Citation needed, even in states where they are legal under state law. The first wave was the legalization by 27 states of laetrile in the late 1970s. This drug was used as a treatment for cancer, but scientific studies both before and after this legislative trend found it to be ineffective. The second wave concerned medical marijuana in the 1990s and 2000s. Though Virginia passed a law with limited effect in 1979, a more widespread trend began in California in 1996.

21st century reforms

Critical Path Initiative

The Critical Path Initiative[283] is FDA's effort to stimulate and facilitate a national effort to modernize the sciences through which FDA-regulated products are developed, evaluated, and manufactured. The Initiative was launched in March 2004, with the release of a report entitled Innovation/Stagnation: Challenge and Opportunity on the Critical Path to New Medical Products.[284]

Patients' rights to access unapproved drugs

A 2006 court case, *Abigail Alliance v. von Eschenbach*, would have forced radical changes in FDA regulation of unapproved drugs. The Abigail Alliance argued that the FDA must license drugs for use by terminally ill patients with "desperate diagnoses," after they have completed Phase I testing. The case won an initial appeal in May 2006, but that decision was reversed by a March 2007 rehearing. The US Supreme Court declined to hear the case, and the final decision denied the existence of a right to unapproved medications.

Critics of the FDA's regulatory power argue that the FDA takes too long to approve drugs that might ease pain and human suffering faster if brought to market sooner. The AIDS crisis created some political efforts to streamline the approval process. However, these limited reforms were targeted for AIDS drugs, not for the broader market. This has led to the call for more robust and enduring reforms that would allow patients, under the care of their doctors, access to drugs that have passed the first round of clinical trials.

Post-marketing drug safety monitoring

The widely publicized recall of Vioxx, a non-steroidal anti-inflammatory drug now estimated to have contributed to fatal heart attacks in thousands of Americans, played a strong role in driving a new wave of safety reforms at both the FDA rulemaking and statutory levels. Vioxx was approved by the FDA in 1999, and was initially hoped to be safer than previous NSAIDs, due to its reduced risk of intestinal tract bleeding. However, a number of pre- and post-marketing studies suggested that Vioxx might increase the risk of myocardial infarction, and this was conclusively demonstrated by results from the APPROVe trial in 2004.

Faced with numerous lawsuits, the manufacturer voluntarily withdrew it from the market. The example of Vioxx has been prominent in an ongoing debate over whether new drugs should be evaluated on the basis of their absolute safety, or their safety relative to existing treatments for a given condition. In the wake of the Vioxx recall, there were widespread calls by major newspapers, medical journals, consumer advocacy organizations, lawmakers, and FDA officials[285] for reforms in the FDA's procedures for pre- and post- market drug safety regulation.

In 2006, a congressionally requested committee was appointed by the Institute of Medicine to review pharmaceutical safety regulation in the U.S. and to issue recommendations for improvements. The committee was composed of 16 experts, including leaders in clinical medicinemedical research, economics, biostatistics, law, public policy, public health, and the allied health professions, as well as current and former executives from the pharmaceutical, hospital, and health insurance industries. The authors found major deficiencies in the current FDA system for ensuring the safety of drugs on the American market. Overall, the authors called for an increase in the regulatory powers, funding, and independence of the FDA.[286,287] Some of the committee's recommendations have been incorporated into drafts of the PDUFA IV bill, which was signed into law in 2007.

As of 2011, Risk Minimization Action Plans (RiskMAPS) have been created to ensure risks of a drug never outweigh the benefits of that drug within the postmarketing period. This program requires that manufacturers design and implement periodic assessments of their programs' effectiveness. The Risk Minimization Action Plans are set in place depending on the overall level of risk a prescription drug is likely to pose to the public.

Pediatric drug testing

Prior to the 1990s, only 20% of all drugs prescribed for children in the United States were tested for safety or efficacy in a pediatric population. This became a major concern of pediatricians as evidence accumulated that the physiological response of children to many drugs differed significantly from those drugs' effects on adults. Children react different to the drugs because of many reason, including size, weight, etc. There were several reasons that not many medical trials were done with children. For many drugs, children represented such a small proportion of the potential market, that drug manufacturers did not see such testing as cost-effective.

Also, because children were thought to be ethically restricted in their ability to give informed consent, there were increased governmental and institutional hurdles to approval of these clinical trials, as well as greater concerns about legal liability. Thus, for decades, most medicines prescribed to children in the U.S. were done so in a non-FDA-approved, "off-label" manner, with dosages "extrapolated" from adult data through body weight and body-surface-area calculations.

An initial attempt by the FDA to address this issue was the 1994 FDA Final Rule on Pediatric Labeling and Extrapolation, which allowed manufacturers to add pediatric labeling information, but required drugs that had not been tested for pediatric safety and efficacy to bear a disclaimer to that effect. However, this rule failed to motivate many drug companies to conduct additional pediatric drug trials. In 1997, the FDA proposed a rule to require pediatric drug trials from the sponsors of New Drug Applications. However, this new rule was successfully preempted in federal court as exceeding the FDA's statutory authority.

While this debate was unfolding, Congress used the 1997 Food and Drug Administration Modernization Act to pass incentives that gave pharmaceutical manufacturers a six-month patent term extension on new drugs submitted with pediatric trial data. The act reauthorizing these provisions, the 2002 Best Pharmaceuticals for Children Act, allowed the FDA to request NIH-sponsored testing for pediatric drug testing, although these requests are subject to NIH funding constraints. In the Pediatric Research Equity Act of 2003, Congress codified the FDA's authority to mandate manufacturer-sponsored pediatric drug trials for certain drugs as a "last resort" if incentives and publicly funded mechanisms proved inadequate.

Rules for generic biologics

Since the 1990s, many successful new drugs for the treatment of cancer, autoimmune diseases, and other conditions have been protein-based biotechnology drugs, regulated by the Center for Biologics Evaluation and Research. Many of these drugs are extremely expensive; for example, the anti-cancer drug Avastin costs $55,000 for a year of treatment, while the enzyme replacement therapy drug Cerezyme costs $200,000 per year, and must be taken by Gaucher's Disease patients for life.

Biotechnology drugs do not have the simple, readily verifiable chemical structures of conventional drugs, and are produced through complex, often proprietary techniques, such as transgenic mammalian cell cultures. Because of these complexities, the 1984 Hatch-Waxman Act did not include biologics in the Abbreviated New Drug Application (ANDA) process, in essence precluding the possibility of generic drug competition for biotechnology drugs. In February 2007, identical bills were introduced into the House to create an ANDA process for the approval of generic biologics, but were not passed.

Mobile medical applications

In 2013, a guidance was issued to regulate mobile medical applications and protect users from their unintended use. This guidance distinguishes the apps subjected to regulation based on the marketing claims of the apps. Incorporation of the guidelines during the development phase of such app has been proposed for expedite market entry and clearance.

Criticisms

Main article: Criticism of the Food and Drug Administration

 Wikinews has related news: *Obama calls food safety system a 'hazard to public health'*

The FDA has regulatory oversight over a large array of products that affect the health and life of American citizens. As a result, the FDA's powers and decisions are carefully monitored by several governmental and non-governmental organizations. A $1.8 million 2006 Institute of Medicine report on pharmaceutical regulation in the U.S. found major deficiencies in the current FDA system for ensuring the safety of drugs on the American market. Overall, the authors called for an increase in the regulatory powers, funding, and independence of the FDA.[288,289]

Nine FDA scientists appealed to then president-elect Barack Obama over pressures from management, experienced during the George W. Bush presidency, to manipulate data, including in relation to the review process for medical devices. Characterized as "corrupted and distorted by current FDA managers, thereby placing the American people at risk," these concerns were also highlighted in the 2006 report on the agency as well.

The FDA has also been criticized from the opposite viewpoint, as being too tough on industry. According to an analysis published on the website of the libertarian Mercatus Center as well as published statements by economists, medical practitioners, and concerned consumers, many feel the FDA oversteps its regulatory powers and undermines small business and small farms in favor of large corporations. Three of the FDA restrictions under analysis are the permitting of new drugs and devices, the control of manufacturer speech, and the imposition of prescription requirements. The authors argue that in the increasingly complex and diverse food marketplace, the FDA is not equipped to adequately regulate or inspect food.Wikipedia:Verifiability

However, in an indicator that the FDA may be too lax in their approval process, in particular for medical devices, a 2011 study by Dr. Diana Zuckerman and Paul Brown of the National Research Center for Women and Families, and Dr. Steven Nissen of the Cleveland Clinic, published in the Archives of Internal Medicine, showed that most medical devices recalled in the last five years for "serious health problems or death" had been previously approved by the FDA using the less stringent, and cheaper, 510(k) process. In a few cases the devices had been deemed so low-risk that they did not need FDA regulation. Of the 113 devices recalled, 35 were for cardiovascular health purposes.

Further reading

- Givel, Michael (December 2005). "Philip Morris' FDA Gambit: Good for Public Health?" *Journal of Public Health Policy* (26): pp. 450–468
- Henninger, Daniel (2002). "Drug Lag"[290]. In David R. Henderson (ed.). *Concise Encyclopedia of Economics* (1st ed.). Library of Economics and Liberty. OCLC 317650570[291], 50016270[292] and 163149563[293]
- Hilts, Philip J. (2003). *Protecting America's Health: The FDA, Business, and One Hundred Years of Regulation.* New York: Alfred E. Knopf. ISBN 0-375-40466-X
- Madden, Bartley (2010) *Free To Choose Medicine: How Faster Access to New Drugs Would Save Countless Lives and End Needless Suffering* Chicago: The Heartland Institute. ISBN 978-1-934791-32-5
- Moore, Thomas J. (1998). *Prescription for Disaster: The Hidden Dangers in Your Medicine Cabinet.* New York: Simon & Schuster. ISBN 0-684-82998-3

- Kevin Fain, Matthew Daubresse, G. Caleb Alexander (2013). "The Food and Drug Administration Amendments Act and Postmarketing Commitments." "JAMA" 310(2): 202-204 doi:10.1001/jama.2013.7900.

External links

 Wikimedia Commons has media related to *Food and Drug Administration (United States)*.

 Wikinews has news related to: *Food and Drug Administration*

- Official website[266]
- Food and Drug Administration[294] in the Federal Register
- FDA Organizational Hierarchy Chart[295] in PDF format
- Strategic Plan[296]

Coordinates: 39°02′07″N 76°58′59″W[297]

Pharmaceutical industry

The **pharmaceutical industry** develops, produces, and markets drugs or pharmaceuticals for use as medications.[298] Pharmaceutical companies may deal in generic or brand medications and medical devices. They are subject to a variety of laws and regulations that govern the patenting, testing, safety, efficacy and marketing of drugs.

History

Mid-1800s – 1945: From botanicals to the first synthetic drugs

The modern pharmaceutical industry traces its roots to two sources. The first of these were local apothecaries that expanded from their traditional role distributing botanical drugs such as morphine and quinine to wholesale manufacture in the mid 1800s. Multinational corporations including Merck, Hoffman-La Roche, Burroughs-Wellcome (now part of Glaxo Smith Kline), Abbott Laboratories, Eli Lilly and Upjohn (now part of Pfizer) began as local apothecary shops in the mid-1800s. By the late 1880s, German dye manufacturers had perfected the purification of individual organic compounds from coal tar and

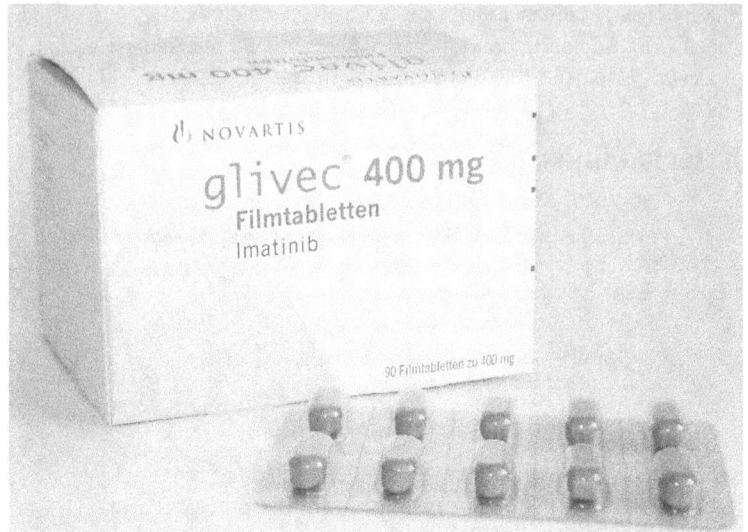

Figure 25: *Gleevec, a drug used in the treatment of several cancers, is marketed by Novartis, one of the world's major pharmaceutical companies.*

other mineral sources and had also established rudimentary methods in organic chemical synthesis. The development of synthetic chemical methods allowed scientists to systematically vary the structure of chemical substances, and growth in the emerging science of pharmacology expanded their ability to evaluate the biological effects of these structural changes.

Epinephrine, norepinephrine, and amphetamine

By the 1890s the profound effect of adrenal extracts on many different tissue types had been discovered, setting off a search both for the mechanism of chemical signalling and efforts to exploit these observations for the development of new drugs. The blood pressure raising and vasoconstrictive effects of adrenal extracts were of particular interest to surgeons as hemostatic agents and as treatment for shock, and a number of companies developed products based on adrenal extracts containing varying purities of the active substance. In 1897 John Abel of Johns Hopkins University identified the active principle as epinephrine, which he isolated in an impure state as the sulfate salt. Industrial chemist Jokichi Takamine later developed a method for obtaining epinephrine in a pure state, and licensed the technology to Parke Davis. Parke Davis marketed epinephrine under the trade name Adrenalin. Injected epinephrine proved to be especially efficacious for the acute treatment of asthma attacks, and an inhaled version was sold in the United States

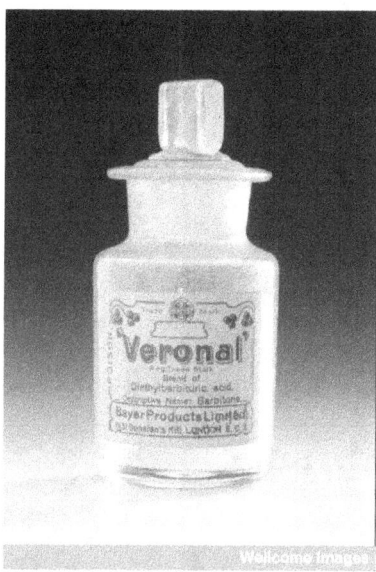

Figure 26: *Diethylbarbituric acid was the first marketed barbiturate. It was sold by Bayer under the trade name Veronal*

until 2011 (Primatene Mist). By 1929 epinephrine had been formulated into an inhaler for use in the treatment of nasal congestion.

While highly effective, the requirement for injection limited the use of norepinephrineWikipedia:Please clarify and orally active derivatives were sought. A structurally similar compound, ephedrine, was identified by Japanese chemists in the *Ma Huang* plant and marketed by Eli Lilly as an oral treatment for asthma. Following the work of Henry Dale and George Barger at Burroughs-Wellcome, academic chemist Gordon Alles synthesized amphetamine and tested it in asthma patients in 1929. The drug proved to have only modest anti-asthma effects, but produced sensations of exhilaration and palpitations. Amphetamine was developed by Smith, Kline and French as a nasal decongestant under the trade name Benzedrine Inhaler. Amphetamine was eventually developed for the treatment of narcolepsy, post-encepheletic parkinsonism, and mood elevation in depression and other psychiatric indications. It received approval as a New and Nonofficial Remedy from the American Medical Association for these uses in 1937 and remained in common use for depression until the development of tricyclic antidepressants in the 1960s.

Discovery and development of the barbiturates

In 1903 Hermann Emil Fischer and Joseph von Mering disclosed their discovery that diethylbarbituric acid, formed from the reaction of diethylmalonic acid, phosphorus oxychloride and urea, induces sleep in dogs. The discovery was patented and licensed to Bayer pharmaceuticals, which marketed the compound under the trade name Veronal as a sleep aid beginning in 1904. Systematic investigations of the effect of structural changes on potency and duration of action led to the discovery of phenobarbital at Bayer in 1911 and the discovery of its potent anti-epileptic activity in 1912. Phenobarbital was among the most widely used drugs for the treatment of epilepsy through the 1970s, and as of 2014, remains on the World Health Organizations list of essential medications. The 1950s and 1960s saw increased awareness of the addictive properties and abuse potential of barbiturates and amphetamines and led to increasing restrictions on their use and growing government oversight of prescribers. Today, amphetamine is largely restricted to use in the treatment of attention deficit disorder and phenobarbital in the treatment of epilepsy.

Insulin

A series of experiments performed from the late 1800s to the early 1900s revealed that diabetes is caused by the absence of a substance normally produced by the pancreas. In 1869, Oskar Minkowski and Joseph von Mering found that diabetes could be induced in dogs by surgical removal of the pancreas. In 1921, Canadian professor Frederick Banting and his student Charles Best repeated this study, and found that injections of pancreatic extract reversed the symptoms produced by pancreas removal. Soon, the extract was demonstrated to work in people, but development of insulin therapy as a routine medical procedure was delayed by difficulties in producing the material in sufficient quantity and with reproducible purity. The researchers sought assistance from industrial collaborators at Eli Lilly and Co. based on the company's experience with large scale purification of biological materials. Chemist George Walden of Eli Lilly and Company found that careful adjustment of the pH of the extract allowed a relatively pure grade of insulin to be produced. Under pressure from Toronto University and a potential patent challenge by academic scientists who had independently developed a similar purification method, an agreement was reached for non-exclusive production of insulin by multiple companies. Prior to the discovery and widespread availability of insulin therapy the life expectancy of diabetics was only a few months.

Early anti-infective research: Salvarsan, Prontosil, Penicillin and vaccines

The development of drugs for the treatment of infectious diseases was a major focus of early research and development efforts; in 1900 pneumonia, tuberculosis, and diarrhea were the three leading causes of death in the United States and mortality in the first year of life exceeded 10%.

In 1911 arsphenamine, the first synthetic anti-infective drug, was developed by Paul Ehrlich and chemist Alfred Bertheim of the Institute of Experimental Therapy in Berlin. The drug was given the commercial name Salvarsan. Ehrlich, noting both the general toxicity of arsenic and the selective absorption of certain dyes by bacteria, hypothesized that an arsenic-containing dye with similar selective absorption properties could be used to treat bacterial infections. Arsphenamine was prepared as part of a campaign to synthesize a series of such compounds, and found to exhibit partially selective toxicity. Arsphenamine proved to be the first effective treatment for syphilis, a disease which prior to that time was incurable and led inexorably to severe skin ulceration, neurological damage, and death.

Ehrlich's approach of systematically varying the chemical structure of synthetic compounds and measuring the effects of these changes on biological activity was pursued broadly by industrial scientists, including Bayer scientists Josef Klarer, Fritz Mietzsch, and Gerhard Domagk. This work, also based in the testing of compounds available from the German dye industry, led to the development of Prontosil, the first representative of the sulfonamide class of antibiotics. Compared to arsphenamine, the sulfonamides had a broader spectrum of activity and were far less toxic, rendering them useful for infections caused by pathogens such as streptococci. In 1939, Domagk received the Nobel Prize in Medicine for this discovery.[299,300] Nonetheless, the dramatic decrease in deaths from infectious diseases that occurred prior to World War II was primarily the result of improved public health measures such as clean water and less crowded housing, and the impact of anti-infective drugs and vaccines was significant mainly after World War II.

In 1928, Alexander Fleming discovered the antibacterial effects of penicillin, but its exploitation for the treatment of human disease awaited the development of methods for its large scale production and purification. These were developed by a U.S. and British government-led consortium of pharmaceutical companies during the Second World War.[301]

Early progress toward the development of vaccines occurred throughout this period, primarily in the form of academic and government-funded basic research directed toward the identification of the pathogens responsible for common communicable diseases. In 1885 Louis Pasteur and Pierre Paul Émile

Figure 27: *In 1937 over 100 people died after ingesting a solution of the antibacterial sulfanilamide formulated in the toxic solvent diethylene glycol*

Roux created the first rabies vaccine. The first diphtheria vaccines were produced in 1914 from a mixture of diphtheria toxin and antitoxin (produced from the serum of an inoculated animal), but the safety of the inoculation was marginal and it was not widely used. The United States recorded 206,000 cases of diphtheria in 1921 resulting in 15,520 deaths. In 1923 parallel efforts by Gaston Ramon at the Pasteur Institute and Alexander Glenny at the Wellcome Research Laboratories (later part of GlaxoSmithKline) led to the discovery that a safer vaccine could be produced by treating diphtheria toxin with formaldehyde. In 1944, Maurice Hilleman of Squibb Pharmaceuticals developed the first vaccine against Japanese encephelitis. Hilleman would later move to Merck where he would play a key role in the development of vaccines against measles, mumps, chickenpox, rubella, hepatitis A, hepatitis B, and meningitis.

Unsafe drugs and early industry regulation

Prior to the 20th century drugs were generally produced by small scale manufacturers with little regulatory control over manufacturing or claims of safety and efficacy. To the extent that such laws did exist, enforcement was lax. In the United States, increased regulation of vaccines and other biological drugs was spurred by tetanus outbreaks and deaths caused by the distribution of contaminated smallpox vaccine and diphtheria antitoxin. The Biologics Control Act of 1902 required that federal government grant premarket approval for every biological drug and for the process and facility producing such drugs. This was followed in 1906 by the Pure Food and Drugs Act, which forbade the interstate distribution of adulterated or misbranded foods and drugs. A drug was considered misbranded if it contained alcohol, morphine, opium, cocaine, or any of several other potentially dangerous or addictive drugs, and if its label failed to indicate the quantity or proportion of such drugs. The government's attempts to use the law to prosecute manufacturers for making unsupported claims of efficacy were undercut by a Supreme Court ruling restricting the federal government's enforcement powers to cases of incorrect specification of the drug's ingredients.

In 1937 over 100 people died after ingesting "Elixir Sulfanilamide" manufactured by S.E. Massengill Company of Tennessee. The product was formulated in diethylene glycol, a highly toxic solvent that is now widely used as antifreeze. Under the laws extant at that time, prosecution of the manufacturer was possible only under the technicality that the product had been called an "elixir", which literally implied a solution in ethanol. In response to this episode, the U.S. Congress passed the Federal Food, Drug, and Cosmetic Act of 1938, which for the first time required pre-market demonstration of safety before a drug could be sold, and explicitly prohibited false therapeutic claims.

The post-war years, 1945–1970

Further advances in anti-infective research

The aftermath of World War II saw an explosion in the discovery of new classes of antibacterial drugs including the cephalosporins (developed by Eli Lilly based on the seminal work of Giuseppe Brotzu and Edward Abraham), streptomycin (discovered during a Merck-funded research program in Selman Waksman's laboratory), the tetracyclines (discovered at Lederle Laboratories, now a part of Pfizer), erythromycin (discovered at Eli Lilly and Co.) and their extension to an increasingly wide range of bacterial pathogens. Streptomycin, discovered during a Merck-funded research program in Selman Waksman's laboratory at Rutgers in 1943, became the first effective treatment for tuberculosis. At the time of its discovery, sanitoriums for the isolation of tuberculosis-infected people were an ubiquitous feature of cities in developed countries, with 50% dying within 5 years of admission.[302]

A Federal Trade Commission report issued in 1958 attempted to quantify the effect of antibiotic development on American public health. The report found that over the period 1946-1955, there was a 42% drop in the incidence of

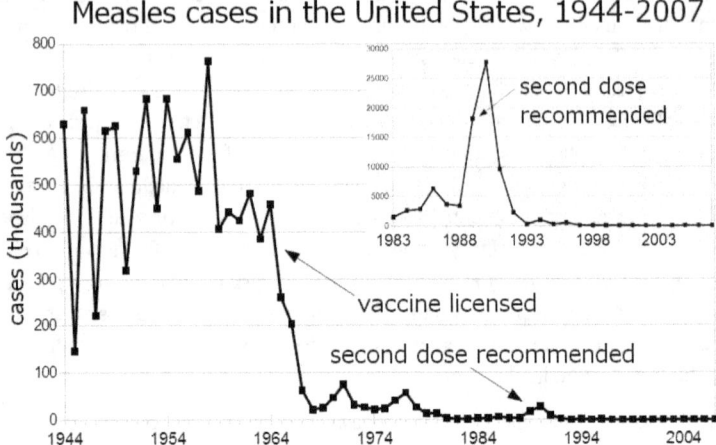

Figure 28: *Measles cases reported in the United States before and after introduction of the vaccine.*

diseases for which antibiotics were effective and only a 20% drop in those for which antibiotics were not effective. The report concluded that "it appears that the use of antibiotics, early diagnosis, and other factors have limited the epidemic spread and thus the number of these diseases which have occurred". The study further examined mortality rates for eight common diseases for which antibiotics offered effective therapy (syphilis, tuberculosis, dysentery, scarlet fever, whooping cough, meningococcal infections, and pneumonia), and found a 56% decline over the same period.[303] Notable among these was a 75% decline in deaths due to tuberculosis.[304]

During the years 1940-1955, the rate of decline in the U.S. death rate accelerated from 2% per year to 8% per year, then returned to the historical rate of 2% per year. The dramatic decline in the immediate post-war years has been attributed to the rapid development of new treatments and vaccines for infectious disease that occurred during these years. Vaccine development continued to accelerate, with the most notable achievement of the period being Jonas Salk's 1954 development of the polio vaccine under the funding of the non-profit National Foundation for Infantile Paralysis. The vaccine process was never patented, but was instead given to pharmaceutical companies to manufacture as a low-cost generic. In 1960 Maurice Hilleman of Merck Sharp & Dohme identified the SV40 virus, which was later shown to cause tumors in many mammalian species. It was later determined that SV40 was present as a contaminant in polio vaccine lots that had been administered to 90% of the

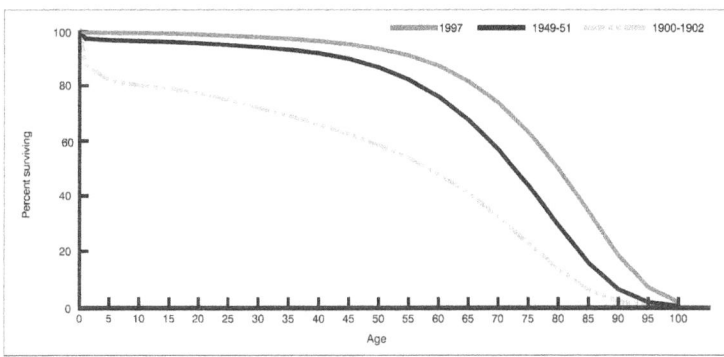

Figure 29: *Percent surviving by age in 1900, 1950, and 1997.*

children in the United States. The contamination appears to have originated both in the original cell stock and in monkey tissue used for production. In 2004 the United States Cancer Institute announced that it had concluded that SV40 is not associated with cancer in people.

Other notable new vaccines of the period include those for measles (1962, John Franklin Enders of Children's Medical Center Boston, later refined by Maurice Hilleman at Merck), Rubella (1969, Hilleman, Merck) and mumps (1967, Hilleman, Merck) The United States incidences of rubella, congenital rubella syndrome, measles, and mumps all fell by >95% in the immediate aftermath of widespread vaccination. The first 20 years of licensed measles vaccination in the U.S. prevented an estimated 52 million cases of the disease, 17,400 cases of mental retardation, and 5,200 deaths.

Development and marketing of antihypertensive drugs

Hypertension is a risk factor for atherosclerosis, heart failure, coronary artery disease, stroke, renal disease, and peripheral arterial disease, and is the most important risk factor for cardiovascular morbidity and mortality, in industrialized countries. Prior to 1940 approximately 23% of all deaths among persons over age 50 were attributed to hypertension. Severe cases of hypertension were treated by surgery.

Early developments in the field of treating hypertension included quaternary ammonium ion sympathetic nervous system blocking agents, but these compounds were never widely used due to their severe side effects, because the long term health consequences of high blood pressure had not yet been established, and because they had to be administered by injection.

In 1952 researchers at Ciba discovered the first orally available vasodilator, hydralazine. A major shortcoming of hydralazine monotherapy was that it lost its effectiveness over time (tachyphylaxis). In the mid-1950s Karl H. Beyer, James M. Sprague, John E. Baer, and Frederick C. Novello of Merck and Co. discovered and developed chlorothiazide, which remains the most widely used antihypertensive drug today. This development was associated with a substantial decline in the mortality rate among people with hypertension. The inventors were recognized by a Public Health Lasker Award in 1975 for "the saving of untold thousands of lives and the alleviation of the suffering of millions of victims of hypertension".

A 2009 Cochrane review concluded that thiazide antihypertensive drugs reduce the risk of death (RR 0.89), stroke (RR 0.63), coronary heart disease (RR 0.84), and cardiovascular events (RR 0.70) in people with high blood pressure. In the ensuring years other classes of antihypertensive drug were developed and found wide acceptance in combination therapy, including loop diuretics (Lasix/furosemide, Hoechst Pharmaceuticals, 1963), beta blockers (ICI Pharmaceuticals, 1964) ACE inhibitors, and angiotensin receptor blockers. ACE inhibitors reduce the risk of new onset kidney disease [RR 0.71] and death [RR 0.84] in diabetic patients, irrespective of whether they have hypertension.

Oral Contraceptives

Prior to the second world war, birth control was prohibited in many countries, and in the United States even the discussion of contraceptive methods sometimes led to prosecution under Comstock laws. The history of the development of oral contraceptives is thus closely tied to the birth control movement and the efforts of activists Margaret Sanger, Mary Dennett, and Emma Goldman. Based on fundamental research performed by Gregory Pincus and synthetic methods for progesterone developed by Carl Djerassi at Syntex and by Frank Colton at G.D. Searle & Co., the first oral contraceptive, Enovid, was developed by E.D. Searle and Co. and approved by the FDA in 1960. The original formulation incorporated vastly excessive doses of hormones, and caused severe side effects. Nonetheless, by 1962, 1.2 million American women were on the pill, and by 1965 the number had increased to 6.5 million. The availability of a convenient form of temporary contraceptive led to dramatic changes in social mores including expanding the range of lifestyle options available to women, reducing the reliance of women on men for contraceptive practice, encouraging the delay of marriage, and increasing pre-marital co-habitation.

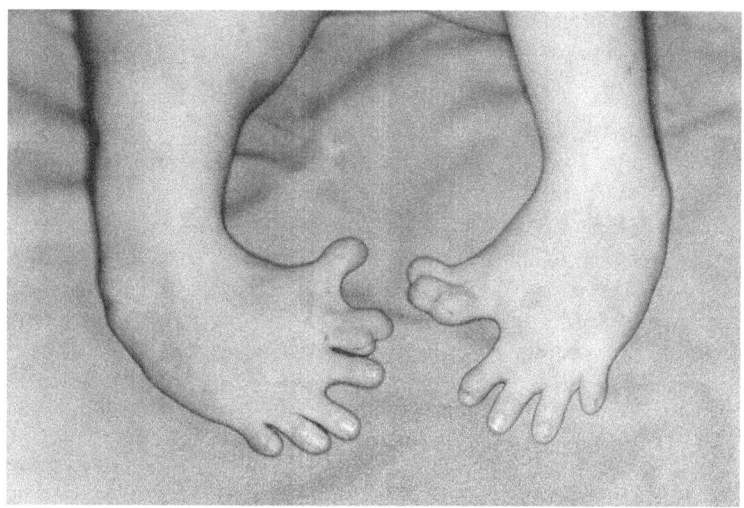

Figure 30: *Baby born to a mother who had taken thalidomide while pregnant.*

Thalidomide and the Kefauver-Harris Amendments

In the U.S., a push for revisions of the FD&C Act emerged from Congressional hearings led by Senator Estes Kefauver of Tennessee in 1959. The hearings covered a wide range of policy issues, including advertising abuses, questionable efficacy of drugs, and the need for greater regulation of the industry. While momentum for new legislation temporarily flagged under extended debate, a new tragedy emerged that underscored the need for more comprehensive regulation and provided the driving force for the passage of new laws.

On September 12, 1960, an American licensee, the William S. Merrell Company of Cincinnati, submitted to FDA a new drug application for Kevadon (thalidomide), the brand name of a sedative that had been marketed in Europe since 1956: thalidomide. The FDA medical officer in charge of this review, Frances Kelsey, believed the data were too incomplete to support the safety of this drug.

The firm continued to pressure Kelsey and the agency to approve the application—until November 1961, when the drug was pulled off the German market because of its association with grave congenital abnormalities. Several thousand newborns in Europe and elsewhere suffered the teratogenic effects of thalidomide. Though the drug was never approved in the USA, the firm distributed Kevadon to over 1,000 physicians there under the guise of investigational use. Over 20,000 Americans received thalidomide in this "study," including 624 pregnant patients, and about 17 known newborns suffered the effects of the drug.wikipedia:Citation needed

The thalidomide tragedy resurrected Kefauver's bill to enhance drug regulation that had stalled in Congress, and the Kefauver-Harris Amendment became law on October 10, 1962. Manufacturers henceforth had to prove to FDA that their drugs were effective as well as safe before they could go on the US market. The FDA received authority to regulate advertising of prescription drugs and to establish good manufacturing practices. The law required that all drugs introduced between 1938 and 1962 had to be effective. An FDA - National Academy of Sciences collaborative study showed that nearly 40 percent of these products were not effective. A similarly comprehensive study of over-the-counter products began ten years later.

1970–1980s

Statins

In 1971, Akira Endo, a Japanese biochemist working for the pharmaceutical company Sankyo, identified mevastatin (ML-236B), a molecule produced by the fungus Penicillium citrinum, as an inhibitor of HMG-CoA reductase, a critical enzyme used by the body to produce cholesterol. Animal trials showed very good inhibitory effect as in clinical trials, however a long term study in dogs found toxic effects at higher doses and as a result mevastatin was believed to be too toxic for human use. Mevastatin was never marketed, because of its adverse effects of tumors, muscle deterioration, and sometimes death in laboratory dogs.

P. Roy Vagelos, chief scientist and later CEO of Merck & Co, was interested, and made several trips to Japan starting in 1975. By 1978, Merck had isolated lovastatin (mevinolin, MK803) from the fungus *Aspergillus terreus*, first marketed in 1987 as Mevacor.[305]

In April 1994, the results of a Merck-sponsored study, the Scandinavian Simvastatin Survival Study, were announced. Researchers tested simvastatin, later sold by Merck as Zocor, on 4,444 patients with high cholesterol and heart disease. After five years, the study concluded the patients saw a 35% reduction in their cholesterol, and their chances of dying of a heart attack were reduced by 42%. In 1995, Zocor and Mevacor both made Merck over US$1 billion. Endo was awarded the 2006 Japan Prize, and the Lasker-DeBakey Clinical Medical Research Award in 2008. For his "pioneering research into a new class of molecules" for "lowering cholesterol,"sentence fragment

Research and development

Main articles: Drug discovery and Drug development

Drug discovery is the process by which potential drugs are discovered or designed. In the past most drugs have been discovered either by isolating the active ingredient from traditional remedies or by serendipitous discovery. Modern biotechnology often focuses on understanding the metabolic pathways related to a disease state or pathogen, and manipulating these pathways using molecular biology or biochemistry. A great deal of early-stage drug discovery has traditionally been carried out by universities and research institutions.

Drug development refers to activities undertaken after a compound is identified as a potential drug in order to establish its suitability as a medication. Objectives of drug development are to determine appropriate formulation and dosing, as well as to establish safety. Research in these areas generally includes a combination of *in vitro* studies, *in vivo* studies, and clinical trials. The cost of late stage development has meant it is usually done by the larger pharmaceutical companies.

Often, large multinational corporations exhibit vertical integration, participating in a broad range of drug discovery and development, manufacturing and quality control, marketing, sales, and distribution. Smaller organizations, on the other hand, often focus on a specific aspect such as discovering drug candidates or developing formulations. Often, collaborative agreements between research organizations and large pharmaceutical companies are formed to explore the potential of new drug substances. More recently, multi-nationals are increasingly relying on contract research organizations to manage drug development.[306]

The cost of innovation

Drug discovery and development is very expensive; of all compounds investigated for use in humans only a small fraction are eventually approved in most nations by government appointed medical institutions or boards, who have to approve new drugs before they can be marketed in those countries. In 2010 18 NMEs (New Molecular Entities) were approved and three biologics by the FDA, or 21 in total, which is down from 26 in 2009 and 24 in 2008. On the other hand, there were only 18 approvals in total in 2007 and 22 back in 2006. Since 2001, the Center for Drug Evaluation and Research has averaged 22.9 approvals a year. This approval comes only after heavy investment in pre-clinical development and clinical trials, as well as a commitment to ongoing safety monitoring. Drugs which fail part-way through this process often incur large costs, while generating no revenue in return. If the cost of these failed drugs is taken into account, the cost of developing a successful new drug (new chemical entity, or NCE), has been estimated at about 1.3 billion USD[307] (not including marketing expenses). Professors Light and Lexchin reported in 2012, however, that the rate of approval for new drugs has been a relatively stable average rate of 15 to 25 for decades.

Industry-wide research and investment reached a record $65.3 billion in 2009.[308] While the cost of research in the U.S. was about $34.2 billion between 1995 and 2010, revenues rose faster (revenues rose by $200.4 billion in that time).

A study by the consulting firm Bain & Company reported that the cost for discovering, developing and launching (which factored in marketing and other business expenses) a new drug (along with the prospective drugs that fail) rose over a five-year period to nearly $1.7 billion in 2003.[309] According to Forbes, by 2010 development costs were between $4 billion to $11 billion per drug.

Some of these estimates also take into account the opportunity cost of investing capital many years before revenues are realized (see Time-value of money). Because of the very long time needed for discovery, development, and approval of pharmaceuticals, these costs can accumulate to nearly half the total expense. A direct consequence within the pharmaceutical industry value chain is that major pharmaceutical multinationals tend to increasingly outsource risks related to fundamental research, which somewhat reshapes the industry ecosystem with biotechnology companies playing an increasingly important role, and overall strategies being redefined accordingly. Some approved drugs, such as those based on re-formulation of an existing active ingredient (also referred to as Line-extensions) are much less expensive to develop.

Controversies

Due to repeated accusations and findings that some clinical trials conducted or funded by pharmaceutical companies may report only positive results for the preferred medication, the industry has been looked at much more closely by independent groups and government agencies.[310]

In response to specific cases in which unfavorable data from pharmaceutical company-sponsored research was not published, the Pharmaceutical Research and Manufacturers of America have published new guidelines urging companies to report all findings and limit the financial involvement in drug companies of researchers.[311] US congress signed into law a bill which requires phase II and phase III clinical trials to be registered by the sponsor on the clinicaltrials.gov[312] website run by the NIH.

Drug researchers not directly employed by pharmaceutical companies often look to companies for grants, and companies often look to researchers for studies that will make their products look favorable. Sponsored researchers are rewarded by drug companies, for example with support for their conference/symposium costs. Lecture scripts and even journal articles presented by academic researchers may actually be "ghost-written" by pharmaceutical companies.

An investigation by ProPublica found that at least 21 doctors have been paid more than $500,000 for speeches and consulting by drugs manufacturers since 2009, with half of the top earners working in psychiatry, and about $2 billion in total paid to doctors for such services. AstraZeneca, Johnson & Johnson and Eli Lilly have paid billions of dollars in federal settlements over allegations that they paid doctors to promote drugs for unapproved uses. Some prominent medical schools have since tightened rules on faculty acceptance of such payments by drug companies.[313]

In contrast to this viewpoint, an article and associated editorial in the New England Journal of Medicine in May 2015 emphasized the importance of pharmaceutical industry-physician interactions for the development of novel treatments, and argued that moral outrage over industry malfeasance had unjustifiably led many to overemphasize the problems created by financial conflicts of interest. The article noted that major healthcare organizations such as National Center for Advancing Translational Sciences of the National Institutes of Health, the President's Council of Advisors on Science and Technology, the World Economic Forum, the Gates Foundation, the Wellcome Trust, and the Food and Drug Administration had encouraged greater interactions between physicians and industry in order to bring greater benefits to patients.

Product approval

In the United States, new pharmaceutical products must be approved by the Food and Drug Administration (FDA) as being both safe and effective. This process generally involves submission of an Investigational New Drug filing with sufficient pre-clinical data to support proceeding with human trials. Following IND approval, three phases of progressively larger human clinical trials may be conducted. Phase I generally studies toxicity using healthy volunteers. Phase II can include pharmacokinetics and dosing in patients, and Phase III is a very large study of efficacy in the intended patient population. Following the successful completion of phase III testing, a New Drug Application is submitted to the FDA. The FDA review the data and if the product is seen as having a positive benefit-risk assessment, approval to market the product in the US is granted.

A fourth phase of post-approval surveillance is also often required due to the fact that even the largest clinical trials cannot effectively predict the prevalence of rare side-effects. Postmarketing surveillance ensures that after marketing the safety of a drug is monitored closely. In certain instances, its indication may need to be limited to particular patient groups, and in others the substance is withdrawn from the market completely.

The FDA provides information about approved drugs at the Orange Book site.

In the UK, the Medicines and Healthcare Products Regulatory Agency approves drugs for use, though the evaluation is done by the European Medicines Agency, an agency of the European Union based in London. Normally an approval in the UK and other European countries comes later than one in the USA. Then it is the National Institute for Health and Care Excellence (NICE), for England and Wales, who decides if and how the National Health Service (NHS) will allow (in the sense of paying for) their use. The British National Formulary is the core guide for pharmacists and clinicians.

In many non-US western countries a 'fourth hurdle' of cost effectiveness analysis has developed before new technologies can be provided. This focuses on the efficiency (in terms of the cost per QALY) of the technologies in question rather than their efficacy. In England and Wales NICE decides whether and in what circumstances drugs and technologies will be made available by the NHS, whilst similar arrangements exist with the Scottish Medicines Consortium in Scotland, and the Pharmaceutical Benefits Advisory Committee in Australia. A product must pass the threshold for cost-effectiveness if it is to be approved. Treatments must represent 'value for money' and a net benefit to society.

Orphan drugs

Main article: Orphan drug

There are special rules for certain rare diseases ("orphan diseases") in several major drug regulatory territories. For example, diseases involving fewer than 200,000 patients in the United States, or larger populations in certain circumstances are subject to the Orphan Drug Act. Because medical research and development of drugs to treat such diseases is financially disadvantageous, companies that do so are rewarded with tax reductions, fee waivers, and market exclusivity on that drug for a limited time (seven years), regardless of whether the drug is protected by patents.

Industry revenues

[314] For the first time ever, in 2011, global spending on prescription drugs topped $954 billion, even as growth slowed somewhat in Europe and North America. The United States accounts for more than a third of the global pharmaceutical market, with $340 billion in annual sales followed by the EU and

Japan. (pdf)[315] Emerging markets such as China, Russia, South Korea and Mexico outpaced that market, growing a huge 81 percent.

The top ten best-selling drugs of 2013 totaled $75.6 billion in sales, with the anti-inflammatory drug Humira being the best-selling drug world wide at $10.7 billion in sales. The second and third best selling were Enbrel and Remicade, respectively.[316] The top three best-selling drugs in the United States in 2013 were Abilify ($6.3 billion,) Nexium ($6 billion) and Humira ($5.4 billion).[317] The best-selling drug ever, Lipitor, averaged $13 billion annually and netted $141 billion total over its lifetime before Pfizer's patent expired in November 2011.

IMS Health publishes an analysis of trends expected in the pharmaceutical industry in 2007, including increasing profits in most sectors despite loss of some patents, and new 'blockbuster' drugs on the horizon.

Teradata Magazine predicted that by 2007, $40 billion in U.S. sales could be lost at the top 10 pharmaceutical companies as a result of slowdown in R&D innovation and the expiry of patents on major products, with 19 blockbuster drugs losing patent. As the number of patents that expire accumulates faster than the number of marketed drugs, this amount is expected to increase even more in the near future.

Patents and generics

Depending on a number of considerations, a company may apply for and be granted a patent for the drug, or the process of producing the drug, granting exclusivity rights typically for about 20 years.[318] However, only after rigorous study and testing, which takes 10 to 15 years on average, will governmental authorities grant permission for the company to market and sell the drug. Patent protection enables the owner of the patent to recover the costs of research and development through high profit margins for the branded drug. When the patent protection for the drug expires, a generic drug is usually developed and sold by a competing company. The development and approval of generics is less expensive, allowing them to be sold at a lower price. Often the owner of the branded drug will introduce a generic version before the patent expires in order to get a head start in the generic market. Restructuring has therefore become routine, driven by the patent expiration of products launched during the industry's "golden era" in the 1990s and companies' failure to develop sufficient new blockbuster products to replace lost revenues.[319]

Prescriptions

In the U.S., the value of prescriptions increased over the period of 1995 to 2005 by 3.4 billion annually, a 61 percent increase. Retail sales of prescription drugs jumped 250 percent from $72 billion to $250 billion, while the average price of prescriptions more than doubled from $30 to $68.[320]

Marketing

Advertising is common in healthcare journals as well as through more mainstream media routes. In some countries, notably the US, they are allowed to advertise directly to the general public. Pharmaceutical companies generally employ sales people (often called 'drug reps' or, an older term, 'detail men') to market directly and personally to physicians and other healthcare providers. In some countries, notably the US, pharmaceutical companies also employ lobbyists to influence politicians. Marketing of prescription drugs in the US is regulated by the federal Prescription Drug Marketing Act of 1987.

To healthcare professionals

The book *Bad Pharma* also discusses the influence of drug representatives, how ghostwriters are employed by the drug companies to write papers for academics to publish, how independent the academic journals really are, how the drug companies finance doctors' continuing education, and how patients' groups are often funded by industry.[321]

Direct to consumer advertising

Main article: Direct-to-consumer advertising

Since the 1980s new methods of marketing for prescription drugs to consumers have become important. Direct-to-consumer media advertising was legalised in the FDA Guidance for Industry on Consumer-Directed Broadcast Advertisements.

Controversy about drug marketing and lobbying

There has been increasing controversy surrounding pharmaceutical marketing and influence. There have been accusations and findings of influence on doctors and other health professionals through drug reps, including the constant provision of marketing 'gifts' and biased information to health professionals; highly prevalent advertising in journals and conferences; funding independent healthcare organizations and health promotion campaigns; lobbying physicians and politicians (more than any other industry in the US); sponsorship of medical schools or nurse training; sponsorship of continuing educational events, with influence on the curriculum;[322] and hiring physicians as paid consultants on medical advisory boards.

Some advocacy groups, such as No Free Lunch, have criticized the effect of drug marketing to physicians because they say it biases physicians to prescribe the marketed drugs even when others might be cheaper or better for the patient.[323]

There have been related accusations of disease mongering[324] (overmedicalising) to expand the market for medications. An inaugural conference on that subject took place in Australia in 2006. In 2009, the Government-funded National Prescribing Service launched the "Finding Evidence – Recognising Hype"[325] program, aimed at educating GPs on methods for independent drug analysis.

A 2005 review by a special committee of the UK government came to all the above conclusions in a European Union context whilst also highlighting the contributions and needs of the industry.

Meta-analyses have shown that psychiatric studies sponsored by pharmaceutical companies are several times more likely to report positive results, and if a drug company employee is involved the effect is even larger. Influence has also extended to the training of doctors and nurses in medical schools, which is being fought.[326]

It has been argued that the design of the Diagnostic and Statistical Manual of Mental Disorders and the expansion of the criteria represents an increasing medicalization of human nature, or "disease mongering", driven by drug company influence on psychiatry. The potential for direct conflict of interest has been raised, partly because roughly half the authors who selected and defined the DSM-IV psychiatric disorders had or previously had financial relationships with the pharmaceutical industry.[327]

In the US, starting in 2013, under the Physician Financial Transparency Reports (part of the Sunshine Act), the Centers for Medicare & Medicaid Services has to collect information from applicable manufacturers and group purchasing organizations in order to report information about their financial relationships with physicians and hospitals. Data are made public in the Centers for Medicare & Medicaid Services website. The expectation is that relationship between doctors and Pharmaceutical industry will become fully transparent.[328]

Regulatory issues

Ben Goldacre has argued that regulators – such as the Medicines and Healthcare products Regulatory Agency (MHRA) in the UK, or the Food and Drug Administration (FDA) in the United States – advance the interests of the drug companies rather than the interests of the public due to revolving door exchange of employees between the regulator and the companies and friendships develop between regulator and company employees.[329] He argues that regulators do not require that new drugs offer an improvement over what is already available, or even that they be particularly effective.[330]

Others have argued that excessive regulation suppresses therapeutic innovation, and that the current cost of regulator-required clinical trials prevents the full exploitation of new genetic and biological knowledge for the treatment of human disease. A 2012 report by the President's Council of Advisors on Science and Technology made several key recommendations to reduce regulatory burdens to new drug development, including 1) expanding the FDA's use of accelerated approval processes, 2) creating an expedited approval pathway for drugs intended for use in narrowly defined populations, and 3) undertaking pilot projects designed to evaluate the feasibility of a new, adaptive drug approval process.

Pharmaceutical fraud

See also: List of largest pharmaceutical settlements in the United States

Pharmaceutical fraud involves activities that result in false claims to insurers or programs such as Medicare in the United States or equivalent state programs for financial gain to a pharmaceutical company. There are several different schemes used to defraud the health care system which are particular to the pharmaceutical industry. These include: Good Manufacturing Practice (GMP) Violations, Off Label Marketing, Best Price Fraud, CME Fraud, Medicaid Price Reporting, and Manufactured Compound Drugs. Of this amount $2.5 billion was recovered through *False Claims Act* cases in FY 2010. Examples of fraud cases include the GlaxoSmithKline $3 billion settlement, Pfizer $2.3 billion settlement and Merck & Co. $650 million settlement. Damages from fraud can be recovered by use of the False Claims Act, most commonly under the *qui tam* provisions which rewards an individual for being a "whistleblower", or relator (law).

Every major company selling the antipsychotics — Bristol-Myers Squibb, Eli Lilly, Pfizer, AstraZeneca and Johnson & Johnson — has either settled recent government cases, under the False Claims Act, for hundreds of millions of dollars or is currently under investigation for possible health care fraud. Following charges of illegal marketing, two of the settlements set records last year for the largest criminal fines ever imposed on corporations. One involved Eli Lilly's antipsychotic Zyprexa, and the other involved Bextra. In the Bextra case, the government also charged Pfizer with illegally marketing another antipsychotic, Geodon; Pfizer settled that part of the claim for $301 million, without admitting any wrongdoing.

On 2 July 2012, GlaxoSmithKline pleaded guilty to criminal charges and agreed to a $3 billion settlement of the largest health-care fraud case in the U.S. and the largest payment by a drug company. The settlement is related to the company's illegal promotion of prescription drugs, its failure to report safety data, bribing doctors, and promoting medicines for uses for which they were not licensed. The drugs involved were Paxil, Wellbutrin, Advair, Lamictal, and Zofran for off-label, non-covered uses. Those and the drugs Imitrex, Lotronex, Flovent, and Valtrex were involved in the kickback scheme.

The following is a list of the four largest settlements reached with pharmaceutical companies from 1991 to 2012, rank ordered by the size of the total settlement. Legal claims against the pharmaceutical industry have varied widely over the past two decades, including Medicare and Medicaid fraud, off-label promotion, and inadequate manufacturing practices.[331]

Company	Settlement	Violation(s)	Year	Product(s)	Laws allegedly violated (if applicable)
GlaxoSmithKline[332]	$3 billion	Off-label promotion/ failure to disclose safety data	2012	Avandia/-Wellbutrin/Paxil	False Claims Act/FDCA
Pfizer[333]	$2.3 billion	Off-label promotion/-kickbacks	2009	Bextra/Geodon/ Zyvox/Lyrica	False Claims Act/FDCA
Abbott Laboratories[334]	$1.5 billion	Off-label promotion	2012	Depakote	False Claims Act/FDCA
Eli Lilly[335]	$1.4 billion	Off-label promotion	2009	Zyprexa	False Claims Act/FDCA

Developing world

Patents

Patents have been criticized in the developing world, as they are thought to reduce access to existing medicines.[336] Reconciling patents and universal access to medicine would require an efficient international policy of price discrimination. Moreover, under the TRIPS agreement of the World Trade Organization, countries must allow pharmaceutical products to be patented. In 2001, the WTO adopted the Doha Declaration, which indicates that the TRIPS agreement should be read with the goals of public health in mind, and allows some methods for circumventing pharmaceutical monopolies: via compulsory licensing or parallel imports, even before patent expiration.[337]

In March 2001, 40 multi-national pharmaceutical companies brought litigation against South Africa for its Medicines Act, which allowed the generic production of antiretroviral drugs (ARVs) for treating HIV, despite the fact that these drugs were on-patent.[338] HIV was and is an epidemic in South Africa, and ARVs at the time cost between 10,000 and 15,000 USD per patient per year. This was unaffordable for most South African citizens, and so the South African government committed to providing ARVs at prices closer to what people could afford. To do so, they would need to ignore the patents on drugs and produce generics within the country (using a compulsory license), or import them from abroad. After international protest in favour of public health rights (including the collection of 250,000 signatures by MSF), the governments of several developed countries (including The Netherlands, Germany, France, and later the US) backed the South African government, and the case was dropped in April of that year.[339]

Charitable programs

Charitable programs and drug discovery & development efforts by pharmaceutical companies include:

- "Merck's Gift", wherein billions of river blindness drugs were donated in Africa[340]
- Pfizer's gift of free/discounted fluconazole and other drugs for AIDS in South Africa[341]
- GSK's commitment to give free albendazole tablets to the WHO for, and until, the elimination of lymphatic filariasis worldwide.
- In 2006, Novartis committed US$755 million in corporate citizenship initiatives around the world, particularly focusing on improved access to medicines in the developing world through its Access to Medicine projects, including donations of medicines to patients affected by leprosy,

tuberculosis, and malaria; Glivec patient assistance programs; and relief to support major humanitarian organisations with emergency medical needs.[342]

Alternative medicine

For other uses of "CAM", see Cam (disambiguation).

Alternative medical systems

- Acupuncture
- Anthroposophic medicine
- Chiropractic
- Homeopathy
- Naturopathy
- Osteopathy

Traditional medicine

- Ayurveda
- Faith healing
- Japanese
- Shamanism
- Siddha
- Chinese
- Korean
- Mongolian
- Tibetan
- Unani

NCCIH domains

- Mind–body interventions
- Biologically based therapies
- Manual therapy
- Energy therapies

- v
- t
- e[343]

Alternative medicine is any practice that is perceived by its users to have the healing effects of medicine, but does not originate from evidence gathered using the scientific method, is not part of biomedicine, or is contradicted by scientific evidence or established science. It consists of a wide range of health care practices, products and therapies, ranging from being biologically plausible but not well tested, to being directly contradicted by evidence and science, or even harmful or toxic. Examples include new and traditional medicine practices such as homeopathy, naturopathy, chiropractic, energy medicine, various forms of acupuncture, traditional Chinese medicine, Ayurvedic medicine, and Christian faith healing. The treatments are those that are not part of the

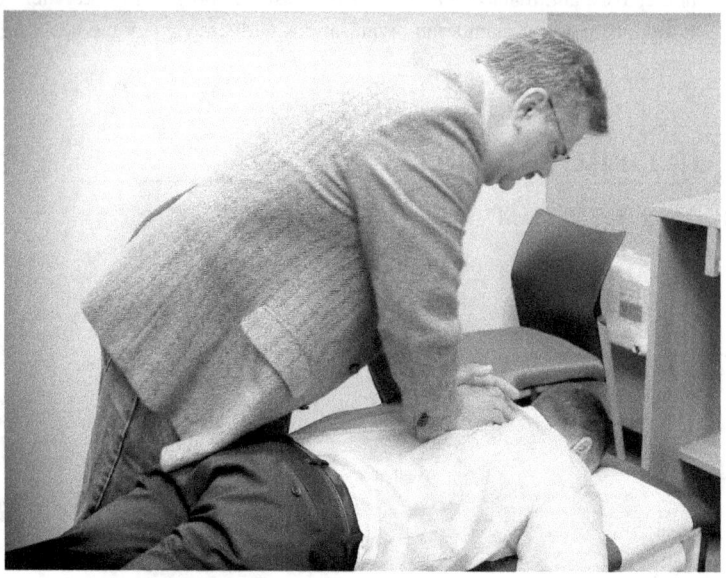

Figure 31: *A Chiropractor manipulating the spine.*

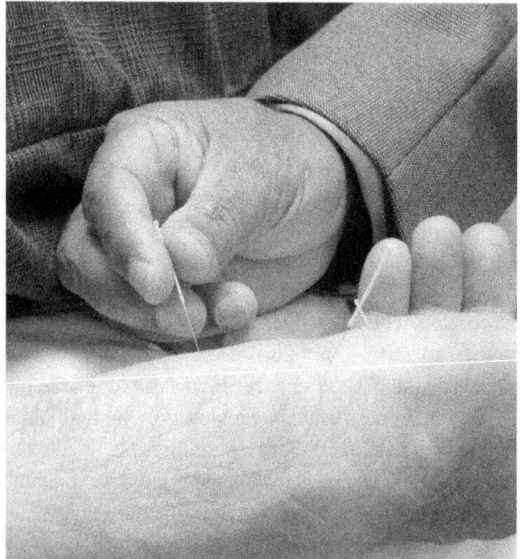

Figure 32: *Acupuncture involves insertion of needles in the body.*

Figure 33: *Christian laying of hands, prayer intervention, and faith healing*

Figure 34: *The science community is critical of alternative medicine for making unproven claims.*

science-based healthcare system, and are not clearly backed by scientific evidence.[344] Despite significant expenditures on testing alternative medicine, including $2.5 billion spent by the United States government, almost none have shown any effectiveness greater than that of false treatments (placebo), and alternative medicine has been criticized by prominent figures in science and medicine as being quackery, nonsense, fraudulent, or unethical.[345]

Complementary medicine is alternative medicine used together with conventional medical treatment in a belief, not established using the scientific method, that it "complements" (improves the efficacy of) the treatment.[346] **CAM** is the abbreviation for **complementary and alternative medicine**. **Integrative medicine** (or integrative health) is the combination of the practices and methods of alternative medicine with conventional medicine.

Alternative medical diagnoses and treatments are not included as science-based treatments that are taught in medical schools, and are not used in medical practice where treatments are based on what is established using the scientific method. Alternative therapies lack such scientific validation, and their effectiveness is either unproved or disproved.[347] Alternative medicine is usually based on religion, tradition, superstition, belief in supernatural energies, pseudoscience, errors in reasoning, propaganda, or fraud. Regulation and licensing of alternative medicine and health care providers varies from country to country, and state to state.

The scientific community has criticized alternative medicine as being based on misleading statements, quackery, pseudoscience, antiscience, fraud, or poor scientific methodology. Promoting alternative medicine has been called dangerous and unethical.[348] Testing alternative medicine has been called a waste of scarce medical research resources. Critics have said "there is really no such thing as alternative medicine, just medicine that works and medicine that doesn't", and "Can there be any reasonable 'alternative' [to medicine based on evidence]?"

Types of alternative medicine

See also: List of forms of alternative medicine

Alternative medicine consists of a wide range of health care practices, products, and therapies. The shared feature is a claim to heal that is not based on the scientific method. Alternative medicine practices are diverse in their foundations and methodologies. Alternative medicine practices may be classified by their cultural origins or by the types of beliefs upon which they are based. Methods may incorporate or base themselves on traditional medicinal practices of a particular culture, folk knowledge, supersition,[349] spiritual beliefs,

Figure 35: *A Botanica of traditional Hispanic medicines may look like a pharmacy of science based medicines. The difference is not in their appearance, but in the basis for belief that the medicines have a healing effect.*

belief in supernatural energies (antiscience), pseudoscience, errors in reasoning, propaganda, fraud, new or different concepts of health and disease, and any bases other than being proven by scientific methods. Different cultures may have their own unique traditional or belief based practices developed recently or over thousands of years, and specific practices or entire systems of practices.

Unscientific belief systems

Alternative medical systems can be based on a common belief systems that are not consistent with facts of science, such as in naturopathy or homeopathy.

Homeopathy

Homeopathy is a system developed in a belief that a substance that causes the symptoms of a disease in healthy people will cure similar symptoms in sick people.[350]</ref> It was developed before knowledge of atoms and molecules, and of basic chemistry, which shows that repeated dilution as practiced in homeopathy produces only water and that homeopathy is scientifically implausible. Homeopathy is considered quackery in the medical community.

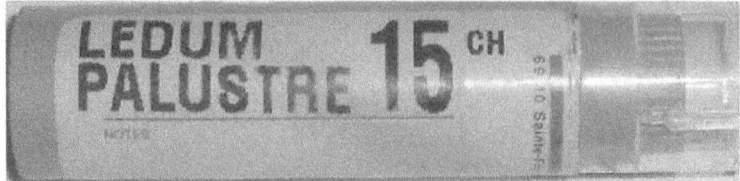

Figure 36: *A homeopathic remedy is unlikely to contain one molecule of the original herb or mineral*

Figure 37: *Traditional N'anga medical doctor in Zimbabwe*

Naturopathic medicine

Naturopathic medicine is based on a belief that the body heals itself using a supernatural vital energy that guides bodily processes, a view in conflict with the paradigm of evidence-based medicine. Many naturopaths have opposed vaccination, and "scientific evidence does not support claims that naturopathic medicine can cure cancer or any other disease".

Traditional ethnic systems

Alternative medical systems may be based on traditional medicine practices, such as Traditional Chinese medicine, Ayurveda in India, or practices of other cultures around the world.

Figure 38: *Ready to drink traditional Chinese medicine mixture*

Traditional Chinese medicine

Traditional Chinese medicine is a combination of traditional practices and beliefs developed over thousands of years in China, together with modifications made by the Communist party. Common practices include herbal medicine, acupuncture (insertion of needles in the body at specified points), massage (Tui na), exercise (qigong), and dietary therapy. The practices are based on belief in a supernatural energy called qi, considerations of Chinese Astrology and Chinese numerology, traditional use of herbs and other substances found in China, a belief that a map of the body is contained on the tongue which reflects changes in the body, and an incorrect model of the anatomy and physiology of internal organs.

The Chinese Communist Party Chairman Mao Zedong, in response to the lack of modern medical practitioners, revived acupuncture and its theory was rewritten to adhere to the political, economic and logistic necessities of providing for the medical needs of China's population.Wikipedia:Citing sources In the 1950s the "history" and theory of Traditional Chinese medicine was rewritten as communist propaganda, at Mao's insistence, to correct the supposed "bourgeois thought of Western doctors of medicine".[351] Acupuncture gained attention in the United States when President Richard Nixon visited China in 1972, and the delegation was shown a patient undergoing major

Figure 39: *Indian Ayurvedic medicine includes a belief that the spiritual balance of mind influences disease.*

surgery while fully awake, ostensibly receiving acupuncture rather than anesthesia. Later it was found that the patients selected for the surgery had both a high pain tolerance and received heavy indoctrination before the operation; these demonstration cases were also frequently receiving morphine surreptitiously through an intravenous drip that observers were told contained only fluids and nutrients. Cochrane reviews found acupuncture is not effective for a wide range of conditions. A systematic review of systematic reviews found that for reducing pain, real acupuncture was no better than sham acupuncture.

Ayurvedic medicine

Ayurvedic medicine is a traditional medicine of India. Ayurveda believes in the existence of three elemental substances, the doshas (called Vata, Pitta and Kapha), and states that a balance of the doshas results in health, while imbalance results in disease. Such disease-inducing imbalances can be adjusted and balanced using traditional herbs, minerals and heavy metals. Ayurveda stresses the use of plant-based medicines and treatments, with some animal products, and added minerals, including sulfur, arsenic, lead, copper sulfate.Wikipedia:Citation needed

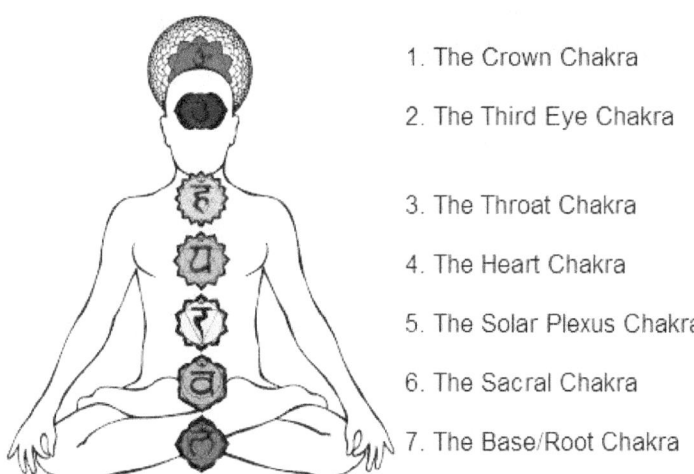

1. The Crown Chakra
2. The Third Eye Chakra
3. The Throat Chakra
4. The Heart Chakra
5. The Solar Plexus Chakra
6. The Sacral Chakra
7. The Base/Root Chakra

Figure 40: *In Japanese Reiki, some other traditional medical systems, and some New Age practices, it is believed that supernatural energies flow from the palms of the healer into the patient near Chakras, influencing disease.*

Safety concerns have been raised about Ayurveda, with two U.S. studies finding about 20 percent of Ayurvedic Indian-manufactured patent medicines contained toxic levels of heavy metals such as lead, mercury and arsenic. Other concerns include the use of herbs containing toxic compounds and the lack of quality control in Ayurvedic facilities. Incidents of heavy metal poisoning have been attributed to the use of these compounds in the United States.[352,353]

Supernatural energies and misunderstanding of energy in physics

Bases of belief may include belief in existence of supernatural energies undetected by the science of physics, as in biofields, or in belief in properties of the energies of physics that are inconsistent with the laws of physics, as in energy medicine.

Biofields

Biofield therapies are intended to influence energy fields that, it is purported, surround and penetrate the body. Writers such as noted astrophysicist and advocate of skeptical thinking (Scientific skepticism) Carl Sagan (1934-1996) have described the lack of empirical evidence to support the existence of the putative energy fields on which these therapies are predicated.[354]

Acupuncture is a component of Traditional Chinese medicine. In acupuncture, it is believed that a supernatural energy called qi flows through the universe and through the body, and helps propel the blood, blockage of which leads to disease. It is believed that insertion of needles at various parts of the body determined by astrological calculations can restore balance to the blocked flows, and thereby cure disease.

Chiropractic was developed in the belief that manipulating the spine affects the flow of a supernatural vital energy and thereby affects health and disease.

In the western version of Japanese Reiki, the palms are placed on the patient near Chakras, believed to be centers of supernatural energies, in a belief that the supernatural energies can transferred from the palms of the practitioner, to heal the patient.

Energy medicines

Bioelectromagnetic-based therapies use verifiable electromagnetic fields, such as pulsed fields, alternating-current, or direct-current fields in an unconventional manner. Magnetic healing does not claim existence of supernatural energies, but asserts that magnets can be used to defy the laws of physics to influence health and disease.

Holistic health and mind body medicine

Mind-body medicine takes a holistic approach to health that explores the interconnection between the mind, body, and spirit. It works under the premise that the mind can affect "bodily functions and symptoms". Mind body medicines includes healing claims made in yoga, meditation, deep-breathing exercises, guided imagery, hypnotherapy, progressive relaxation, qi gong, and tai chi.

Yoga, a method of traditional stretches, exercises, and meditations in Hinduism, may also be classified as an energy medicine insofar as its healing effects are believed to be due to a healing "life energy" that is absorbed into the body through the breath, and is thereby believed to treat a wide variety of illnesses and complaints.

Since the 1990s, tai chi (t'ai chi ch'uan) classes that purely emphasise health have become popular in hospitals, clinics, as well as community and senior centers. This has occurred as the baby boomers generation has aged and the art's reputation as a low-stress training method for seniors has become better known. There has been some divergence between those that say they practice t'ai chi ch'uan primarily for self-defence, those that practice it for its aesthetic appeal (see *wushu* below), and those that are more interested in its benefits to physical and mental health.

Alternative medicine

Figure 41: *Tai chi*

Figure 42: *Yoga class*

Figure 43: *Qigong practitioners in Manhattan*

Qigong, chi kung, or chi gung, is a practice of aligning body, breath, and mind for health, meditation, and martial arts training. With roots in Chinese Traditional Chinese Medicine, philosophy, and martial arts, qigong is traditionally viewed as a practice to cultivate and balance qi (chi) or what has been translated as "life energy".

Herbal remedies and other substances used

Substance based practices use substances found in nature such as herbs, foods, non-vitamin supplements and megavitamins, animal and fungal products, and minerals, including use of these products in traditional medical practices that may also incorporate other methods. Examples include healing claims for non-vitamin supplements, fish oil, Omega-3 fatty acid, glucosamine, echinacea, flaxseed oil, and ginseng. Herbal medicine, or phytotherapy, includes not just the use of plant products, but may also include the use of animal and mineral products. It is among the most commercially successful branches of alternative medicine, and includes the tablets, powders and elixirs that are sold as "nutritional supplements". Only a very small percentage of these have been shown to have any efficacy, and there is little regulation as to standards and safety of their contents. This may include use of known toxic substances, such as use of the poison lead in Traditional Chinese Medicine.

Alternative medicine 163

Figure 44: *Medicinal herbs in a traditional Spanish market*

Figure 45: *Traditional medicines in Madagascar*

Figure 46: *Assorted dried plant and animal parts used in traditional Chinese medicine*

Body manipulation

Manipulative and body-based practices feature the manipulation or movement of body parts, such as is done in bodywork and chiropractic manipulation.

Osteopathic manipulative medicine, also known as osteopathic manipulative treatment, is a core set of techniques of osteopathy and osteopathic medicine distinguishing these fields from mainstream medicine.

Religion, faith healing, and prayer

Religion based healing practices, such as use of prayer and the laying of hands in Christian faith healing, and shamanism, rely on belief in divine or spiritual intervention for healing.

Shamanism is a practice of many cultures around the world, in which a practitioner reaches an altered states of consciousness in order to encounter and interact with the spirit world or channel supernatural energies in the belief they can heal.[355]

Figure 47: *Shaman healer in Sonora, Mexico.*

Alternative medicines based on exploitation of ignorance and flawed reasoning

Some alternative medicine practices may be based on pseudoscience, ignorance, or flawed reasoning. This can lead to fraud.

Practitioners of electricity and magnetism based healing methods may deliberately exploit a patient's ignorance of physics in order to defraud them.

Definitions and terminology

"Alternative medicine" is a loosely defined set of products, practices, and theories that are believed or perceived by their users to have the healing effects of medicine,[356,357]</ref> but whose effectiveness has not been clearly established using scientific methods,[358] whose theory and practice is not part of biomedicine,[359]</ref>[360,361] or whose theories or practices are directly contradicted by scientific evidence or scientific principles used in biomedicine. "Biomedicine" is that part of medical science that applies principles of biology, physiology, molecular biology, biophysics, and other natural sciences to clinical practice, using scientific methods to establish the effectiveness of that practice. Alternative medicine is a diverse group of medical and health care systems, practices, and products that originate outside of biomedicine, are not considered part of biomedicine,[362] are not widely used by the biomedical healthcare professions, and are not taught as skills practiced in biomedicine. Unlike biomedicine, an alternative medicine product or practice does not originate from the sciences or from using scientific methodology, but may instead be based on testimonials, religion, tradition, superstition, belief in supernatural energies, pseudoscience, errors in reasoning, propaganda, fraud, or other unscientific sources. The expression "alternative medicine" refers to a very diverse range of related and unrelated products, practices, and theories, originating from widely varying sources, cultures, theories, and belief systems, and ranging from biologically plausible practices and products and practices with some evidence, to practices and theories that are directly contradicted by basic science or clear evidence, and products that have proven to be ineffective or even toxic and harmful.

"Complementary medicine" refers to use of alternative medicine alongside conventional medicine, in the belief that it increases the effectiveness of the science-based medicine. An example of "complementary medicine" is use of acupuncture (sticking needles in the body to influence the flow of a supernatural energy), along with using science-based medicine, in the belief that the acupuncture increases the effectiveness or "complements" the science-based medicine. "CAM" is an abbreviation for "complementary and alternative medicine". The expression "integrative medicine" (or "integrated medicine") is used in two different ways. One use refers to a belief that medicine based on science can be "integrated" with practices that are not. Another use refers only to a combination of alternative medical treatments with conventional treatments that have some scientific proof of efficacy, in which case it is identical with CAM. "holistic medicine" (or holistic health) is an alternative medicine practice which claim to treat the "whole person" and not just the illness itself.

"Alternative medicine", "complementary medicine", "holistic medicine", "natural medicine", "unorthodox medicine", "fringe medicine", "unconventional medicine", and "new age medicine" may be used interchangeably as having the same meaning (synonyms) in some contexts, but may have different meanings in other contexts, for example, unorthodox medicine may refer to biomedicine that is different from what is commonly practiced, and fringe medicine may refer to biomedicine that is based on fringe science, which may be scientifically valid but is not mainstream.

"Traditional medicine" and "folk medicine" refer to prescientific practices of a culture, not to what is traditionally practiced in cultures where medical science dominates. "Eastern medicine" typically refers to prescientific traditional medicines of Asia. "Western medicine", when referring to modern practice, typically refers to medical science, and not to alternative medicines practiced in the west (Europe and the Americas). "Western medicine", "biomedicine", "mainstream medicine", "medical science", "science-based medicine", "evidence-based medicine", "conventional medicine", "standard medicine", "orthodox medicine", "allopathic medicine", "dominant health system", and "medicine", are sometimes used interchangeably as having the same meaning, when contrasted with alternative medicine, but these terms may have different meanings in some contexts, e.g., some practices in medical science are not supported by rigorous scientific testing so "medical science" is not strictly identical with "science-based medicine", and "standard medical care" may refer to "best practice" when contrasted with other biomedicine that is less used or less recommended.[363,364]

The meaning of the term "alternative" in the expression "alternative medicine", is not that it is an actual effective alternative to medical science, although some alternative medicine promoters may use the loose terminology to give the appearance of effectiveness. Loose terminology may also be used to suggest meaning that a dichotomy exists when it does not, e.g., the use of the expressions "western medicine" and "eastern medicine" to suggest that the difference is a cultural difference between the Asiatic east and the European west, rather than that the difference is between evidence based medicine and treatments which don't work.

Problems with defining alternative medicine

Prominent members of the science and biomedical science community assert that it is not meaningful to define an alternative medicine that is separate from a conventional medicine, that the expressions "conventional medicine", "alternative medicine", "complementary medicine", "integrative medicine", and "holistic medicine" do not refer to anything at all. Their criticisms of trying to make such artificially definitions include: "There's no such thing as conventional or alternative or complementary or integrative or holistic medicine. There's only medicine that works and medicine that doesn't;" "By definition, alternative medicine has either not been proved to work, or been proved not to work. You know what they call alternative medicine that's been proved to work? Medicine;" "There cannot be two kinds of medicine – conventional and alternative. There is only medicine that has been adequately tested and medicine that has not, medicine that works and medicine that may or may not work. Once a treatment has been tested rigorously, it no longer matters whether it was considered alternative at the outset. If it is found to be reasonably safe and effective, it will be accepted;" and "There is no alternative medicine. There is only scientifically proven, evidence-based medicine supported by solid data or unproven medicine, for which scientific evidence is lacking."

Others in both the biomedical and CAM communities point out that CAM *cannot* be precisely defined because of the diversity of theories and practices it includes, and because the boundaries between CAM and biomedicine overlap, are porous, and change.[364,365] The expression "complementary and alternative medicine" (CAM) resists easy definition because the health systems and practices to which it refers are diffuse and its boundaries are poorly defined.[366,367]</ref> Healthcare practices categorized as alternative may differ in their historical origin, theoretical basis, diagnostic technique, therapeutic practice and in their relationship to the medical mainstream.[368] Some alternative therapies, including traditional Chinese Medicine (TCM) and Ayurveda, have antique origins in East or South Asia and are entirely alternative medical systems;[369] others, such as homeopathy and chiropractic, have origins in Europe or the United States and emerged in the eighteenth and nineteenth centuries.[370] Some, such as osteopathy and chiropractic, employ manipulative physical methods of treatment; others, such as meditation and prayer, are based on mind-body interventions.[371] Treatments considered alternative in one location may be considered conventional in another. Thus, chiropractic is not considered alternative in Denmark and likewise osteopathic medicine is no longer thought of as an alternative therapy in the United States.

Different types of definitions

One common feature of all definitions of alternative medicine is its designation as "other than" conventional medicine.[372] For example, the widely referenced[373] descriptive definition of complementary and alternative medicine devised by the US National Center for Complementary and Integrative Health (NCCIH) of the National Institutes of Health (NIH), states that it is "a group of diverse medical and health care systems, practices, and products that are not generally considered part of conventional medicine." For conventional medical practitioners, it does not necessarily follow that either it or its practitioners would no longer be considered alternative.[374]

Some definitions seek to specify alternative medicine in terms of its social and political marginality to mainstream healthcare. This can refer to the lack of support that alternative therapies receive from the medical establishment and related bodies regarding access to research funding, sympathetic coverage in the medical press, or inclusion in the standard medical curriculum. In 1993, the British Medical Association (BMA), one among many professional organizations who have attempted to define alternative medicine, stated that it[375] referred to "those forms of treatment which are not widely used by the conventional healthcare professions, and the skills of which are not taught as part of the undergraduate curriculum of conventional medical and paramedical healthcare courses". In a US context, an influential definition coined in 1993 by the Harvard-based physician, David M. Eisenberg, characterized alternative medicine "as interventions neither taught widely in medical schools nor generally available in US hospitals".[376] These descriptive definitions are inadequate in the present-day when some conventional doctors offer alternative medical treatments and CAM introductory courses or modules can be offered as part of standard undergraduate medical training; alternative medicine is taught in more than 50 per cent of US medical schools and increasingly US health insurers are willing to provide reimbursement for CAM therapies.[377] In 1999, 7.7% of US hospitals reported using some form of CAM therapy; this proportion had risen to 37.7% by 2008.

An expert panel at a conference hosted in 1995 by the US Office for Alternative Medicine (OAM),[378] devised a theoretical definition of alternative medicine as "a broad domain of healing resources ... other than those intrinsic to the politically dominant health system of a particular society or culture in a given historical period." This definition has been widely adopted by CAM researchers, cited by official government bodies such as the UK Department of Health, attributed as the definition used by the Cochrane Collaboration, and, with some modification,Wikipedia:Disputed statement was preferred in the 2005 consensus report of the US Institute of Medicine, *Complementary and Alternative Medicine in the United States*.

The 1995 OAM conference definition, an expansion of Eisenberg's 1993 formulation, is silent regarding questions of the medical effectiveness of alternative therapies. Its proponents hold that it thus avoids relativism about differing forms of medical knowledge and, while it is an essentially political definition, this should not imply that the dominance of mainstream biomedicine is solely due to political forces. According to this definition, alternative and mainstream medicine can only be differentiated with reference to what is "intrinsic to the politically dominant health system of a particular society of culture". However, there is neither a reliable method to distinguish between cultures and subcultures, nor to attribute them as dominant or subordinate, nor any accepted criteria to determine the dominance of a cultural entity. If the culture of a politically dominant healthcare system is held to be equivalent to the perspectives of those charged with the medical management of leading healthcare institutions and programs, the definition fails to recognize the potential for division either within such an elite or between a healthcare elite and the wider population.

Normative definitions distinguish alternative medicine from the biomedical mainstream in its provision of therapies that are unproven, unvalidated or ineffective and support of theories which have no recognized scientific basis.[379] These definitions characterize practices as constituting alternative medicine when, used independently or in place of evidence-based medicine, they are put forward as having the healing effects of medicine, but which are not based on evidence gathered with the scientific method. Exemplifying this perspective, a 1998 editorial co-authored by Marcia Angell, a former editor of the *New England Journal of Medicine*, argued that:

> "It is time for the scientific community to stop giving alternative medicine a free ride. There cannot be two kinds of medicine – conventional and alternative. There is only medicine that has been adequately tested and medicine that has not, medicine that works and medicine that may or may not work. Once a treatment has been tested rigorously, it no longer matters whether it was considered alternative at the outset. If it is found to be reasonably safe and effective, it will be accepted. But assertions, speculation, and testimonials do not substitute for evidence. Alternative treatments should be subjected to scientific testing no less rigorous than that required for conventional treatments."

This line of division has been subject to criticism, however, as not all forms of standard medical practice have adequately demonstrated evidence of benefit,[380] and it is also unlikely in most instances that conventional therapies, if proven to be ineffective, would ever be classified as CAM.

Regional definitions

Public information websites maintained by the governments of the US and of the UK make a distinction between "alternative medicine" and "complementary medicine", but mention that these two overlap. The National Center for Complementary and Integrative Health (NCCIH) of the National Institutes of Health (NIH) (a part of the US Department of Health and Human Services) states that "alternative medicine" refers to using a non-mainstream approach in place of conventional medicine and that "complementary medicine" generally refers to using a non-mainstream approach together with conventional medicine, and comments that the boundaries between complementary and conventional medicine overlap and change with time.

The National Health Service (NHS) website *NHS Choices* (owned by the UK Department of Health), adopting the terminology of NCCIH, states that when a treatment is used alongside conventional treatments, to help a patient cope with a health condition, and not as an alternative to conventional treatment, this use of treatments can be called "complementary medicine"; but when a treatment is used instead of conventional medicine, with the intention of treating or curing a health condition, the use can be called "alternative medicine".

Similarly, the public information website maintained by the National Health and Medical Research Council (NHMRC) of the Commonwealth of Australia uses the acronym "CAM" for a wide range of health care practices, therapies, procedures and devices not within the domain of conventional medicine. In the Australian context this is stated to include acupuncture; aromatherapy; chiropractic; homeopathy; massage; meditation and relaxation therapies; naturopathy; osteopathy; reflexology, traditional Chinese medicine; and the use of vitamin supplements.

The Danish National Board of Health's "Council for Alternative Medicine" (Sundhedsstyrelsens Råd for Alternativ Behandling (SRAB)), an independent institution under the National Board of Health (Danish: *Sundhedsstyrelsen*), uses the term "alternative medicine" for:

- Treatments performed by therapists that are not authorized healthcare professionals.
- Treatments performed by authorized healthcare professionals, but those based on methods otherwise used mainly outside the healthcare system. People without a healthcare authorisation are [also] allowed to perform the treatments.

Definitions based on national traditions or dominant practices

In *General Guidelines for Methodologies on Research and Evaluation of Traditional Medicine*, published in 2000 by the World Health Organization (WHO), complementary and alternative medicine were there defined as a broad set of health care practices that are not part of that country's own tradition and are not integrated into the dominant health care system.[381]

Some herbal therapies are mainstream in Europe but are alternative in the US.

History

The history of alternative medicine may refer to the history of a group of diverse medical practices that were collectively promoted as "alternative medicine" beginning in the 1970s, to the collection of individual histories of members of that group, or to the history of western medical practices that were labeled "irregular practices" by the western medical establishment.[382,383,384] It includes the histories of complementary medicine and of integrative medicine. Before the 1970s, western practitioners that were not part of the increasingly science-based medical establishment were referred to "irregular practitioners", and were dismissed by the medical establishment as unscientific and as practicing quackery. Until the 1970's, irregular practice became increasingly marginalized as quackery and fraud, as western medicine increasingly incorporated scientific methods and discoveries, and had a corresponding increase in success of its treatments. In the 1970s, irregular practices were grouped with traditional practices of nonwestern cultures and with other unproven or disproven practices that were not part of biomedicine, with the entire group collectively marketed and promoted under the single expression "alternative medicine".[385]

Use of alternative medicine in the west began to rise following the counterculture movement of the 1960s, as part of the rising new age movement of the 1970s.[386] This was due to misleading mass marketing of "alternative medicine" being an effective "alternative" to biomedicine, changing social attitudes about not using chemicals and challenging the establishment and authority of any kind, sensitivity to giving equal measure to beliefs and practices of other cultures (cultural relativism), and growing frustration and desperation by patients about limitations and side effects of science-based medicine. At the same time, in 1975, the American Medical Association, which played the central role in fighting quackery in the United States, abolished its quackery committee and closed down its Department of Investigation.:xxi[387] By the early to mid 1970s the expression "alternative medicine" came into widespread use, and the expression became mass marketed as a collection of "natural" and effective treatment "alternatives" to science-based biomedicine.[388,389] By 1983, mass marketing of "alternative medicine" was so pervasive that the British Medical Journal (BMJ) pointed to "an apparently endless stream of books, articles, and radio and television programmes urge on the public the virtues of (alternative medicine) treatments ranging from meditation to drilling a hole in the skull to let in more oxygen". In this 1983 article, the BMJ wrote, "one of the few growth industries in contemporary Britain is alternative medicine", noting that by 1983, "33% of patients with rheumatoid arthritis and 39% of those with backache admitted to having consulted an alternative practitioner".

By about 1990, the American alternative medicine industry had grown to a $27 Billion per year, with polls showing 30% of Americans were using it. Moreover, polls showed that Americans made more visits for alternative therapies than the total number of visits to primary care doctors, and American out-of-pocket spending (non-insurance spending) on alternative medicine was about equal to spending on biomedical doctors.:172 In 1991, Time magazine ran a cover story, "The New Age of Alternative Medicine: Why New Age Medicine Is Catching On".[390] In 1993, the New England Journal of Medicine reported one in three Americans as using alternative medicine. In 1993, the Public Broadcasting System ran a Bill Moyers special, Healing and the Mind, with Moyers commenting that "...people by the tens of millions are using alternative medicine. If established medicine does not understand that, they are going to lose their clients."

Another explosive growth began in the 1990s, when senior level political figures began promoting alternative medicine, investing large sums of

Figure 48: *Sen. Tom Harkin at a press conference.*

government medical research funds into testing alternative medicine, including testing of scientifically implausible treatments, and relaxing government regulation of alternative medicine products as compared to biomedical products.:xxi391,392,393 Beginning with a 1991 appropriation of $2 million for funding research of alternative medicine research, federal spending grew to a cumulative total of about $2.5 billion by 2009, with 50% of Americans using alternative medicine by 2013.

In 1991, pointing to a need for testing because of the widespread use of alternative medicine without authoritative information on its efficacy, United States Senator Thomas Harkin used $2 million of his discretionary funds to create the Office for the Study of Unconventional Medical Practices (OSUMP), later renamed to be the Office of Alternative Medicine (OAM).:170 The OAM was created to be within the National Institute of Health (NIH), the scientifically prestigious primary agency of the United States government responsible for biomedical and health-related research.:170 The mandate was to investigate, evaluate, and validate effective alternative medicine treatments, and alert the public as the results of testing its efficacy.394,395,396

Sen. Harkin had become convinced his allergies were cured by taking bee pollen pills, and was urged to make the spending by two of his influential constituents. Bedell, a longtime friend of Sen. Harkin, was a former member of the United States House of Representatives who believed that alternative medicine had twice cured him of diseases after mainstream medicine

Figure 49: *Prince Charles in 2012.*

had failed, claiming that cow's milk colostrum cured his Lyme disease, and an herbal derivative from camphor had prevented post surgical recurrence of his prostate cancer. Wiewel was a promoter of unproven cancer treatments involving a mixture of blood sera that the Food and Drug Administration had banned from being imported. Both Bedell and Wiewel became members of the advisory panel for the OAM. The company that sold the bee pollen was later fined by the Federal Trade Commission for making false health claims about their bee-pollen products reversing the aging process, curing allergies, and helping with weight loss.[397]

In 1993, Brittan's Prince Charles, who claimed that homeopathy and other alternative medicine was an effective alternative to biomedicine, established the Foundation for Integrated Health (FIH), as a charity to explore "how safe, proven complementary therapies can work in conjunction with mainstream medicine". The FIH received government funding through grants from Brittan's Department of Health.

In 1994, Sen. Harkin (D) and Senator Orrin Hatch (R) introduced the Dietary Supplement Health and Education Act (DSHEA). The act reduced authority of the FDA to monitor products sold as "natural" treatments. Labeling standards were reduced to allow health claims for supplements based only on unconfirmed preliminary studies that were not subjected to scientific peer review, and the act made it more difficult for the FDA to promptly seize products or demand proof of safety where there was evidence of a product being dangerous.[398] The Act became known as the "The 1993 Snake Oil Protection Act" following a New York Times editorial under that name.

Senator Harkin complained about the "unbendable rules of randomized clinical trials", citing his use of bee pollen to treat his allergies, which he claimed to be effective even though it was biologically implausible and efficacy was not established using scientific methods. Sen. Harkin asserted that claims for alternative medicine efficacy be allowed not only without conventional scientific testing, even when they are biologically implausible, "It is not necessary for the scientific community to understand the process before the American public can benefit from these therapies." Following passage of the act, sales rose from about $4 billion in 1994, to $20 billion by the end of 2000, at the same time as evidence of their lack of efficacy or harmful effects grew.[399] Senator Harkin came into open public conflict with the first OAM Director Joseph M. Jacobs and OAM board members from the scientific and biomedical community. Jacobs' insistence on rigorous scientific methodology caused friction with Senator Harkin.[400,401] Increasing political resistance to the use of scientific methodology was publicly criticized by Dr. Jacobs and another OAM board member complained that "nonsense has trickled down to every aspect of this office". In 1994, Senator Harkin appeared on television with cancer patients who blamed Dr. Jacobs for blocking their access to untested cancer treatment, leading Jacobs to resign in frustration.

In 1995, Wayne Jonas, a promoter of homeopathy and political ally of Senator Harkin, became the director of the OAM, and continued in that role until 1999.[402] In 1997, the NCCAM budget was increased from $12 million to $20 million annually. From 1990 to 1997, use of alternative medicine in the US increased by 25%, with a corresponding 50% increase in expenditures. The OAM drew increasing criticism from eminent members of the scientific community with letters to the Senate Appropriations Committee when discussion of renewal of funding OAM came up.:[175] Nobel laureate Paul Berg wrote that prestigious NIH should not be degraded to act as a cover for quackery, calling the OAM "an embarrassment to serious scientists.":[175] The president of the American Physical Society wrote complaining that the government was spending money on testing products and practices that "violate basic laws of physics and more clearly resemble witchcraft".:[175][403] In 1998, the President of the North Carolina Medical Association publicly called for shutting down the OAM.[404]

In 1998, NIH director and Nobel laureate Harold Varmus came into conflict with Senator Harkin by pushing to have more NIH control of alternative medicine research. The NIH Director placed the OAM under more strict scientific NIH control. Senator Harkin responded by elevating OAM into an independent NIH "center", just short of being its own "institute", and renamed to be the National Center for Complementary and Alternative Medicine (NCCAM). NCCAM had a mandate to promote a more rigorous and scientific approach to the study of alternative medicine, research training and career development, outreach, and "integration". In 1999, the NCCAM budget was increased from $20 million to $50 million. The United States Congress approved the appropriations without dissent. In 2000, the budget was increased to about $68 million, in 2001 to $90 million, in 2002 to $104 million, and in 2003, to $113 million.

In 2004, modifications of the European Parliament's 2001 Directive 2001/83/EC, regulating all medicine products, were made with the expectation of influencing development of the European market for alternative medicine products. Regulation of alternative medicine in Europe was loosened with "a simplified registration procedure" for traditional herbal medicinal products. Plausible "efficacy" for traditional medicine was redefined to be based on long term popularity and testimonials ("the pharmacological effects or efficacy of the medicinal product are plausible on the basis of long-standing use and experience."), without scientific testing.[405] The Committee on Herbal Medicinal Products (HMPC) was created within the European Medicines Agency in London (EMEA). A special working group was established for homeopathic remedies under the Heads of Medicines Agencies.

Through 2004, alternative medicine that was traditional to Germany continued to be a regular part of the health care system, including homeopathy and anthroposophic medicine.[406] The German Medicines Act mandated that science-based medical authorities consider the "particular characteristics" of complementary and alternative medicines. By 2004, homeopathy had grown to be the most used alternative therapy in France, growing from 16% of the population using homeopathic medicine in 1982, to 29% by 1987, 36% percent by 1992, and 62% of French mothers using homeopathic medicines by 2004, with 94.5% of French pharmacists advising pregnant women to use homeopathic remedies.[407] As of 2004, 100 million people in India depended solely on traditional German homeopathic remedies for their medical care.[408] As of 2010, homeopathic remedies continued to be the leading alternative treatment used by European physicians. By 2005, sales of homeopathic remedies and anthroposophical medicine had grown to $930 million Euros, a 60% increase from 1995.[409]

In 2008, London's *The Times* published a letter from Edzard Ernst that asked the FIH to recall two guides promoting alternative medicine, saying: "the majority of alternative therapies appear to be clinically ineffective, and many are

Figure 50: *Edzard Ernst in 2012*

downright dangerous." In 2010, Brittan's FIH closed after allegations of fraud and money laundering led to arrests of its officials.

In 2009, after a history of 17 years of government testing and spending of nearly $2.5 billion on research had produced almost no clearly proven efficacy of alternative therapies, Senator Harkin complained, "One of the purposes of this center was to investigate and validate alternative approaches. Quite frankly, I must say publicly that it has fallen short. It think quite frankly that in this center and in the office previously before it, most of its focus has been on disproving things rather than seeking out and approving."[410,411] Members of the scientific community criticized this comment as showing Senator Harkin did not understand the basics of scientific inquiry, which tests hypotheses, but never intentionally attempts to "validate approaches". Members of the scientific and biomedical communities complained that after a history of 17 years of being tested, at a cost of over $2.5 Billion on testing scientifically and biologically implausible practices, almost no alternative therapy showed clear efficacy. In 2009, the NCCAM's budget was increased to about $122 million.[412] Overall NIH funding for CAM research increased to $300 Million by 2009. By 2009, Americans were spending $34 Billion annually on CAM.[413]

In 2012, the Journal of the American Medical Association (JAMA) published a criticism that study after study had been funded by NCCAM, but "failed to prove that complementary or alternative therapies are anything more than placebos". The JAMA criticism pointed to large wasting of research money on testing scientifically implausible treatments, citing "NCCAM officials spending $374,000 to find that inhaling lemon and lavender scents does not promote wound healing; $750,000 to find that prayer does not cure AIDS or hasten recovery from breast-reconstruction surgery; $390,000 to find that ancient Indian remedies do not control type 2 diabetes; $700,000 to find that magnets do not treat arthritis, carpal tunnel syndrome, or migraine headaches; and $406,000 to find that coffee enemas do not cure pancreatic cancer."[414] It was pointed out that negative results from testing were generally ignored by the public, that people continue to "believe what they want to believe, arguing that it does not matter what the data show: They know what works for them". Continued increasing use of CAM products was also blamed on the lack of FDA ability to regulate alternative products, where negative studies do not result in FDA warnings or FDA-mandated changes on labeling, whereby few consumers are aware that many claims of many supplements were found not to have not to be supported.

By 2013, 50% of Americans were using CAM.[415] As of 2013, CAM medicinal products in Europe continued to be exempted from documented efficacy standards required of other medicinal products.[416]

In 2014 the NCCAM was renamed to the National Center for Complementary and Integrative Health (NCCIH) with a new charter requiring that 12 of the 18 council members shall be selected with a preference to selecting leading representatives of complementary and alternative medicine, 9 of the members must be licensed practitioners of alternative medicine, 6 members must be general public leaders in the fields of public policy, law, health policy, economics, and management, and 3 members must represent the interests of individual consumers of complementary and alternative medicine.[417]

Histories of individual systems and practices

Much of what is now categorized as alternative medicine was developed as independent, complete medical systems. These were developed long before biomedicine and use of scientific methods. Each system was developed in relatively isolated regions of the world where there was little or no medical contact with pre-scientific western medicine, or with each others' systems. Examples are Traditional Chinese medicine and the Ayurvedic medicine of India.

Other alternative medicine practices, such as homeopathy, were developed in western Europe and in opposition to western medicine, at a time when western medicine was based on unscientific theories that were dogmatically imposed by western religious authorities. Homeopathy was developed prior to discovery of the basic principles of chemistry, which proved homeopathic remedies contained nothing but water. But homeopathy, with its remedies made of water, was harmless compared to the unscientific and dangerous orthodox western medicine practiced at that time, which included use of toxins and draining of blood, often resulting in permanent disfigurement or death.

Other alternative practices such as chiropractic and osteopathic manipulative medicine were developed in the United States at a time that western medicine was beginning to incorporate scientific methods and theories, but the biomedical model was not yet totally dominant. Practices such as chiropractic and osteopathic, each considered to be irregular practices by the western medical establishment, also opposed each other, both rhetorically and politically with licensing legislation. Osteopathic practitioners added the courses and training of biomedicine to their licensing, and licensed Doctor of Osteopathic Medicine holders began diminishing use of the unscientific origins of the field. Without the original nonscientific practices and theories, osteopathic medicine is now considered the same as biomedicine.

History of "irregular practitioners"

Main article: History of alternative medicine

Further information: Rise of modern medicine

Until the 1970s, western practitioners that were not part of the medical establishment were referred to "irregular practitioners", and were dismissed by the medical establishment as unscientific, as practicing quackery. Irregular practice became increasingly marginalized as quackery and fraud, as western medicine increasingly incorporated scientific methods and discoveries, and had a corresponding increase in success of its treatments.

Dating from the 1970s, medical professionals, sociologists, anthropologists and other commentators noted the increasing visibility of a wide variety of health practices that had neither derived directly from nor been verified by biomedical science. Since that time, those who have analyzed this trend have deliberated over the most apt language with which to describe this emergent health field. A variety of terms have been used, including heterodox, irregular, fringe and alternative medicine while others, particularly medical commentators, have been satisfied to label them as instances of quackery. The most persistent term has been alternative medicine but its use is problematic as it assumes a value-laden dichotomy between a medical fringe, implicitly of borderline acceptability at best, and a privileged medical orthodoxy, associated with validated medico-scientific norms. The use of the category of alternative medicine has also been criticized as it cannot be studied as an independent entity but must be understood in terms of a regionally and temporally specific medical orthodoxy. Its use can also be misleading as it may erroneously imply that a real medical alternative exists. As with near-synonymous expressions, such as unorthodox, complementary, marginal, or quackery, these linguistic devices have served, in the context of processes of professionalisation and market competition, to establish the authority of official medicine and police the boundary between it and its unconventional rivals.

An early instance of the influence of this modern, or western, scientific medicine outside Europe and North America is Peking Union Medical College.[418,419]

From a historical perspective, the emergence of alternative medicine, if not the term itself, is typically dated to the 19th century. This is despite the fact that there are variants of Western non-conventional medicine that arose in the late-eighteenth century or earlier and some non-Western medical traditions, currently considered alternative in the West and elsewhere, which boast extended historical pedigrees. Alternative medical systems, however, can only be said to exist when there is an identifiable, regularized and authoritative standard medical practice, such as arose in the West during the nineteenth-century, to which they can function as an alternative.[420]

During the late eighteenth and nineteenth centuries regular and irregular medical practitioners became more clearly differentiated throughout much of Europe and, as the nineteenth century progressed, most Western states converged in the creation of legally delimited and semi-protected medical markets. It is at this point that an "official" medicine, created in cooperation with the state and employing a scientific rhetoric of legitimacy, emerges as a recognizable entity and that the concept of alternative medicine as a historical category becomes tenable.

As part of this process, professional adherents of mainstream medicine in countries such as Germany, France, and Britain increasingly invoked the scientific basis of their discipline as a means of engendering internal professional unity and of external differentiation in the face of sustained market competition from homeopaths, naturopaths, mesmerists and other nonconventional medical practitioners, finally achieving a degree of imperfect dominance through alliance with the state and the passage of regulatory legislation. In the US the Johns Hopkins University School of Medicine, based in Baltimore, Maryland, opened in 1893,with William H. Welch and William Osler among the founding physicians, and was the first medical school devoted to teaching "German scientific medicine".

Buttressed by the increased authority arising from significant advances in the medical sciences of the late 19th century onwards—including the development and application of the germ theory of disease by the chemist Louis Pasteur and the surgeon Joseph Lister, of microbiology co-founded by Robert Koch (in 1885 appointed professor of hygiene at the University of Berlin), and of the use of X-rays (Röntgen rays)—the 1910 Flexner Report called upon American medical schools to follow the model set by the Johns Hopkins School of Medicine and adhere to mainstream science in their teaching and research. This was in a belief, mentioned in the Report's introduction, that the preliminary and professional training then prevailing in medical schools should be reformed in view of the new means for diagnosing and combating disease being made available to physicians and surgeons by the sciences on which medicine depended.[421]

Among putative medical practices available at the time which later became known as "alternative medicine" were homeopathy (founded in Germany in the early 19c.) and chiropractic (founded in North America in the late 19c.). These conflicted in principle with the developments in medical science upon which the Flexner reforms were based, and they have not become compatible with further advances of medical science such as listed in Timeline of medicine and medical technology, 1900–1999 and 2000–present, nor have Ayurveda, acupuncture or other kinds of alternative medicine.Wikipedia:Citation needed

At the same time "Tropical medicine" was being developed as a specialist branch of western medicine in research establishments such as Liverpool School of Tropical Medicine founded in 1898 by Alfred Lewis Jones, London School of Hygiene & Tropical Medicine, founded in 1899 by Patrick Manson and Tulane University School of Public Health and Tropical Medicine, instituted in 1912. A distinction was being made between western scientific medicine and indigenous systems. An example is given by an official report about indigenous systems of medicine in India, including Ayurveda, submitted by Mohammad Usman of Madras and others in 1923. This stated that the first question the Committee considered was "to decide whether the indigenous systems of medicine were scientific or not".[422]

By the later twentieth century the term 'alternative medicine' entered public discourse,[423] but it was not always being used with the same meaning by all parties. Arnold S. Relman remarked in 1998 that in the best kind of medical practice, all proposed treatments must be tested objectively, and that in the end there will only be treatments that pass and those that do not, those that are proven worthwhile and those that are not. He asked 'Can there be any reasonable "alternative"?' But also in 1998 the then Surgeon General of the United States, David Satcher, issued public information about eight common alternative treatments (including acupuncture, holistic and massage), together with information about common diseases and conditions, on nutrition, diet, and lifestyle changes, and about helping consumers to decipher fraud and quackery, and to find healthcare centers and doctors who practiced alternative medicine.

By 1990, approximately 60 million Americans had used one or more complementary or alternative therapies to address health issues, according to a nationwide survey in the US published in 1993 by David Eisenberg. A study published in the November 11, 1998 issue of the Journal of the American Medical Association reported that 42% of Americans had used complementary and alternative therapies, up from 34% in 1990. However, despite the growth in patient demand for complementary medicine, most of the early alternative/complementary medical centers failed.

Medical education since 1910

Mainly as a result of reforms following the Flexner Report of 1910 medical education in established medical schools in the US has generally not included alternative medicine as a teaching topic.[424] Typically, their teaching is based on current practice and scientific knowledge about: anatomy, physiology, histology, embryology, neuroanatomy, pathology, pharmacology, microbiology and immunology. Medical schools' teaching includes such topics as doctor-patient communication, ethics, the art of medicine, and engaging in complex clinical reasoning (medical decision-making). Writing in 2002, Snyderman and Weil remarked that by the early twentieth century the Flexner model had helped to create the 20th-century academic health center in which education, research and practice were inseparable. While this had much improved medical practice by defining with increasing certainty the pathophysiological basis of disease, a single-minded focus on the pathophysiological had diverted much of mainstream American medicine from clinical conditions which were not well understood in mechanistic terms and were not effectively treated by conventional therapies.

By 2001 some form of CAM training was being offered by at least 75 out of 125 medical schools in the US. Exceptionally, the School of Medicine of the University of Maryland, Baltimore includes a research institute for integrative medicine (a member entity of the Cochrane Collaboration). Medical schools are responsible for conferring medical degrees, but a physician typically may not legally practice medicine until licensed by the local government authority. Licensed physicians in the US who have attended one of the established medical schools there have usually graduated Doctor of Medicine (MD). All states require that applicants for MD licensure be graduates of an approved medical school and complete the United States Medical Licensing Exam (USMLE).

The British Medical Association, in its publication *Complementary Medicine, New Approach to Good Practice* (1993), gave as a working definition of non-conventional therapies (including acupuncture, chiropractic and homeopathy):

"those forms of treatment which are not widely used by the orthodox healthcare professions, and the skills of which are not part of the undergraduate curriculum of orthodox medical and paramedical health-care courses".[425] By 2000 some medical schools in the UK were offering CAM familiarisation courses to undergraduate medical students while some were also offering modules specifically on CAM.

Proponents and opponents

The Cochrane Collaboration Complementary Medicine Field explains its "Scope and Topics" by giving a broad and general definition for complementary medicine as including practices and ideas which are outside the domain of conventional medicine in several countries and defined by its users as preventing or treating illness, or promoting health and well being, and which complement mainstream medicine in three ways: by contributing to a common whole, by satisfying a demand not met by conventional practices, and by diversifying the conceptual framework of medicine.

Proponents of an evidence-base for medicine[426] such as the Cochrane Collaboration (founded in 1993 and from 2011 providing input for WHO resolutions) take a position that *all* systematic reviews of treatments, whether "mainstream" or "alternative", ought to be held to the current standards of scientific method. In a study titled *Development and classification of an operational definition of complementary and alternative medicine for the Cochrane Collaboration* (2011) it was proposed that indicators that a therapy is accepted include government licensing of practitioners, coverage by health insurance, statements of approval by government agencies, and recommendation as part of a practice guideline; and that if something is currently a standard, accepted therapy, then it is not likely to be widely considered as CAM.

That alternative medicine has been on the rise "in countries where Western science and scientific method generally are accepted as the major foundations for healthcare, and 'evidence-based' practice is the dominant paradigm" was described as an "enigma" in the Medical Journal of Australia.

Critics in the US say the expression is deceptive because it implies there is an effective alternative to science-based medicine, and that *complementary* is deceptive because the word implies that the treatment increases the effectiveness of (complements) science-based medicine, while alternative medicines which have been tested nearly always have no measurable positive effect compared to a placebo.

Some opponents, focused upon health fraud, misinformation, and quackery as public health problems in the US, are highly critical of alternative medicine, notably Wallace Sampson and Paul Kurtz founders of Scientific Review of

Alternative Medicine and Stephen Barrett, co-founder of The National Council Against Health Fraud and webmaster of Quackwatch. Grounds for opposing alternative medicine which have been stated in the US and elsewhere are:

- that it is usually based on religion, tradition, superstition, belief in supernatural energies, pseudoscience, errors in reasoning, propaganda, or fraud.
- that alternative therapies typically lack any scientific validation, and their effectiveness is either unproved or disproved.Wikipedia:Disputed statement
- that the treatments are those that are not part of the conventional, science-based healthcare system.[427]
- that research on alternative medicine is frequently of low quality and methodologically flawed.[428]Wikipedia:Citing sources#What information to include
- that where alternative treatments are used in place of conventional science-based medicine, even with the very safest alternative medicines, failure to use or delay in using conventional science-based medicine has resulted in deaths.
- that methods may incorporate or base themselves on traditional medicine, folk knowledge, spiritual beliefs, ignorance or misunderstanding of scientific principles, errors in reasoning, or newly conceived approaches claiming to heal.

Paul Offit has proposed four ways that "alternative medicine becomes quackery":

1. "...by recommending against conventional therapies that are helpful."
2. "...by promoting potentially harmful therapies without adequate warning."
3. "...by draining patients' bank accounts,..."
4. "...by promoting magical thinking,..."

The NCCIH classification system

A United States government agency, the National Center on Complementary and Integrative Health (NCCIH), has created its own classification system for branches of complementary and alternative medicine. It classifies complementary and alternative therapies into five major groups, which have some overlap and two types of energy medicine are distinguished: one, "Veritable" involving scientifically observable energy, including magnet therapy, colorpuncture and light therapy; the other "Putative" which invoke physically undetectable or unverifiable energy.

Alternative medicine practices and beliefs are diverse in their foundations and methodologies. The wide range of treatments and practices referred to as alternative medicine includes some stemming from nineteenth century North America, such as chiropractic and naturopathy, others, mentioned by Jütte, that originated in eighteenth- and nineteenth-century Germany, such as homeopathy and hydropathy, and some that have originated in China or India, while African, Caribbean, Pacific Island, Native American, and other regional cultures have traditional medical systems as diverse as their diversity of cultures.

Examples of CAM as a broader term for unorthodox treatment and diagnosis of illnesses, disease, infections, etc., include yoga, acupuncture, aromatherapy, chiropractic, herbalism, homeopathy, hypnotherapy, massage, osteopathy, reflexology, relaxation therapies, spiritual healing and tai chi. CAM differs from conventional medicine. It is normally private medicine and not covered by health insurance. It is paid out of pocket by the patient and is an expensive treatment. CAM tends to be a treatment for upper class or more educated people.

The NCCIH classification system is -

1. Whole medical systems: cut across more than one of the other groups; examples include traditional Chinese medicine, naturopathy, homeopathy, and ayurveda
2. Mind-body interventions: explore the interconnection between the mind, body, and spirit, under the premise that the mind can affect "bodily functions and symptoms"
3. "Biology"-based practices: use substances found in nature such as herbs, foods, vitamins, and other natural substances. (Note that as used here, "biology" does *not* refer to the science of biology, but is a usage newly coined by NCCIH in the primary source used for this article. "Biology-based" as coined by NCCIH may refer to chemicals from a nonbiological source, such as use of the poison lead in Traditional Chinese Medicine, and to other nonbiological substances.)
4. Manipulative and body-based practices: feature manipulation or movement of body parts, such as is done in chiropractic and osteopathic manipulation
5. Energy medicine: is a domain that deals with putative and verifiable energy fields:
   - Biofield therapies are intended to influence energy fields that, it is purported, surround and penetrate the body. No empirical evidence has been found to support the existence of the putative energy fields on which these therapies are predicated.

- Bioelectromagnetic-based therapies use verifiable electromagnetic fields, such as pulsed fields, alternating-current, or direct-current fields in an unconventional manner.

Examples classified under the NCCIH system

Alternative therapies based on electricity or magnetism use verifiable electromagnetic fields, such as pulsed fields, alternating-current, or direct-current fields in an unconventional manner rather than claiming the existence of imponderable or supernatural energies.

Substance based practices use substances found in nature such as herbs, foods, non-vitamin supplements and megavitamins, and minerals, and includes traditional herbal remedies with herbs specific to regions in which the cultural practices arose. Nonvitamin supplements include fish oil, Omega-3 fatty acid, glucosamine, echinacea, flaxseed oil or pills, and ginseng, when used under a claim to have healing effects.

Mind-body interventions, working under the premise that the mind can affect "bodily functions and symptoms", include healing claims made in hypnotherapy, and in guided imagery, meditation, progressive relaxation, qi gong, tai chi and yoga. Meditation practices including mantra meditation, mindfulness meditation, yoga, tai chi, and qi gong have many uncertainties. According to an AHRQ review, the available evidence on meditation practices through September 2005 is of poor methodological quality and definite conclusions on the effects of meditation in healthcare cannot be made using existing research.

Naturopathy is based on a belief in vitalism, which posits that a special energy called vital energy or vital force guides bodily processes such as metabolism, reproduction, growth, and adaptation. The term was coined in 1895 by John Scheel and popularized by Benedict Lust, the "father of U.S. naturopathy". Today, naturopathy is primarily practiced in the United States and Canada. Naturopaths in unregulated jurisdictions may use the Naturopathic Doctor designation or other titles regardless of level of education.

Traditional Chinese medicine is based on a concept of vital energy, or Qi, flowing in the body along specific pathways. These purported pathways consist of 12 primary meridians. TCM has many branches including, acupuncture, massage, feng shui, herbs, as well as Chinese astrology. TCM diagnosis is primarily based on looking at the tongue, which is claimed to show the condition of the organs, as well as feeling the pulse of the radial artery, which is also claimed to show the condition of the organs.

Criticism

'There is no alternative medicine. There is only scientifically proven, evidence-based medicine supported by solid data or unproven medicine, for which scientific evidence is lacking. - P.B. Fontanarosa, Journal of the American Medical Association *(1998)*

Legitimacy

"CAM", meaning "complementary and alternative medicine", is not as well researched as conventional medicine which undergoes intense research before being released to the public. Funding for research is also sparse making it difficult to do further research for effectiveness of CAM. Most funding for CAM is funded by government agencies. Proposed research for CAM are rejected by most private funding agencies because the results of research are not reliable. The research for CAM has to meet certain standards from research ethics committees which most CAM researchers find almost impossible to meet. Because the results of CAM are not quantifiable, it is hard to prove its effectiveness and it appears to work in a more holistic sense. CAM is thought to help the patient in a mental or psychological sense since the research for CAM is hit and miss. Even with the little research done on it, CAM has not been proven to be effective. This creates an issue of whether the patient is receiving all the information about the treatment that is necessary for the patient to be well informed.

Another critic, with reference to government funding studies of integrating alternative medicine techniques into the mainstream, Steven Novella, a neurologist at Yale School of Medicine, wrote that it "is used to lend an appearance of legitimacy to treatments that are not legitimate." Another, Marcia Angell, argued that it was "a new name for snake oil." Angell considered that critics felt that healthcare practices should be classified based solely on scientific evidence, and if a treatment had been rigorously tested and found safe and effective, science based medicine will adopt it regardless of whether it was considered "alternative" to begin with. It was thus possible for a method to change categories (proven vs. unproven), based on increased knowledge of its effectiveness or lack thereof. Prominent supporters of this position include George D. Lundberg, former editor of the Journal of the American Medical Association (JAMA).

In an article first published in *CA: A Cancer Journal for Clinicians* in 1999, "Evaluating complementary and alternative therapies for cancer patients.", Barrie R. Cassileth mentioned that a 1997 letter to the US Senate Subcommittee on Public Health and Safety, which had deplored the lack of critical thinking and scientific rigor in OAM-supported research, had been signed by four Nobel Laureates and other prominent scientists. (This was supported by the National Institutes of Health (NIH).)

In March 2009 a *Washington Post* staff writer reported that the impending national discussion about broadening access to health care, improving medical practice and saving money was giving a group of scientists an opening to propose shutting down the National Center for Complementary and Alternative Medicine, quoting one of them, Steven Salzberg, a genome researcher and computational biologist at the University of Maryland, saying "One of our concerns is that NIH is funding pseudoscience." They argued that the vast majority of studies were based on fundamental misunderstandings of physiology and disease, and have shown little or no effect.

Writers such as Carl Sagan (1934-1996), a noted astrophysicist, advocate of skeptical thinking (Scientific skepticism) and the author of *The Demon–Haunted World: Science as a Candle in the Dark* (1996), have described the lack of empirical evidence to support the existence of the putative energy fields on which these therapies are predicated.[354]

The NCCIH budget has been criticized because, despite the duration and intensity of studies to measure the efficacy of alternative medicine, there had been no effective CAM treatments supported by scientific evidence as of 2002[429], according to the QuackWatch website; the NCCIH budget has been on a sharp and sustained rise. Critics of the Center argue that the plausibility of interventions such as botanical remedies, diet, relaxation therapies and yoga should not be used to support research on implausible interventions based on superstition and belief in the supernatural, and that the plausible methods can be studied just as well in other parts of NIH, where they should be made to compete on an equal footing with other research projects.

Sampson has also pointed out that CAM tolerated contradiction without thorough reason and experiment. Barrett has pointed out that there is a policy at the NIH of never saying something doesn't work only that a different version or dose might give different results. Barrett also expressed concern that, just because some "alternatives" have merit, there is the impression that the rest deserve equal consideration and respect even though most are worthless, since they are all classified under the one heading of alternative medicine.

A 2002 report on public attitudes and understanding issued by the US National Science Foundation defines the term "alternative medicine" as treatments that had not been proven effective using scientific methods, and described them as giving more weight to ancient traditions and anecdotes over biological science and clinical trials.

Richard Dawkins, an English evolutionary biologist and author, in an essay in his book *A Devil's Chaplain* (2003) (chapter 4.4), has defined alternative medicine as a "set of practices that cannot be tested, refuse to be tested, or consistently fail tests." Another essay in the same book (chapter 1.4) quoted from an article by John Diamond in *The Independent*: "There is really no such thing as alternative medicine, just medicine that works and medicine that doesn't." Dawkins has argued that, if a technique is demonstrated effective in properly performed trials, it ceases to be alternative and simply becomes medicine.

Terminology

Use of the terms "Complementary and alternative medicine (CAM)" and "alternative medicine" have been criticized.

Criticisms have come from individuals such as Wallace Sampson in an article in Annals of the New York Academy of Sciences, June 1995. Sampson argued that proponents of alternative medicine often used terminology which was loose or ambiguous to create the appearance that a choice between "alternative" effective treatments existed when it did not, or that there was effectiveness or scientific validity when it did not exist, or to suggest that a dichotomy existed when it did not, or to suggest that consistency with science existed when it might not; that the term "**alternative**" was to suggest that a patient had a choice between effective treatments when there was not; that use of the word "**conventional**" or "**mainstream**" was to suggest that the difference between alternative medicine and science based medicine was the prevalence of use, rather than lack of a scientific basis of alternative medicine as compared to "conventional" or "mainstream" science based medicine; that use of the term "**complementary**" or "**integrative**" was to suggest that purported supernatural energies of alternative medicine could complement or be integrated into science based medicine. "*Integrative medicine*" or "integrated medicine" is used to refer to the belief that medicine based on science would be improved by "integration" with alternative medical treatments practices that are not, and is substantially similar in use to the term "complementary and alternative medicine". Sampson has also written that CAM is the "propagation of the absurd", and argues that *alternative* and *complementary* have been substituted for *quackery*, *dubious*, and *implausible*.

Stephen Barrett, founder and operator of Quackwatch, has argued that practices labeled "alternative" should be reclassified as either genuine, experimental, or questionable. Here he defines genuine as being methods that have sound evidence for safety and effectiveness, experimental as being unproven but with a plausible rationale for effectiveness, and questionable as groundless without a scientifically plausible rationale.

Ethics

CAM is not as well regulated as conventional medicine. There are ethical concerns about whether people who perform CAM have the proper knowledge to perform the treatments they give to patients. CAM is often done by non-physicians and does not operate with the same medical licensing laws as conventional medicine. It is an issue of non-maleficence.

According to two writers, Wallace Sampson and K. Butler, marketing is part of the medical training required in chiropractic education, and propaganda methods in alternative medicine have been traced back to those used by Hitler and Goebels in their promotion of pseudoscience in medicine.

In November 2011 Edzard Ernst stated that the "level of misinformation about alternative medicine has now reached the point where it has become dangerous and unethical. So far, alternative medicine has remained an ethics-free zone. It is time to change this." Ernst requested that Prince Charles recall two guides to alternative medicine published by the Foundation for Integrated Health, on the grounds that "[t]hey both contain numerous misleading and inaccurate claims concerning the supposed benefits of alternative medicine" and that "[t]he nation cannot be served by promoting ineffective and sometimes dangerous alternative treatments." In general, he believes that CAM can and should be subjected to scientific testing.[430]</ref>

Placebo effect

A research methods expert and author of "Snake Oil Science", R. Barker Bausell, has stated that "it's become politically correct to investigate nonsense." There are concerns that just having NIH support is being used to give unfounded "legitimacy to treatments that are not legitimate."

Use of placebos in order to achieve a placebo effect in integrative medicine has been criticized as "diverting research time, money, and other resources from more fruitful lines of investigation in order to pursue a theory that has no basis in biology".

Another critic has argued that academic proponents of integrative medicine sometimes recommend misleading patients by using known placebo treatments in order to achieve a placebo effect.[431] However, a 2010 survey of family physicians found that 56% of respondents said they had used a placebo in clinical practice as well. Eighty-five percent of respondents believed placebos can have both psychological and physical benefits.

Integrative medicine has been criticized in that its practitioners, trained in science based medicine, deliberately mislead patients by pretending placebos are not. "quackademic medicine" is a pejorative term used for "integrative medicine", which is considered to be an infiltration of quackery into academic science-based medicine.

An analysis of trends in the criticism of complementary and alternative medicine (CAM) in five prestigious American medical journals during the period of reorganization within medicine (1965-1999) was reported as showing that the medical profession had responded to the growth of CAM in three phases, and that in each phase there had been changes in the medical marketplace which influenced the type of response in the journals. Changes included relaxed medical licensing, the development of managed care, rising consumerism, and the establishment of the USA Office of Alternative Medicine (now National Center for Complementary and Alternative Medicine).[432]</ref> In the "condemnation" phase, from the late 1960s to the early 1970s, authors had ridiculed, exaggerated the risks, and petitioned the state to contain CAM; in the "reassessment" phase (mid-1970s through early 1990s), when increased consumer utilization of CAM was prompting concern, authors had pondered whether patient dissatisfaction and shortcomings in conventional care contributed to the trend; in the "integration" phase of the 1990s physicians began learning to work around or administer CAM, and the subjugation of CAM to scientific scrutiny had become the primary means of control.

Use and regulation

Prevalence of use

Complementary and alternative medicine (CAM) has been described as a broad domain of healing resources that encompasses all health systems, modalities, and practices and their accompanying theories and beliefs, other than those intrinsic to the politically dominant health system of a particular society or culture in a given historical period. CAM includes all such practices and ideas self-defined by their users as preventing or treating illness or promoting health and well-being. Boundaries within CAM and between the CAM domain and that of the dominant system are not always sharp or fixed.Wikipedia:Disputed statement

About 50% of people in developed countries use some kind of complementary and alternative medicine other than prayer for health. A British telephone survey by the BBC of 1209 adults in 1998 shows that around 20% of adults in Britain had used alternative medicine in the past 12 months. About 40% of cancer patients use some form of CAM.

In developing nations, access to essential medicines is severely restricted by lack of resources and poverty. Traditional remedies, often closely resembling or forming the basis for alternative remedies, may comprise primary healthcare or be integrated into the healthcare system. In Africa, traditional medicine is used for 80% of primary healthcare, and in developing nations as a whole over one-third of the population lack access to essential medicines.

In the US

In the United States, the 1974 Child Abuse Prevention and Treatment Act (CAPTA) required states to grant religious exemptions to child neglect and abuse laws, regarding religion-based healing practices, in order to receive federal money. Thirty-one states have child-abuse religious exemptions.

In respect of taxation in the US, the Internal Revenue Service has discriminated in favour of medical expenses for acupuncture and chiropractic (and others including Christian Science practitioners) but against homeopathy and the use of non-prescription required medicine.^{433}</ref>

The use of alternative medicine in the US has increased, with a 50 percent increase in expenditures and a 25 percent increase in the use of alternative therapies between 1990 and 1997 in America. Americans spend many billions on the therapies annually. Most Americans used CAM to treat and/or prevent musculoskeletal conditions or other conditions associated with chronic or recurring pain. In America, women were more likely than men to use CAM, with the biggest difference in use of mind-body therapies including prayer specifically for health reasons". In 2008, more than 37% of American hospitals offered alternative therapies, up from 26.5 percent in 2005, and 25% in 2004. More than 70% of the hospitals offering CAM were in urban areas.

A survey of Americans found that 88 percent agreed that "there are some good ways of treating sickness that medical science does not recognize". Use of magnets was the most common tool in energy medicine in America, and among users of it, 58 percent described it as at least "sort of scientific", when it is not at all scientific. In 2002, at least 60 percent of US medical schools have at least some class time spent teaching alternative therapies. "Therapeutic touch", was taught at more than 100 colleges and universities in 75 countries before the practice was debunked by a nine-year-old child for a school science project.

A 1997 survey found that 13.7% of respondents in the US had sought the services of both a medical doctor and an alternative medicine practitioner. The same survey found that 96% of respondents who sought the services of an alternative medicine practitioner also sought the services of a medical doctor in the past 12 months. Medical doctors are often unaware of their patient's use of alternative medical treatments as only 38.5% of the patients alternative therapies were discussed with their medical doctor.

According to Michael H. Cohen, US regulation of alternative includes state licensing of healthcare providers and scope of practice limits on practice by non-MD healthcare professionals; state-law malpractice rules (standard of care limits on professional negligence); discipline of practitioners by state regulatory boards; and federal regulation such as food and drug law.[434] He argues that US regulation of alternative medicine "seeks to integrate biomedical, holistic, and social models of health care in ways that maximize patients' well-being [w]hile still protecting patients from fraud."[435]

Prevalence of use of specific therapies

The most common CAM therapies used in the US in 2002 were prayer (45.2%), herbalism (18.9%), breathing meditation (11.6%), meditation (7.6%), chiropractic medicine (7.5%), yoga (5.1%-6.1%), body work (5.0%), diet-based therapy (3.5%), progressive relaxation (3.0%), mega-vitamin therapy (2.8%) and Visualization (2.1%)

In Britain, the most often used alternative therapies were Alexander technique, Aromatherapy, Bach and other flower remedies, Body work therapies including massage, Counseling stress therapies, hypnotherapy, Meditation, Reflexology, Shiatsu, Ayurvedic medicine, Nutritional medicine, and Yoga.[436] Ayurvedic medicine remedies are mainly plant based with some use of animal materials.[437] Safety concerns include the use of herbs containing toxic compounds and the lack of quality control in Ayurvedic facilities.

According to the National Health Service (England), the most commonly used complementary and alternative medicines (CAM) supported by the NHS in the UK are: acupuncture, aromatherapy, chiropractic, homeopathy, massage, osteopathy and clinical hypnotherapy.

"Complementary medicine treatments used for pain include: acupuncture, low-level laser therapy, meditation, aroma therapy, Chinese medicine, dance therapy, music therapy, massage, herbalism, therapeutic touch, yoga, osteopathy, chiropractic, naturopathy, and homeopathy."

In palliative care

Complementary therapies are often used in palliative care or by practitioners attempting to manage chronic pain in patients. Integrative medicine is considered more acceptable in the interdisciplinary approach used in palliative care than in other areas of medicine. "From its early experiences of care for the dying, palliative care took for granted the necessity of placing patient values and lifestyle habits at the core of any design and delivery of quality care at the end of life. If the patient desired complementary therapies, and as long as such treatments provided additional support and did not endanger the patient, they were considered acceptable." The non-pharmacologic interventions

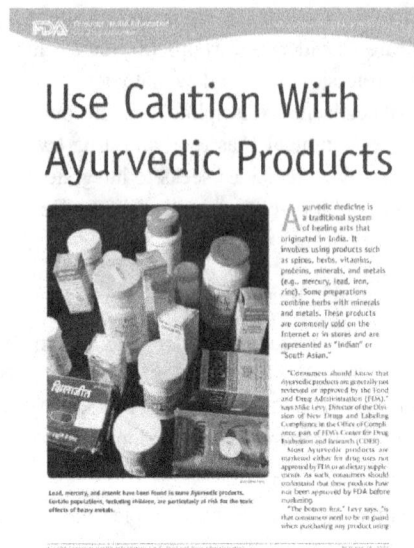

Figure 51: *Health campaign flyers, as in this example from the Food and Drug Administration, warn the public about unsafe products.*

of complementary medicine can employ mind-body interventions designed to "reduce pain and concomitant mood disturbance and increase quality of life."

Regulation

Further information: Regulation of alternative medicine and Regulation and prevalence of homeopathy

In Austria and Germany complementary and alternative medicine is mainly in the hands of doctors with MDs, and half or more of the American alternative practitioners are licensed MDs. In Germany herbs are tightly regulated: half are prescribed by doctors and covered by health insurance.

Some professions of complementary/traditional/alternative medicine, such as chiropractic, have achieved full regulation in North America and other parts of the world[438] and are regulated in a manner similar to that governing science-based medicine. In contrast, other approaches may be partially recognized and others have no regulation at all. Regulation and licensing of alternative medicine ranges widely from country to country, and state to state.[438]

Government bodies in the USA and elsewhere have published information or guidance about alternative medicine. The U.S. Food and Drug Administration (FDA), has issued online warnings for consumers about medication health fraud. This includes a section on Alternative Medicine Fraud, such as a warning that Ayurvedic products generally have not been approved by the FDA before marketing.[439]

Efficacy

Alternative therapies lack the requisite scientific validation, and their effectiveness is either unproved or disproved. Many of the claims regarding the efficacy of alternative medicines are controversial, since research on them is frequently of low quality and methodologically flawed.[428] Wikipedia:Citing sources#What information to include Selective publication of results (misleading results from only publishing positive results, and not all results), marked differences in product quality and standardisation, and some companies making unsubstantiated claims, call into question the claims of efficacy of isolated examples where herbs may have some evidence of containing chemicals that may affect health. *The Scientific Review of Alternative Medicine* points to confusions in the general population - a person may attribute symptomatic relief to an otherwise-ineffective therapy just because they are taking something (the placebo effect); the natural recovery from or the cyclical nature of an illness (the regression fallacy) gets misattributed to an alternative medicine being taken; a person not diagnosed with science based medicine may never originally have had a true illness diagnosed as an alternative disease category.

Edzard Ernst characterized the evidence for many alternative techniques as weak, nonexistent, or negative and in 2011 published his estimate that about 7.4% were based on "sound evidence", although he believes that may be an overestimate due to various reasons. Ernst has concluded that 95% of the alternative treatments he and his team studied, including acupuncture, herbal medicine, homeopathy, and reflexology, are "statistically indistinguishable from placebo treatments", but he also believes there is something that conventional doctors can usefully learn from the chiropractors and homeopath: this is the therapeutic value of the placebo effect, one of the strangest phenomena in medicine.

In 2003, a project funded by the CDC identified 208 condition-treatment pairs, of which 58% had been studied by at least one randomized controlled trial (RCT), and 23% had been assessed with a meta-analysis. According to a 2005 book by a US Institute of Medicine panel, the number of RCTs focused on CAM has risen dramatically. The book cites Vickers (1998), who found that many of the CAM-related RCTs are in the Cochrane register, but 19% of these trials were not in MEDLINE, and 84% were in conventional medical journals.[440]

As of 2005[429], the Cochrane Library had 145 CAM-related Cochrane systematic reviews and 340 non-Cochrane systematic reviews. An analysis of the conclusions of only the 145 Cochrane reviews was done by two readers. In 83% of the cases, the readers agreed. In the 17% in which they disagreed, a third reader agreed with one of the initial readers to set a rating. These studies found that, for CAM, 38.4% concluded positive effect or possibly positive (12.4%), 4.8% concluded no effect, 0.69% concluded harmful effect, and 56.6% concluded insufficient evidence. An assessment of conventional treatments found that 41.3% concluded positive or possibly positive effect, 20% concluded no effect, 8.1% concluded net harmful effects, and 21.3% concluded insufficient evidence. However, the CAM review used the more developed 2004 Cochrane database, while the conventional review used the initial 1998 Cochrane database.[441]

Most alternative medical treatments are not patentable,Wikipedia:Citation needed which may lead to less research funding from the private sector. In addition, in most countries, alternative treatments (in contrast to pharmaceuticals) can be marketed without any proof of efficacy—also a disincentive for manufacturers to fund scientific research. Some have proposed adopting a prize system to reward medical research. However, public funding for research exists. Increasing the funding for research on alternative medicine techniques is the purpose of the US National Center for Complementary and Alternative Medicine. NCCIH and its predecessor, the Office of Alternative Medicine, have spent more than $2.5 billion on such research since 1992; this research has largely not demonstrated the efficacy of alternative treatments.

In the same way as for conventional therapies, drugs, and interventions, it can be difficult to test the efficacy of alternative medicine in clinical trials. In instances where an established, effective, treatment for a condition is already available, the Helsinki Declaration states that withholding such treatment is unethical in most circumstances. Use of standard-of-care treatment in addition to an alternative technique being tested may produce confounded or difficult-to-interpret results.

Cancer researcher Andrew J. Vickers has stated:

> "Contrary to much popular and scientific writing, many alternative cancer treatments have been investigated in good-quality clinical trials, and they have been shown to be ineffective. In this article, clinical trial data on a number of alternative cancer cures including Livingston-Wheeler, Di Bella Multitherapy, antineoplastons, vitamin C, hydrazine sulfate, Laetrile, and psychotherapy are reviewed. The label 'unproven' is inappropriate for such therapies; it is time to assert that many alternative cancer therapies have been 'disproven'."

Homeopathy is based on the belief that a disease can be cured by a very low dose of substance that creates similar symptoms in a healthy person. This conflicts with fundamental concepts of physics and chemistry and there is no good evidence from reviews of research to support its use.

Conflicts of interest

Some commentators have said that special consideration must be given to the issue of conflicts of interest in alternative medicine. Edzard Ernst has said that most researchers into alternative medicine are at risk of "unidirectional bias" because of a generally uncritical belief in their chosen subject. Ernst cites as evidence the phenomenon whereby 100% of a sample of acupuncture trials originating in China had positive conclusions. David Gorski contrasts evidence-based medicine, in which researchers try to disprove hyphotheses, with what he says is the frequent practice in pseudoscience-based research, of striving to confirm pre-existing notions. Harriet A. Hall writes that there is a contrast between the circumstances of alternative medicine practitioners and disinterested scientists: in the case of acupuncture, for example, an acupuncturist would have "a great deal to lose" if acupuncture were rejected by research; but the disinterested skeptic would not lose anything if its effects were confirmed; rather their change of mind would enhance their skeptical credentials.

Safety

See also: List of herbs with known adverse effects

Adequacy of regulation and CAM safety

Many of the claims regarding the safety and efficacy of alternative medicine are controversial. Some alternative treatments have been associated with unexpected side effects, which can be fatal.

One of the commonly voiced concerns about complementary alternative medicine (CAM) is the manner in which is regulated. There have been significant developments in how CAMs should be assessed prior to re-sale in the United Kingdom and the European Union (EU) in the last 2 years. Despite this, it has been suggested that current regulatory bodies have been ineffective in preventing deception of patients as many companies have re-labelled their drugs to avoid the new laws. There is no general consensus about how to balance consumer protection (from false claims, toxicity, and advertising) with freedom to choose remedies.

Advocates of CAM suggest that regulation of the industry will adversely affect patients looking for alternative ways to manage their symptoms, even if many of the benefits may represent the placebo affect. Some contend that alternative medicines should not require any more regulation than over-the-counter medicines that can also be toxic in overdose (such as paracetamol).

Interactions with conventional pharmaceuticals

Forms of alternative medicine that are biologically active can be dangerous even when used in conjunction with conventional medicine. Examples include immuno-augmentation therapy, shark cartilage, bioresonance therapy, oxygen and ozone therapies, insulin potentiation therapy. Some herbal remedies can cause dangerous interactions with chemotherapy drugs, radiation therapy, or anesthetics during surgery, among other problems. An anecdotal example of these dangers was reported by Associate Professor Alastair MacLennan of Adelaide University, Australia regarding a patient who almost bled to death on the operating table after neglecting to mention that she had been taking "natural" potions to "build up her strength" before the operation, including a powerful anticoagulant that nearly caused her death.

To *ABC Online*, MacLennan also gives another possible mechanism:

> And lastly [sic] there's the cynicism and disappointment and depression that some patients get from going on from one alternative medicine to the next, and they find after three months the placebo effect wears off, and they're disappointed and they move on to the next one, and they're disappointed and disillusioned, and that can create depression and make the eventual treatment of the patient with anything effective difficult, because you may not get compliance, because they've seen the failure so often in the past.

Potential side-effects

Conventional treatments are subjected to testing for undesired side-effects, whereas alternative treatments, in general, are not subjected to such testing at all. Any treatment – whether conventional or alternative – that has a biological or psychological effect on a patient may also have potential to possess dangerous biological or psychological side-effects. Attempts to refute this fact with regard to alternative treatments sometimes use the *appeal to nature* fallacy, i.e., "that which is natural cannot be harmful". Specific groups of patients such as patients with impaired hepatic or renal function are more susceptible to side effects of alternative remedies.

An exception to the normal thinking regarding side-effects is Homeopathy. Since 1938, the U.S. Food and Drug Administration (FDA) has regulated homeopathic products in "several significantly different ways from other drugs." Homeopathic preparations, termed "remedies", are extremely dilute, often far beyond the point where a single molecule of the original active (and possibly toxic) ingredient is likely to remain. They are, thus, considered safe on that count, but "their products are exempt from good manufacturing practice requirements related to expiration dating and from finished product testing for identity and strength", and their alcohol concentration may be much higher than allowed in conventional drugs.

Treatment delay

Those having experienced or perceived success with one alternative therapy for a minor ailment may be convinced of its efficacy and persuaded to extrapolate that success to some other alternative therapy for a more serious, possibly life-threatening illness. For this reason, critics argue that therapies that rely on the placebo effect to define success are very dangerous. According to mental health journalist Scott Lilienfeld in 2002, "unvalidated or scientifically unsupported mental health practices can lead individuals to forgo effective treatments" and refers to this as "opportunity cost". Individuals who spend large amounts of time and money on ineffective treatments may be left with precious little of either, and may forfeit the opportunity to obtain treatments that could be more helpful. In short, even innocuous treatments can indirectly produce negative outcomes. Between 2001 and 2003, four children died in Australia because their parents chose ineffective naturopathic, homeopathic, or other alternative medicines and diets rather than conventional therapies.

Unconventional cancer "cures"

There have always been "many therapies offered outside of conventional cancer treatment centers and based on theories not found in biomedicine. These alternative cancer cures have often been described as 'unproven,' suggesting that appropriate clinical trials have not been conducted and that the therapeutic value of the treatment is unknown." However, "many alternative cancer treatments have been investigated in good-quality clinical trials, and they have been shown to be ineffective....The label 'unproven' is inappropriate for such therapies; it is time to assert that many alternative cancer therapies have been 'disproven'."

Edzard Ernst has stated:

"... any alternative cancer cure is bogus by definition. There will never be an alternative cancer cure. Why? Because if something looked halfway promising, then mainstream oncology would scrutinize it, and if there is anything to it, it would become mainstream almost automatically and very quickly. All curative "alternative cancer cures" are based on false claims, are bogus, and, I would say, even criminal."

Research funding

Funding for research into effectiveness of alternative treatments comes from a variety of public and private sources. In the USA, one conduit for funding and information is the National Center for Complementary and Integrative Medicine (NCCIH). Other governments have various levels of funding; the Dutch government funded CAM research between 1986 and 2003, but formally ended it in 2006.

Appeal

Physicians who practice complementary medicine usually discuss and advise patients as to available complementary therapies. Patients often express interest in mind-body complementary therapies because they offer a non-drug approach to treating some health conditions. Some mind-body techniques, such as cognitive-behavioral therapy, were once considered complementary medicine, but are now a part of conventional medicine in the United States.

Against alternative medicine it has been argued that in addition to the social-cultural underpinnings of the popularity of alternative medicine, there are several psychological issues that are critical to its growth. One of the most critical is the placebo effect, which is a well-established observation in medicine. Related to it are similar psychological effects such as the will to believe, cognitive biases that help maintain self-esteem and promote harmonious social functioning, and the *post hoc, ergo propter hoc* fallacy.

In the UK

CAM's popularity may be related to other factors which Edzard Ernst mentioned in an interview in *The Independent*:

> Why is it so popular, then? Ernst blames the providers, customers and the doctors whose neglect, he says, has created the opening into which alternative therapists have stepped. "People are told lies. There are 40 million websites and 39.9 million tell lies, sometimes outrageous lies. They mislead cancer patients, who are encouraged not only to pay their last penny but to be treated with something that shortens their lives. "At the same time, people are gullible. It needs gullibility for the industry to succeed. It doesn't make me popular with the public, but it's the truth.

In a paper published in October 2010 entitled *The public's enthusiasm for complementary and alternative medicine amounts to a critique of mainstream medicine*, Ernst described these views in greater detail and concluded:

> [CAM] is popular. An analysis of the reasons why this is so points towards the therapeutic relationship as a key factor. Providers of CAM

tend to build better therapeutic relationships than mainstream healthcare professionals. In turn, this implies that much of the popularity of CAM is a poignant criticism of the failure of mainstream healthcare. We should consider it seriously with a view of improving our service to patients.

In the USA and Canada

A study published in 1998 indicates that a majority of alternative medicine use was in conjunction with standard medical treatments. Approximately 4.4 percent of those studied used alternative medicine as a replacement for conventional medicine. The research found that those having used alternative medicine tended to have higher education or report poorer health status. Dissatisfaction with conventional medicine was not a meaningful factor in the choice, but rather the majority of alternative medicine users appear to be doing so largely because "they find these healthcare alternatives to be more congruent with their own values, beliefs, and philosophical orientations toward health and life." In particular, subjects reported a holistic orientation to health, a transformational experience that changed their worldview, identification with a number of groups committed to environmentalism, feminism, psychology, and/or spirituality and personal growth, or that they were suffering from a variety of common and minor ailments – notable ones being anxiety, back problems, and chronic pain.

Authors have speculated on the socio-cultural and psychological reasons for the appeal of alternative medicines among that minority using them *in lieu* of conventional medicine. There are several socio-cultural reasons for the interest in these treatments centered on the low level of scientific literacy among the public at large and a concomitant increase in antiscientific attitudes and new age mysticism. Related to this are vigorous marketing of extravagant claims by the alternative medical community combined with inadequate media scrutiny and attacks on critics.

There is also an increase in conspiracy theories toward conventional medicine and pharmaceutical companies, mistrust of traditional authority figures, such as the physician, and a dislike of the current delivery methods of scientific biomedicine, all of which have led patients to seek out alternative medicine to treat a variety of ailments. Many patients lack access to contemporary medicine, due to a lack of private or public health insurance, which leads them to seek out lower-cost alternative medicine. Medical doctors are also aggressively marketing alternative medicine to profit from this market.

Patients can also be averse to the painful, unpleasant, and sometimes-dangerous side effects of biomedical treatments. Treatments for severe diseases such as cancer and HIV infection have well-known, significant side-effects. Even low-risk medications such as antibiotics can have potential to cause life-threatening anaphylactic reactions in a very few individuals. Also, many medications may cause minor but bothersome symptoms such as cough or upset stomach. In all of these cases, patients may be seeking out alternative treatments to avoid the adverse effects of conventional treatments.

Schofield and others, in a systematic review published in 2011, make ten recommendations which they think may increase the effectiveness of consultations in a conventional (here: oncology) setting, such as "Ask questions about CAM use at critical points in the illness trajectory"; "Respond to the person's emotional state"; and "Provide balanced, evidence-based advice". They suggest that this approach may address "... concerns surrounding CAM use [and] encourage informed decision-making about CAM and ultimately, improve outcomes for patients".

References

Bibliography

- Bivins, R. (2007). *Alternative Medicine? A History*. Oxford University Press. ISBN 9780199218875.
- Board of Science and Education, British Medical Association (1993). *Complementary Medicine: New Approaches to Good Practice*. Oxford University Press. ISBN 9780192861665.
- Callahan, D., ed. (2004). *The Role of Complementary and Alternative Medicine: Accommodating Pluralism*. Washington, D.C.: Georgetown University Press. ISBN 9781589014640.
- Cohen, Michael H. (1998). *Complementary & Alternative Medicine: Legal Boundaries and Regulatory Perspectives*. Baltimore: Johns Hopkins University Press. ISBN 9780801856891.
- Committee on the Use of Complementary and Alternative Medicine by the American Public, Board on Health Promotion and Disease Prevention, Institute of Medicine, US National Academies (2005). *Complementary and Alternative Medicine in the United States*[442]. Washington, D.C.: National Academy Press. ISBN 0309092701.
- Gevitz, N. (1997) [1993]. "Chapter 28: Unorthodox Medical Theories". In Bynum, W.F.; Porter, R.S. *Companion Encyclopedia of the History of Medicine*. Vol. 1. New York & London: Routledge. ISBN 9780415164191.
- Hahnemann, S. (1833). *The Homœopathic Medical Doctrine, or "Organon of the Healing Art"*. Translation by Devrient, C.H. Annotated by Stratten, S. Dublin: W.F. Wakeman.

- Kasper, Dennis L; Fauci, Anthony S.; Hauser, Stephen L.; Longo, Dan L.; Jameson, J. Larry; Loscalzo, Joseph (2015). *Harrison's Principles of Internal Medicine* (19th ed.). New York: McGraw Hill Education. ISBN 9780071802154.
- Mishra, Lakshmi Chandra (2004). *Scientific Basis for Ayurvedic Therapies*. Boca Raton: CRC Press. ISBN 0-8493-1366-X.
- O'Connor, Bonnie Blair (1995). *Healing Traditions: Alternative Medicine and the Health Professions*. Philadelphia: University of Pennsylvania Press. ISBN 9780812213980.
- Ruggie, M. (2004). *Marginal to Mainstream: Alternative Medicine in America*. Cambridge University Press. ISBN 9780521834292.
- Sagan, C. (1996). *The Demon-Haunted World: Science As a Candle in the Dark*. New York: Random House. ISBN 9780394535128.
- Saks, M. (2003). *Orthodox and Alternative Medicine: Politics, Professionalization and Health Care*. Sage Publications. ISBN 9781446265369.
- Sointu, E. (2012). *Theorizing Complementary and Alternative Medicines: Wellbeing, Self, Gender, Class*. Basingstoke, England: Palgrave Macmillan. ISBN 9780230309319.
- Walton, J., Sir; Science and Technology Committee, House of Lords, Parliament of the United Kingdom (2000) [Session 1999-2000, HL 123]. *Sixth Report: Complementary and Alternative Medicine*[443]. London: The Stationery Office. ISBN 9780104831007.
- Taylor, Kim (2005). *Chinese Medicine in Early Communist China, 1945–63: a Medicine of Revolution*. Needham Research Institute Studies. London and New York: RoutledgeCurzon. ISBN 0-415-34512-X.
- Wujastyk, D., ed. (2003). *The Roots of Ayurveda: Selections from Sanskrit Medical Writings*. Translated by D. Wujastyk. London and New York: Penguin Books. ISBN 0140448241.

Further reading

- Bausell, R.B (2007). *Snake oil science : the truth about complementary and alternative medicine*. Oxford University Press. ISBN 9780195313680.
- Benedetti, F. et al. (2003). "Open versus hidden medical treatments: The patient's knowledge about a therapy affects the therapy outcome". *Prevention & Treatment* **6** (1). doi: 10.1037/1522-3736.6.1.61a[444].
- Dawkins, R. (2001). "Foreword". In Diamond, J. *Snake Oil and Other Preoccupations*. London: Vintage. ISBN 9780099428336. Reprinted in Dawkins 2003.

- Downing AM, Hunter DG (2003). "Validating clinical reasoning: A question of perspective, but whose perspective?". *Manual Therapy* **8** (2): 117–9. doi: 10.1016/S1356-689X(02)00077-2[445]. PMID 12890440[446].
- Eisenberg DM (July 1997). "Advising patients who seek alternative medical therapies". *Annals of Internal Medicine* **127** (1): 61–9. doi: 10.1059/0003-4819-127-1-199707010-00010[447]. PMID 9214254[448].
- Gunn IP (December 1998). "A critique of Michael L. Millenson's book, *Demanding Medical Excellence: Doctors and Accountability in the Information Age, and its Relevance to CRNAs and Nursing*". AANA Journal (American Association of Nurse Anesthetists) **66** (6): 575–82. ISSN 0094-6354[449]. PMID 10488264[450].
- Hand, W.D. (1980). "Folk Magical Medicine and Symbolism in the West". *Magical Medicine*. Berkeley: University of California Press. pp. 305–19. ISBN 9780520041295. OCLC 6420468[451].
- Illich, I. (1976). *Limits to Medicine: Medical Nemesis: The Expropriation of Health*. Penguin. ISBN 9780140220094. OCLC 4134656[452].
- Mayo Clinic (2007). *Mayo Clinic Book of Alternative Medicine: The New Approach to Using the Best of Natural Therapies and Conventional Medicine*. Parsippany, New Jersey: Time Home Entertainment. ISBN 9781933405926.
- Stevens, P., Jr. (November–December 2001). "Magical thinking in complementary and alternative medicine"[453]. *Skeptical Inquirer*.
- Planer, F.E. (1988). *Superstition* (Rev. ed.). Buffalo, New York: Prometheus Books. ISBN 9780879754945. OCLC 18616238[454].
- Rosenfeld, A. (c. 2000). "Where Do Americans Go for Healthcare?"[455]. Cleveland, Ohio: Case Western Reserve University. Retrieved 2010-09-23.
- Singh, S.; Ernst, E. (2008). *Trick or treatment : the undeniable facts about alternative medicine*. W. W. Norton & Company. ISBN 9780393066616. OCLC 181139440[456]. preview[457] via Google Books.
- Tonelli MR (2001). "The limits of evidence-based medicine". *Respiratory Care* **46** (12): 1435–40; discussion 1440–1. PMID 11728302[458].
- Trivieri, L., Jr. (2002). Anderson, J.W., ed. *Alternative Medicine: The Definitive Guide*. Berkeley: Ten Speed Press. ISBN 9781587611414.
- Wisneski, L.A. et al. (2005). *The scientific basis of integrative medicine*. CRC Press. ISBN 9780849320811.
- Zalewski, Z. (1999). "Importance of philosophy of science to the history of medical thinking"[459]. *CMJ* **40** (1): 8–13. Archived from the original[460] on 2004-02-06.

World Health Organization publications

- *General Guidelines for Methodologies on Research and Evaluation of Traditional Medicine*[461] (PDF). WHO/EDM/TRM/2001.1. Geneva: World Health Organization (WHO). 2000. <q>This document is not a formal publication of the WHO. The views expressed in documents by named authors are solely the responsibility of those authors.</q>
- *WHO Guidelines on Basic Training and Safety in Chiropractic*[462] (PDF). Geneva: WHO. 2005. ISBN 9241593717.
- WHO Kobe Centre; Bodeker, G. et al. (2005). *WHO Global Atlas of Traditional, Complementary and Alternative Medicine*. WHO. ISBN 9789241562867. Summary.[463]

Journals dedicated to alternative medicine research

- Alternative Therapies in Health and Medicine. Aliso Viejo, California : InnoVision Communications, c1995- NLM ID: 9502013[464]
- Alternative Medicine Review: A Journal of Clinical Therapeutics[465]. Sandpoint, Idaho : Thorne Research, c1996- NLM ID: 9705340[466]
- BMC Complementary and Alternative Medicine[467]. London: BioMed Central, 2001- NLM ID: 101088661[468]
- Complementary Therapies in Medicine. Edinburgh ; New York : Churchill Livingstone, c1993- NLM ID: 9308777[469]
- Evidence Based Complementary and Alternative Medicine: eCAM[470]. New York: Hindawi, c2004 NLM ID: 101215021[471]
- Forschende Komplementärmedizin / Research in Complementary Medicine[472]
- Journal of Integrative Medicine[473]
- Journal for Alternative and Complementary Medicine[474] New York : Mary Ann Liebert, c1995
- Scientific Review of Alternative Medicine (SRAM)[475]

External links

- Alternative medicine[476] at DMOZ
- The National Center for Complementary and Integrative Health[477]: US National Institutes of Health
- The Office of Cancer Complementary and Alternative Medicine[478]: US National Cancer Institute, National Institutes of Health
- Knowledge and Research Center for Alternative Medicine[479]: Denmark, the Ministry of the Interior and Health
- Guidelines For Using Complementary and Alternative Methods[480]: from the American Cancer Society

- Complementary and Alternative Medicine Index[481]: from the University of Maryland Medical Center
- Integrative Medicine Podcasts and Handouts[482]: Teaching modules from the University of Wisconsin Integrative Medicine Program
- "Alternative Medicine"[483]: A BBC/Open University television series that examines the evidence scientifically
- "Complementary and alternative medicine: What is it?"[484]: from the Mayo Clinic
- Natural Standard Research Collaboration[485]
- A Different Way to Heal?[486] and Videos[487]: from PBS and Scientific American Frontiers
- Who Gets to Validate Alternative Medicine?[488]: from PBS

Criticism

- What is Complementary and Alternative Medicine?[489] – Steven Novella, Maryland
- "Alternative" health practice[490] – Skeptic's Dictionary
- Quackwatch.org[491] – Stephen Barrett (See also: Quackwatch)
- Purday, K.M. (2009-01-27). "Review - *Healing, Hype, or Harm? A Critical Analysis of Complementary or Alternative Medicine*, by Edzard Ernst (Editor)"[492]. *Metapsychology online reviews* **13** (5).
- What's the harm?[493] Website created by Tim Farley listing cases of people harmed by various alternative treatments

Fraud

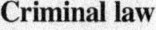 Criminal law
Part of the common law series
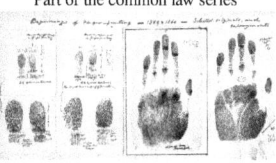
Elements
• *Actus reus* • *Mens rea* • Causation • Concurrence
Scope of criminal liability
• Complicity • Corporate • Vicarious
Seriousness of offense
• Felony • Infraction (also called Violation) • Misdemeanor
Inchoate offenses
• Attempt • Conspiracy • Incitement • Solicitation
Offence against the person
• Alienation of affection • Assassination • Assault • Battery • Bigamy • Criminal negligence • Exhibitionism • False imprisonment • Home invasion • Homicide • Kidnapping • Manslaughter (corporate) • Mayhem • Murder   • corporate • Negligent homicide • Public indecency • Rape • Robbery • Sexual assault • Statutory rape • Vehicular homicide • Voyeurism

Crimes against property

- Arson
- Blackmail
- Bribery
- Burglary
- Embezzlement
- Extortion
- False pretenses
- Fraud
- Larceny
- Payola
- Pickpocketing
- Possessing stolen property
- Robbery
- Smuggling
- Tax evasion
- Theft

Crimes against justice

- Compounding
- Malfeasance in office
- Miscarriage of justice
- Misprision
- Obstruction
- Perjury
- Perverting the course of justice

Victimless crimes

- Adultery
- Apostasy
- Blasphemy
- Buggery
- Providing Contraception information (Comstock law)
- Criminal conversation
- Dueling
- Fornication
- Gambling
- Incest
- Interracial marriage
- Lewd and lascivious behavior
- Masturbation
- Creation of Obscenity
- Prostitution

- Recreational drug use (including alcohol, when prohibited)
- Sale of sex toys
- Sodomy
- Labor strike
- Suicide

Crimes against animals

- Cruelty to animals
- Wildlife smuggling
- Bestiality

Defences to liability

- Automatism
- Consent
- Defence of property
- Diminished responsibility
- Duress
- Entrapment
- *Ignorantia juris non excusat*
- Infancy
- Insanity
- Justification
- Mistake (of law)
- Necessity
- Provocation
- Self-defence

Other common-law areas

- Contracts
- Evidence
- Property
- Torts
- Wills, trusts and estates

Portals

- Criminal justice
- Law

- v
- t
- e[494]

Part of the common law series
Tort law
Intentional torts
- Assault
- Battery
- False imprisonment
- Intentional infliction of emotional distress
- Transferred intent
Property torts
- Trespass
- land
- chattels
- Conversion
- Detinue
- Replevin
- Trover
Defenses
- Assumption of risk
- Comparative negligence
- Contributory negligence
- Consent
- Necessity
- Statute of limitations
- Self-defense
- Defense of others
- Defense of property
- Shopkeeper's privilege
Negligence
- Duty of / standard of care
- Proximate cause
- Res ipsa loquitur
- Calculus of negligence
- Rescue doctrine
- Duty to rescue
- Negligent infliction of emotional distress
- Employment-related
- Entrustment
- Malpractice
- legal
- medical
Liability torts
- Product liability
- Quasi-tort
- Ultrahazardous activity
Nuisance
- Public nuisance
- *Rylands v Fletcher*

Dignitary torts
- Defamation
- Invasion of privacy
- False light
- Breach of confidence
- Abuse of process
- Malicious prosecution
- Alienation of affections
- Criminal conversation
- Seduction
- Breach of promise
Economic torts
- Fraud
- Tortious interference
- Conspiracy
- Restraint of trade
Liability and remedies
- Last clear chance
- Eggshell skull
- Vicarious liability
- Volenti non fit injuria
- Ex turpi causa non oritur actio
- Neutral reportage
- Damages
- Injunction
- Torts and conflict of laws
- Joint and several liability
- Comparative responsibility
- Market share liability
Duty to visitors
- Trespassers
- Licensees
- Invitees
- Attractive nuisance
Other common law areas
- Contracts
- Criminal law
- Evidence
- Property
- Wills, trusts, and estates
- **Law portal**

- v
- t
- e[495]

In law, **fraud** is deliberate deception to secure unfair or unlawful gain. Fraud is both a civil wrong (i.e., a fraud victim may sue the fraud perpetrator to avoid the fraud and/or recover monetary compensation) and a criminal wrong (i.e., a fraud perpetrator may be prosecuted and imprisoned by governmental authorities). The purpose of fraud may be monetary gain or other benefits, such as obtaining a drivers license by way of false statements.

A hoax is a distinct concept that involves deception without the intention of gain or of materially damaging or depriving the victim.

As a civil wrong

In common law jurisdictions, as a civil wrong, fraud is referred to as a tort. While the precise definitions and requirements of proof vary among jurisdictions, the requisite elements of fraud as a tort generally are the intentional misrepresentation or concealment of an important fact upon which the victim is meant to rely, and in fact does rely, to the harm of the victim. Proving fraud in a court of law is often said to be difficult.[496] That difficulty is found, for instance, in that each and every one of the elements of fraud must be proven, that the elements include proving the states of mind of the perpetrator and the victim, and that some jurisdictions require the victim to prove fraud with so-called clear and convincing evidence.[497]

The remedies for fraud may include rescission (i.e., reversal) of a fraudulently obtained agreement or transaction, the recovery of a monetary award to compensate for the harm caused, punitive damages to punish or deter the misconduct, and possibly others.

In cases of a fraudulently induced contract, fraud may serve as a defense in a civil action for breach of contract or specific performance of contract.

Fraud may serve as a basis for a court to invoke its equitable jurisdiction.

As a criminal offence

In common law jurisdictions, as a criminal offence, fraud takes many different forms, some general (e.g., theft by false pretense) and some specific to particular categories of victims or misconduct (e.g., bank fraud, insurance fraud, forgery). The elements of fraud as a crime similarly vary. The requisite elements of perhaps most general form of criminal fraud, theft by false pretense, are the intentional deception of a victim by false representation or pretense with the intent of persuading the victim to part with property and with the victim parting with property in reliance on the representation or pretense and with the perpetrator intending to keep the property from the victim.

In non-common law systems

In civil law systems and other legal systems, the concept of fraud seems to exist, but its elements and application may or may not vary substantially from the common law system concepts discussed in this article.

By region

Canada

Section 380(1) of the Criminal Code of Canada provides the general definition for fraud in Canada:

> *380. (1) Every one who, by deceit, falsehood or other fraudulent means, whether or not it is a false pretence within the meaning of this Act, defrauds the public or any person, whether ascertained or not, of any property, money or valuable security or any service,*
>
> > *(a) is guilty of an indictable offence and liable to a term of imprisonment not exceeding fourteen years, where the subject-matter of the offence is a testamentary instrument or the value of the subject-matter of the offence exceeds five thousand dollars; or*
> >
> > *(b) is guilty*
> >
> > > *(i) of an indictable offence and is liable to imprisonment for a term not exceeding two years, or*
> > >
> > > *(ii) of an offence punishable on summary conviction,*
> >
> > *where the value of the subject-matter of the offence does not exceed five thousand dollars.*

In addition to the penalties outlined above, the court can also issue a prohibition order under s. 380.2 (preventing a person from "seeking, obtaining or continuing any employment, or becoming or being a volunteer in any capacity, that involves having authority over the real property, money or valuable security of another person"). It can also make a restitution order under s. 380.3.

The Canadian courts have held that the offence consists of two distinct elements:

- A prohibited act of deceit, falsehood or other fraudulent means. In the absence of deceit or falsehood, the courts will look objectively for a "dishonest act"; and
- The deprivation must be caused by the prohibited act, and deprivation must relate to property, money, valuable security, or any service.

The Supreme Court of Canada has held that deprivation is satisfied on proof of detriment, prejudice or risk of prejudice; it is not essential that there be actual loss.[498] Deprivation of confidential information, in the nature of a trade secret or copyrighted material that has commercial value, has also been held to fall within the scope of the offence.[499]

United Kingdom

England and Wales and Northern Ireland

Main article: Fraud Act 2006

The BBC World service reported in 2012 that the estimated value lost through fraud in the UK was $100 billion (£66 billion) a year.[500]

The Fraud Act 2006 (c 35) is an Act of the Parliament of the United Kingdom. It affects England and Wales and Northern Ireland. It was given Royal Assent on 8 November 2006, and came into effect on 15 January 2007.[501]

The Act gives a statutory definition of the criminal offence of fraud, defining it in three classes—fraud by false representation, fraud by failing to disclose information, and fraud by abuse of position. It provides that a person found guilty of fraud was liable to a fine or imprisonment for up to twelve months on summary conviction (six months in Northern Ireland), or a fine or imprisonment for up to ten years on conviction on indictment. This Act largely replaces the laws relating to obtaining property by deception, obtaining a pecuniary advantage and other offences that were created under the Theft Act 1978.

Serious Fraud Office

See Serious Fraud Office (United Kingdom) is an arm of the Government of the United Kingdom, accountable to the Attorney-General.

National Fraud Authority

The National Fraud Authority (NFA) is the government agency co-ordinating the counter-fraud response in the UK.

CIFAS - The UK's Fraud Prevention Service

CIFAS - The UK's Fraud Prevention Service, is a not-for-profit membership association representing the private and public sectors. CIFAS is dedicated to the prevention of fraud, including staff fraud, and the identification of financial and related crime.

United States

The U.S. government's 2006 fraud review concluded that fraud is a significantly under-reported crime, and while various agencies and organizations were attempting to tackle the issue, greater co-operation was needed to achieve a real impact in the public sector. The scale of the problem pointed to the need for a small but high-powered body to bring together the numerous counter-fraud initiatives that existed.

To establish a claim of fraud, most jurisdictions in the United States require that each element be plead with particularity and be proved with clear, cogent, and convincing evidence (very probable evidence). The measure of damages in fraud cases is computed using the "benefit of bargain" rule, which is the difference between the value of the property had it been as represented and its actual value. Special damages may be allowed if shown proximately caused by defendant's fraud and the damage amounts are proved with specificity.

Cost

The typical organization loses five percent of its annual revenue to fraud, with a median loss of $160,000. Frauds committed by owners and executives were more than nine times as costly as employee fraud. The industries most commonly affected are banking, manufacturing, and government.

Types of fraudulent acts

See also: Types of fraud

Fraud can be committed through many media, including mail, wire, phone, and the Internet (computer crime and Internet fraud). International dimensions of the web and ease with which users can hide their location, the difficulty of checking identity and legitimacy online, and the simplicity with which hackers can divert browsers to dishonest sites and steal credit card details have all contributed to the very rapid growth of Internet fraud. In some countries, tax fraud is also prosecuted under false billing or tax forgery.[502] There have also been fraudulent "discoveries", e.g., in science, to gain prestige rather than immediate monetary gain.Wikipedia:Citation needed

Figure 52: *A possibly fraudulent "work from home" advertisement.*

Anti-fraud movements

Beyond laws that aim at prevention of fraud, there are also governmental and non-governmental organizations that aim to fight fraud. Between 1911 and 1933, 47 states adopted the so-called Blue Sky Laws status. These laws were enacted and enforced at the state level and regulated the offering and sale of securities to protect the public from fraud. Though the specific provisions of these laws varied among states, they all required the registration of all securities offerings and sales, as well as of every US stockbroker and brokerage firm. However, these Blue Sky laws were generally found to be ineffective. To increase public trust in the capital markets the President of the United States, Franklin D. Roosevelt, established the U.S. Securities and Exchange Commission (SEC). The main reason for the creation of the SEC was to regulate the stock market and prevent corporate abuses relating to the offering and sale of securities and corporate reporting. The SEC was given the power to license and regulate stock exchanges, the companies whose securities traded on them, and the brokers and dealers who conducted the trading.

Figure 53: *A fraudulent Manufacturer's Suggested Retail Price on a speaker.*

Detection

For detection of fraudulent activities on the large scale, massive use of (online) data analysis is required, in particular predictive analytics or forensic analytics. Forensic analytics is the use of electronic data to reconstruct or detect financial fraud. The steps in the process are data collection, data preparation, data analysis, and the preparation of a report and possibly a presentation of the results. Using computer-based analytic methods Nigrini's wider goal is the detection of fraud, errors, anomalies, inefficiencies, and biases which refer to people gravitating to certain dollar amounts to get past internal control thresholds.

The analytic tests usually start with high-level data overview tests to spot highly significant irregularities. In a recent purchasing card application these tests identified a purchasing card transaction for 3,000,000 Costa Rica Colons. This was neither a fraud nor an error, but it was a highly unusual amount for a purchasing card transaction. These high-level tests include tests related to Benford's Law and possibly also those statistics known as descriptive statistics. These high-tests are always followed by more focused tests to look for small samples of highly irregular transactions. The familiar methods of correlation and time-series analysis can also be used to detect fraud and other irregularities. Forensic analytics also includes the use of a fraud risk-scoring model to identify high risk forensic units (customers, employees, locations, insurance claims and so on). Forensic analytics also includes suggested tests to identify financial statement irregularities, but the general rule is that analytic methods alone are not too successful at detecting financial statement fraud.>

Notable fraudsters

- Frank Abagnale Jr., US impostor who wrote bad checks and falsely represented himself as a qualified member of professions such as airline pilot, doctor, attorney, and teacher. The film *Catch Me If You Can* is based on his life.
- John Bodkin Adams, British doctor and suspected serial killer, but only found guilty of forging wills and prescriptions
- Eddie Antar, founder of Crazy Eddie, who has about $1 billion worth of judgments against him stemming from fraudulent accounting practices at that company.
- Jordan Belfort, "The Wolf of Wall Street, who swindled over $200 million via a penny stock boiler room operation.
- Cassie Chadwick, who pretended to be Andrew Carnegie's illegitimate daughter to get loans.
- Columbia/HCA Medicare fraud. Columbia/HCA pleaded guilty to 14 felony counts and paid out more than $2 billion to settle lawsuits arising from the fraud. The company's board of directors forced then–Chairman and CEO Rick Scott to resign at the beginning of the federal investigation; Scott was subsequently elected Governor of Florida in 2010.
- Salim Damji is a convicted fraudster who stole millions of dollars in an affinity fraud. The money came mostly from relatives and members of the close-knit Ismaili community. His $78 million scam was among the largest in Canadian history.
- Charles Dawson, an amateur British archeologist who claimed to have found the Piltdown Man.
- Edward Davenport self-styled "Lord", nicknamed "Fast Eddie", from 2005 to 2009 he was the "ringmaster" of a series of advance-fee fraud schemes that defrauded dozens of individuals out of millions of pounds. He is said to have made £34.5 million through his various frauds.
- Marc Dreier, Managing founder of Attorney firm Dreir LLP, a $700 million Ponzi scheme.[503]
- Enric Durán defrauded Spanish banks and then gave away the loaned money to anti-growth organizations.
- Bernard Ebbers, founder of WorldCom, which inflated its asset statements by about $11 billion.

- Mehran "Ron" Farhadi, Los Angeles real estate magnate, adjudicated to be lead conspirator in multimillion dollar fraud centered on collapse of Los Angeles-area chain of automobile dealerships[504]
- Ramón Báez Figueroa, banker from the Dominican Republic and former President of Banco Intercontinental. He was sentenced on October 21, 2007 to 10 years in prison for a US $2.2 billion fraud case that drove the Caribbean nation into economic crisis in 2003.
- Martin Frankel, former U.S. financier, convicted in 2002 of insurance fraud worth $208 million, racketeering and money laundering.
- Samuel Israel III, former hedge fund manager who ran the former fraudulent Bayou Hedge Fund Group, and faked suicide to avoid jail.
- Konrad Kujau, German fraudster and forger responsible for the "Hitler Diaries".
- Kenneth Lay, the American businessman who built energy company Enron. He was one of the highest paid CEOs in the U.S. until he was ousted as Chairman and convicted of fraud and conspiracy, although, as a result of his death, his conviction was vacated.
- Nick Leeson, English trader whose unsupervised speculative trading caused the collapse of Barings Bank.
- James Paul Lewis, Jr., ran one of the biggest ($311 million) and longest running Ponzi Schemes (20 years) in U.S. history.
- Gregor MacGregor, Scottish conman who tried to attract investment and settlers for the non-existent country of Poyais.
- Bernard Madoff, creator of a $65 billion Ponzi scheme – the largest investor fraud ever attributed to a single individual.
- Bill Mastro, sports memorabilia kingpin who altered the famous T206 Honus Wagner card that eventually sold for $2.8 million. He also engaged in the practice of "shill bidding" — artificially raising bids on items in his auction house.
- Matt the Knife, American con artist, card cheat and pickpocket who, from the ages of approximately 14 through 21, bilked dozens of casinos, corporations and at least one Mafia crime family out of untold sums.
- Gaston Means, a professional conman during U.S. President Warren G. Harding's administration.
- Barry Minkow and the *ZZZZ Best* scam.
- Michael Monus, founder of Phar-Mor, which ultimately cost its investors more than $1 billion.
- F. Bam Morrison, who conned the town of Wetumka, Oklahoma by promoting a circus that never came.
- Lou Pearlman, former boy-band manager and operator of a $300 million Ponzi scheme using two shell companies.
- Frederick Emerson Peters, American impersonator who wrote bad checks.

- Thomas Petters is an American masquerading as a business man who turned out to be a con man and was the former CEO and chairman of Petters Group Worldwide.[505] Petters resigned his position as CEO on September 29, 2008, amid mounting criminal investigations. He later was convicted for turning Petters Group Worldwide into a $3.65 billion Ponzi scheme and was sentenced to 50 years in federal prison.
- Charles Ponzi and the Ponzi scheme.
- Alves Reis, who forged documents to print 100,000,000 PTE in official escudo banknotes (adjusted for inflation, it would be worth about US$150 million today).
- John Rigas, cable television entrepreneur, cofounder of Adelphia Communications Corporation and owner of the Buffalo Sabres hockey team, defrauded investors of over $2 billion and was sentenced to a 12-year term in federal prison.
- Christopher Rocancourt, a Rockefeller impersonator who defrauded Hollywood celebrities.
- Scott W. Rothstein, a disbarred lawyer from Ft. Lauderdale, Florida, who perpetrated a Ponzi scheme which defrauded investors of over $1 billion.
- Michael Sabo, best known as a check, stocks and bonds forger. He became notorious in the 1960s throughout the 1990s as a "Great Impostor" with over 100 aliases, and earned millions from such.
- Alfredo Sáenz Abad who lied about bank loans, as a banker so that some customers to the bank went to prison. Later on he was sentenced to prison, but managed to get a pardon and kept his job.
- John Spano, a struggling businessman who faked massive success in an attempt to buy out the New York Islanders of the NHL.
- Allen Stanford Self-styled banker who sold fake certificates of deposit to people in many countries, raking in $7 billion to $8 billion over decades.
- John Stonehouse, the last Postmaster-General of the UK and MP who faked his death to marry his mistress.
- Kevin Trudeau, U.S. writer and billiards promoter, convicted of fraud and larceny in 1991, known for a series of late-night infomercials and his series of books about "Natural Cures "They" Don't Want You to Know About".
- Richard Whitney, who stole from the New York Stock Exchange Gratuity Fund in the 1930s.

Related

Apart from fraud, there are several related categories of intentional deceptions that may or may not include the elements of personal gain or damage to another individual:

- Obstruction of justice
- 18 U.S.C. § 704[506] which criminalizes false representation of having been awarded any decoration or medal authorized by Congress for the Armed Forces of the United States

Further reading

- Fred Cohen *Frauds, Spies, and Lies – and How to Defeat Them*. ISBN 1-878109-36-7 (2006). ASP Press.
- Green, Stuart P. *Lying, Cheating, and Stealing: A Moral Theory of White Collar Crime*. Oxford University Press, 2006. ISBN 978-0199225804
- Review Fraud – Alex Copola[507] Podgor, Ellen S. *Criminal Fraud*, (1999) Vol, 48, No. 4 American Law Review 1.
- The Nature, Extent and Economic Impact of Fraud in the UK. February, 2007.[508]
- *The Fraudsters – How Con Artists Steal Your Money*[509] (ISBN 978-1-903582-82-4) by Eamon Dillon, published September 2008 by Merlin Publishing

External links

 Wikimedia Commons has media related to *Fraud*.

 Wikiquote has quotations related to: *Fraud*

- The dictionary definition of fraud at Wiktionary
- Association of Certified Fraud Examiners[510]
- Immigration Marriage Fraud Amendments of 1986[511]
- FBI Home page for fraud[512]
- U.S. Department of Justice Fraud Section[513]

Appendix

References

[1] http://www.ftc.gov/opa/2008/10/trudeau.shtm

[2] U.S. TV pitchman Trudeau found guilty of criminal contempt http://in.reuters.com/article/2013/11/12/usa-trudeau-pitchman-idINL2N0IQ2BE20131112

[3] http://abclocal.go.com/wls/story?section=news/local/chicago_news&id=9468958

[4] http://articles.chicagotribune.com/2014-04-28/news/ct-kevin-trudeau-infomercials-met-20140428_1_kevin-trudeau-free-money-weight-loss-cure

[5] Revealing the Truth about Natural Cures http://www.livescience.com/health/060725_bad_book.html

[6] "Infomercial king Kevin Trudeau fined $38m for misleading Americans over 'natural cures' for deadly diseases", Daily Mail, December 20, 2011, http://www.dailymail.co.uk/news/article-2076656/Infomercial-king-Kevin-Trudeau-fined-38m-misleading-Americans-natural-cures-deadly-diseases.html Retrieved November 22, 2013

[7] Gell, A. (January 20, 2015). 'That's Not All!' Kevin Trudeau, The World's Greatest Salesman, Makes One Last Pitch. Business Insider http://www.businessinsider.com/kevin-trudeau-interview-2014-12#ixzz3YX2QL7uJ. Retrieved April 27, 2015.

[8] "Author targeted for cure claims",Chicago Tribune, August 30, 2005,http://articles.chicagotribune.com/2005-08-30/business/0508300104_1_natural-cures-kevin-trudeau-cure-claims Retrieved November 23, 1013

[9] Trudeau, Kevin (Host). (2010, May 16).*Your Wish is your Command*[Informercial]. Toronto: CityTV

[10] Cosmic Mind pages 8 through 19 http://www.colorado.edu/philosophy/vstenger/Quantum/01CosmicMind.pdf

[11] The God Particle: If the Universe is the Answer, What is the Question – pages 189 to 198 by Leon Lederman with Dick Teresi (copyright 1993) Houghton Mifflin Company

[12] "Is Trudeau A Charlatan Or Healer?" http://www.cbsnews.com/stories/2005/09/28/earlyshow/leisure/books/main887681.shtml?source=search_story – CBS News, The Early Show

[13] (transcript http://abcnews.go.com/2020/Health/story?id=1527774)

[14] Dateline NBC: From the Inside Out http://www.msnbc.msn.com/id/14856571/ by John Larson

[15] http://vowman.org/pages/1/index.htm

[16] Barrett S, *What They Don't Want You to Know*, Skeptical Inquirer, January 2006. available online http://www.csicop.org/si/2006-01/trudeau.html

[17] Direct Marketing Leaders Donald Barrett and Kevin Trudeau Join Forces http://www.backchannelmedia.com/newsletter/articles/4408/Direct-Marketing-Leaders-Donald-Barrett-and-Kevin-Trudeau-Join-Forces. Retrieved December 21, 2006.

[18] ITV Ventures http://www.itvventures.com/index.asp. Retrieved December 21, 2006.

[19] Kevin Trudeau Banned from Infomercials For Three Years, Ordered to Pay More Than $5 Million for False Claims About Weight-Loss Book http://www.ftc.gov/opa/2008/10/trudeau.shtm, Federal Trade Commission, October 6, 2008.

[20] 1990 Indictment for Credit Card Fraud, filed in USDC District of Massachusetts http://www.casewatch.org/doj/trudeau/indictment1990.shtml

21

[22] Entry for 'Kevin Trudeau' at The Skeptic's Dictionary http://skepdic.com/trudeau.html

23

24

[25] Kevin Trudeau Banned from Infomercials http://www.consumeraffairs.com/news04/trudeau_informercials.html – ConsumerAffairs.com, September 10, 2004

[26] *Trudeau v. FTC* (Appeal) http://caselaw.lp.findlaw.com/data2/circs/dc/055363a.pdf. Retrieved August 7, 2006.

[27] Infomercial king sues New York regulators, Chicago Sun-Times, August 15, 2005 by Stephanie Zimmermann http://findarticles.com/p/articles/mi_qn4155/is_20050815/ai_n15333306

[28] Natasha Korecki. Kevin Trudeau held in criminal contempt, facing jail time. Federal judge in Chicago acts after being flooded with emails prompted by the author-infomercial king http://www.suntimes.com/news/metro/2043065,kevin-trudeau-infomercial-judge-021110.article. *Chicago Sun-Times*, February 11, 2010

[29] Infamous infomercial king Kevin Trudeau's secret global club off the market, sold to highest bidders. KHSB.com archive http://www.kshb.com/news/local-news/investigations/infamous-infomercial-king-kevin-trudeaus-secret-global-club-off-the-market-sold-to-highest-bidders. Retrieved April 15, 2015.

[30] Infomercial Scammer Kevin Trudeau Appeals Conviction (September 10, 2014). Consumerist.com http://consumerist.com/2014/09/10/infomercial-scammer-kevin-trudeau-appeals-conviction/. Retrieved April 15, 2015.

[31] Kevin Trudeau, inmate # 18046-036, Federal Bureau of Prisons, U.S. Dep't of Justice.

[32] (*Natural Cures*, Chapter 1 – "I Should Be Dead by Now")

[33] Firm claims diabetes cure – Allegations fly as company accuses U of C of cover up, Gauntlet News, February 16, 2006, by Nisha Patel (archived August 13, 2011 at theguantlet.ca) http://web.archive.org/web/20110813194647/http://thegauntlet.ca/story/9845

[34] U of C refutes diabetes coverup (January 31, 2006). Calgary *Herald* http://www.canada.com/story.html?id=a2175fba-5488-4d4a-b4d2-1b91117e6b3d. Retrieved April 8, 2015.

[35] Jennifer Ross-Nazzal. "From Farm to Fork": How Space Food Standards Impacted the Food Industry and Changed Food Safety Standards http://history.nasa.gov/sp4801-chapter12.pdf page 226. NASA History Division. Retrieved August 25, 2013.

[36] Richard D. Lyons (December 31, 1969). Ousted F.D.A. Chief Charges 'Pressure' From Drug Industry http://select.nytimes.com/gst/abstract.html?res=F20F17FF3B58127B93C3AA1789D95F4D8685F9 . *New York Times*. Retrieved August 25, 2013.

[37] Best-seller 'Natural Cures' sparks court battle http://www.msnbc.msn.com/id/9006287/ – Bob Sullivan, MSNBC, August 22, 2005

[38] http://www.billiardsdigest.com/current_issue/nov_05/index.php

[39] //www.worldcat.org/issn/0164-761X

[40] http://www.sciam.com/article.cfm?articleID=0007A2C3-4664-13F3-B85583414B7F0101&ref=sciam&chanID=sa006

[41] http://www.nytimes.com/2005/08/28/business/media/28trudeau.html?_r=1&oref=slogin

[42] http://www.quackwatch.org/01QuackeryRelatedTopics/DSH/coral.html

[43] http://www.thesmokinggun.com/archive/0826051trudeau1.html

[44] http://www.consumeraffairs.com/news04/2008/02/trudeau_debt.html

[45] http://heinonline.org/HOL/Page?handle=hein.journals/mislj79&div=44&g_sent=1&collection=journals#1053

[46] http://www.nndb.com/people/754/000103445

[47] http://www.ftc.gov/opa/1998/01/megasyst.htm

[48] Cancer 'Cures' Are Empty Promises in Kevin Trudeau's 'Natural Cures' Book http://www.infomercialwatch.org/reports/nycpb.shtml. New York State Consumer Protection Board News Release, August 5, 2005.

[49] Without Notice to Consumers, Kevin Trudeau is Selling Consumer Names and Addresses from Infomercial Orders - Consumers Also Hit with Unexpected Charges for Trudeau Newsletter and Discount Purchase Program http://www.quackwatch.org/11Ind/trudeaucpb.html. New York State Consumer Protection Board News Release, October 27, 2005.

[50] Shermer, Michael. " Cures and Cons: Natural scams "he" doesn't want you to know about http://www.sciam.com/article.cfm?id=cures-and-cons". *Scientific American*, March 2006.

[51] Warner, Melanie. " After Jail and More, Salesman Scores Big With Cure-All Book http//web.archive.org." *The New York Times*, August 28, 2005.

[52] Kevin Trudeai's Snake Oil Empire http://web.archive.org/web/20070427064012/http://www.corante.com/pipeline/archives/2005/08/25/kevin_trudeaus_snake_oil_empire.php

[53] http://www.detnews.com/2005/money/0509/25/B03-326006.htm

[54] http://www.infomercialwatch.org/tran/trudeau.shtml

[55] http://www.salon.com/2005/07/29/trudeau_4/

[56] http://abcnews.go.com/2020/Health/story?id=1527774

[57] http://www.sciam.com/article.cfm?articleID=0007A2C3-4664-13F3-B85583414B7F0101&ref=sciam&chanID=sa006
[58] http://abcnews.go.com/Nightline/story?id=1503856
[59] http://www.washingtonpost.com/wp-dyn/content/article/2005/10/22/AR2005102201272_pf.html
[60] //www.worldcat.org/oclc/122341864
[61] Kevin Trudeau#Criminal history and legal problems
[62] Kevin Trudeau#No medical training
[63] Federal Trade Commission, Plaintiff v. Kevin Trudeau, Shop America (USA) LLC, Shop America Marketing Group, LLC, Trustar Global Media, Limited, Robert Barefoot, Deonna Enterprises, Inc., and Karbo Enterprises, Inc., Defendants, and K.T. Corporation, Limited, and Trucom, LLC, http://www.ftc.gov/os/caselist/0323064.shtm
[64] FTC: Marketer Kevin Trudeau Violated Prior Court Order - Charges Him with Misrepresenting Contents of Book, September 14, 2007 http://www.ftc.gov/opa/2007/09/trudeau.shtm
[65] Court finds *Natural Cures'* author Trudeau in contempt of 2004 settlement, may be fined again Christopher S. Rugaber, Associated Press, November 19, 2007 http://www.signonsandiego.com/news/business/20071119-1334-ftc-trudeau.html
[66] Order Finding Trudeau in Contempt http://www.ftc.gov/os/caselist/0323064/071121order.pdf
[67] Federal Court Finds Kevin Trudeau in Civil Contempt, FTC website, November 21, 2007 http://www.ftc.gov/opa/2007/11/kt.shtm
[68] Kevin Trudeau Banned from Infomercials For Three Years, Ordered to Pay More Than $5 Million for False Claims About Weight-Loss Book http://www.ftc.gov/opa/2008/10/trudeau.shtm, Federal Trade Commission, October 6, 2008.
[69] http://consumeraffairs.com/health/trudeau.html
[70] "Report: Kevin Trudeau, The Weight Loss Cure" (book review), Pam, Belle Plaine, Kansas, May 2007, webpage R19 http://www.ripoffreport.com/reports/0/240/RipOff0240019.htm
[71] "The Weight Loss Cure They Don't Want You to Know About" (notes), Vitality Fit Corporation, Payson, Arizona, 2007, webpage: Primev-WLC http://www.primev.com/The_Weight_Loss_Cure_They_Dont_Want_You_to_Know_About.htm
[72] "The Rationale for Banning Human Chorionic Gonadotropin and Estrogen Blockers in Sport" (medical analysis), David J. Handelsman, medical report in *The Journal of Clinical Endocrinology & Metabolism*, Vol. 91, No. 5 1646-1653, year 2006, webpage: EJ1646 http://jcem.endojournals.org/cgi/content/full/91/5/1646.
[73] "Tongkat Ali (Eurycoma Longifolia Jack)" (herb tongkat ali), IronMagLabs (Ironmagazine.com LLC), 2007, webpage: IL-tongkat http://www.ironmaglabs.com/articles_tongkat.php.
[74] http://www.csicop.org/specialarticles/show/kevin_trudeaus_18000_weight_loss_plan_a_book_review/
[75] Ten Pounds in Ten Days: A Sampler of Diet Scams and Abuse http://healthresources.caremark.com/topic/dietscams by Laura Fraser.
[76] HCG Worthless as Weight-Loss Aid http://www.dietscam.org/reports/hcg.shtml by Stephen Barrett, M.D.
[77] Ineffectiveness of human chorionic gonadotropin in weight reduction: a double-blind study http://www.ajcn.org/cgi/reprint/29/9/940.pdf American Journal of Clinical Nutrition 29:940–948, 1976.
[78] "Amazon.com: The Weight Loss Cure They Don't Want You to Know..." Amazon.com, April 2007, ISBN 0-9787851-0-X, ISBN 978-0-9787851-0-9, webpage: Am-097878510X http://www.amazon.com/dp/097878510X.
[79] "Amazon.com Bestsellers" (list of book ranks), Amazon, 2007, webpage: Amazon-bestsellerpage http://www.amazon.com/gp/bestsellers/books.
[80] http://jcem.endojournals.org/cgi/content/full/91/5/1646
[81] http://www.happynews.com/news/5112007/lists-best-selling-books.htm
[82] http://www.kansascity.com/211/story/102197.html
[83] http://abcnews.go.com/2020/Health/story?id=1527774
[84] http://www.sciam.com/article.cfm?articleID=0007A2C3-4664-13F3-B85583414B7F0101&ref=sciam&chanID=sa006
[85] http://abcnews.go.com/Nightline/story?id=1503856

[86] http://heinonline.org/HOL/Page?handle=hein.journals/mislj79&div=44&g_sent=1&collection=journals#1053
[87] "Quack" http://dictionary.reference.com/browse/quack – Dictionary.com Unabridged (v 1.1). Random House, Inc. 7 February 2007.
[88] quacksalver http://www.etymonline.com/index.php?search=quacksalver- Online Etymology Dictionary
[89] *German-English Glossary of Idioms* http://accurapid.com/journal/german-glossary.htm – Accurapid.com at "quacksalber"
[90] (also titled "Killing Us Softly: The Sense and Nonsense of Alternative Medicine" in the UK).
[91] Griffenhagen, George B.; James Harvey Young, "Old English Patent Medicines in America," Contributions from the Museum of History and Technology (U.S. National Museum Bulletin 218, Smithsonian Institution: Wash., 1959), 155–83.
[92] British Medical Association, Secret Remedies. What They Cost And What They Contain, 1909
[93] Young, J. H. (1961) The Toadstool Millionaires: A social history of patent medicines in America before federal regulation. Princeton University Press. 282pp.
[94] Hulda Regehr Clark, *The Cure For All Diseases*
[95] Ladimer, Irving "The Health Advertising Program of the National Better Business Bureau" http://www.pubmedcentral.nih.gov/picrender.fcgi?artid=1256406&blobtype=pdf A.J.P.H. Vol. 55, No. 8. August 1965
[96] " Quackery Targets Teens http://www.cfsan.fda.gov/~dms/wh-teen2.html" U.S. FDA
[97] "Rampant Fraud Threat to China's Brisk Ascent" http://www.nytimes.com/2010/10/07/world/asia/07fraud.html article by Andrew Jacobs in *The New York Times* October 6, 2010, accessed October 7, 2010
[98] "Zhang Wuben and the traditional Chinese medicine racket" http://www.danwei.org/health_care_diseases_and_pharmaceuticals/from_laid-off_worker_to_tcm_ma.php post by Eric Mu on Danwei.org June 18, 2010 11:37 AM, accessed October 7, 2010
[99] "Popular diet guru exposed as fraud" http://china.globaltimes.cn/society/2010-05/536844.html article in *Global Times* May 31, 2010, accessed October 7, 2010
[100] Shippee, Tetyana; Henning-Smith, Carrie; Shippee, Nathan; Kemmick Pintor, Jessie; Call, Kathleen T.; McAlpine, Donna; and Johnson, Pamela Jo (2013) "Discrimination in Medical Settings and Attitudes toward Complementary and Alternative Medicine: The Role of Distrust in Conventional Providers," *Journal of Health Disparities Research and Practice*, 6(1):3. http://digitalscholarship.unlv.edu/jhdrp/vol6/iss1/3
[101] , reprinted in
[102] Thomas Blair. Linus Pauling: Nobel Laureate for Peace and Chemistry 1901–1994 http://www.harvardsquarelibrary.org/unitarians/pauling.html
[103] "Great Science Frauds" http://healthland.time.com/2012/01/13/great-science-frauds/. *Time Magazine*, 13 January 2012
[104] http://skepdic.com/
[105] https://www.dmoz.org//Society/Issues/Health/Fraud/Quackery/
[106] http://www.nlm.nih.gov/medlineplus/healthfraud.html
[107] http://www.fda.gov/Fdac/features/1999/699_fraud.html
[108] http://www.ftc.gov/bcp/edu/pubs/consumer/health/hea07.shtm
[109] http://www.museumofquackery.com
[110] http://www.tshaonline.org/handbook/online/articles/smm04
[111] "What Kevin Trudeau doesn't want you to know" http://dir.salon.com/story/books/feature/2005/07/29/trudeau/index.html, Salon.com, July 29, 2005. Retrieved October 27, 2008
[112] Loree Jon Jones Player Bio http://www.internationalpooltour.com/ipt_content/ipt_players/bio/l_jones.asp, *InternationalPoolTour.com*. Retrieved June 22, 2007
[113] "IPT Pool Tour Goes Off With a Bang" http://www.buzzle.com/editorials/12-11-2005-83690.asp, by Pete Williams, *Buzzle.com*, December 11, 2005. Retrieved June 26, 2007
[114] "8-Ball Legends to Compete in World Championship Match: New Pool Tour Launches with Biggest Prize Money In History of Sport" http://www.azbilliards.com/2000pressrelease.cfm?id=432, *AzBilliards.com*, Las Vegas, Nevada, July 21, 2005. Retrieved June 25, 2007
[115] "Magician is King of the Hill" http://www.professorqball.com/viewpress.php?RecordID=46, *ProfessorQball.com*. Retrieved June 25, 2007

[116] *Kevin Trudeau Speaks*, November 29, 2005, Orlando, Florida. Retrieved June 25, 2007

[117] "Big Changes at IPT: Tour to Be Sold, London Event Cancelled" http://www.billiardsdigest.com/new_news/display_article?id=680, *Billiards Digest*, September 3, 2006. Retrieved December 11, 2011

[118] "Trudeau to Anxious Players: Trust Me, the Money's Coming" http://www.billiardsdigest.com/new_news/display_article?id=722, *Billiards Digest*, October 20, 2006. Retrieved December 11, 2011

[119] Prior to 1968, New Mexico U.S. representatives had been elected at-large statewide.

[120] "Edgar Franklin Foreman", *Who's Who in America with World Notables*, Vol, 56 (1970-1971), (Chicago: Marquis Who's Who, 1970), p. 747

[121] http://www.chicagotribune.com/business/breaking/chi-kevin-trudeau-sentenced-20140317,0,832577.story

[122] http://www.gregcaton.com

[123] Greg Caton CV http://www.gregcaton.com/

[124] Shapiro, Rose, *How Alternative Medicine Makes Fools of Us All*, quoted at The Sunday Times Online, February 23, 2008 http://entertainment.timesonline.co.uk/tol/arts_and_entertainment/books/book_extracts/article3418058.ece

[125] Website:Greg Caton http://www.gregcaton.com

[126] List of Lake Charles Amateur Radio Licences http://www.city-data.com/aradio/lic-Lake-Charles-Louisiana.html

[127] Website:PRNewswire Feb 25, 1987 http://www.highbeam.com/doc/1G1-4669633.html

[128] Website PRNewswire Jan 11, 1989 http://www.highbeam.com/doc/1G1-7243789.html

[129] Website:PR Newswire Nov 7, 1995 http://www.highbeam.com/doc/1G1-17558940.html

[130] Dixon, Anna. Doctoral Dissertaion University of Hawaii Health and wealth: Dietary supplements, network marketing and the commodification of health http://scholarspace.manoa.hawaii.edu/bitstream/10125/1250/1/uhm_phd_4386_r.pdf

[131] Website:Skeptic Dictionary - Kevin Trudeau accessed 19 DEC 09 http://www.skepdic.com/trudeau.html

[132] Website:Down line News Archive JAN/FEB 1993, Accessed 21 December 09 http://www.mlmwatchdog.com/Watchdog_1993_January_WhatsHappening.html

[133] Website:Stanford University College of Law, Securities Accessed 18 DEC 09 http://securities.stanford.edu/1012/NFLI/

[134] Website: Mills, Ami Chen, Metroactive Accessed 20DEC09 http://www.metroactive.com/papers/metro/10.03.96/cover/multilevel3-9640.html

[135] Caton, Greg, *Meditopia*, online book, 2004 and subsequent, ongoing project http://www.meditopia.org/toc.htm

[136] Drug Week, June 18, 2004, cited at HighBeam http://www.highbeam.com/doc/1G1-118047779.html

[137] World Net Daily, Banks seizing Y2K supplier funds, 14 APR 1999 http://www.wnd.com/index.php?fa=PAGE.view&pageId=3659

[138] Letter from Caton to WND, 14 APR 1999 http://www.greenspun.com/bboard/q-and-a-fetch-msg.tcl?msg_id=000ia4

[139] Letter from Professor C.S. Prakash, Director of the Center for Plant Biotechnology Research at Tuskegee University and a member of the newly formed USDA Advisory Committee on Agricultural Biotechnology. Published in AgNet 06 FEB 2000 http://archives.foodsafety.ksu.edu/agnet/2000/2-2000/ag-02-07-00-01.txt

[140] Food and Drink Weekly, Health foods manufacturer takes pro-GMO stance, 28 FEB 2000 http://www.allbusiness.com/retail-trade/food-beverage-stores/467480-1.html

[141] Cornell University - Informing the Dialogue about Agricultural Biotechnology Symposium, November 1999 http://www.nysaes.cornell.edu/comm/gmo/ag_symposiumsch.pdf

[142] CropChoice "Lumen's Costumers Come First" 16 August 2000 http://www.cropchoice.com/FL_Archive9896.html?pg=2&ID=8&YR=2000

[143] Magazine: BusinessWeek January 8, 2007, webversion http://www.businessweek.com/magazine/content/07_02/b4016109.htm

[144] Natural Causes Book http://www.amazon.com/Natural-Causes-Politics-Americas-Supplement/dp/0767920422

[145] Website: Meditopia pdf Archive:WISH TV Channel 8 News Story accessed 19 DEC 09 http://www.meditopia.org/docs/wishtv.pdf
[146] Website WISH TV 8, Indianapolis, IN http://www.wishtv.com/Global/story.asp?S=1540595&nav=0Ra7JXqeJXqg
[147] BusinessWeek, Jan. 8, 2007. http://www.businessweek.com/magazine/content/07_02/b4016109.htm
[148] Affidavit by Gilliatt http://www.meditopia.org/gilliatt_affidavit.htm
[149] Meditopia, Ch. 3 http://www.meditopia.org/chap3-1.htm Greg Caton's website
[150] McDaniel S and Goldman GD, *Consequences of Using Escharotic Agents as Primary Treatment for Nonmelanoma Skin Cancer*, Archives of Dermatology 2002;138:1593-1596 http://archderm.ama-assn.org/cgi/content/full/138/12/1593
[151] EDDI, Inc. Security Specialists http://www.eddi-inc.com/news7.html "On September 17, 2003, a federal search warrant was executed at CATON's residence, Lumen Food Corporation, and an industrial site owned by CATON. All of these locations were in Lake Charles, Louisiana."
[152] Health and Medicine Week, September 13, 2004, cited at Highbeam http://www.highbeam.com/doc/1G1-121813821.html
[153] Official Transcript of Pleas Hearing, Docket 04-20075 26 May 2004 http://www.meditopia.org/docs/transcript_plea.pdf
[154] CBS-11 News, June 30, 2004 http//docs.google.com
[155] Web Accessed pdf - Case 2:04-cr-20075-TLM-CMH Document 49 Filed 11/23/2005 http://www.meditopia.org/docs/gc_49.pdf
[156] US Patent Office document dated 19 Sept 2008 - *PDF File* http://www.uspto.gov/ip/boards/bpai/decisions/inform/105617-66.pdf "...on 5 June 2006 Caton began serving a 3 three year period of supervised release..."
[157] Court document dated August 24, 2004 (PDF file) http://www.meditopia.org/docs/04-20075-01.document19.pdf Probation terms
[158] Meditopia, Ch. 3 http://www.meditopia.org/chap3-2.htm "our family permanently moved to Ecuador in the summer of 2007"
[159] US Patent Office document dated 19 Sept 2008 *(PDF File)* http://www.uspto.gov/ip/boards/bpai/decisions/inform/105617-66.pdf "Caton further tells us that because he could not fly to the United States he could not attend 27 October 2007 hearing in the Western District of Louisiana. As a result, Caton was in violation of the conditions of his release."
[160] Website: Patent Interference 105,617 McK INTELLECTUAL CONCEPTS, LLC, (Inventor: Gregory James Caton) v.ZANNIER, INC.,(Inventor: Paul D. Manos) Patent 7,264,847 http://www.uspto.gov/ip/boards/bpai/decisions/inform/105617-66.pdf (This filing was made because Caton was a junior party to a lawsuit regarding his patent with Paul Manos.)
[161] Familia Caton denuncia secuestro http://www.latarde.com.ec/1660-Familia+Caton+denuncia+secuestro.html (Spanish) 2010-01-27
[162] UNITED STATES OF AMERICA, Plaintiff-Appellee,v.GREGORY JAMES CATON, Defendant-Appellant. No. 10-30459, United States Court of Appeals, Fifth Circuit http://www.leagle.com/xmlResult.aspx?xmldoc=In%20FCO%2020110623187.xml&docbase=CSLWAR3-2007-CURR June 23, 2011
[163] IN THE UNITED STATES COURT OF APPEALS FOR THE FIFTH CIRCUIT No. 10-30459 http://www.ca5.uscourts.gov/opinions%5Cunpub%5C10/10-30459.0.wpd.pdf 23 JUN 2011
[164] http://www.altcancer.com
[165] Official website of Reno R. Rollé http://www.renorolle.com
[166] Official website of BōKU International http://www.bokusuperfood.com
[167] National Lampoon http://nationallampoon.com
[168] Home Shopping Network http://www.hsn.co
[169] Rollé Beach Blankets http://rollebeachblanket.com
[170] http://www.drhoffman.com/podcasts/
[171] http://www.drhoffman.com/
[172] http://www.wor710.com/pages/3600642.php
[173] RobertBarefoot.com http://www.robertbarefoot.com/t-RobertBarefoot.aspx

[174] Jaroff, Leon (Mar. 14, 2003). Coral Calcium: A Barefoot Scam. http://www.time.com/time/columnist/jaroff/article/0,9565,433084,00.html *Time*

[175] Maryland Attorney General (May 10, 2000). Curran Orders Aloe Company to Stop "Miracle Cure" Claims and to Pay Restitution and $3.7 Million in Civil Penalties. http://www.oag.state.md.us/Press/pr356.htm

[176] Rodowsky J. Opinion in T-Up, Inc, et al. v. Consumer Protection Division, Office of the Attorney General. http://caselaw.lp.findlaw.com/data2/marylandstatecases/cosa/2002/64s01.pdf In the Court of Special Appeals of Maryland, No. 0064, September Term, 2001.

[177] http://www.barefootcureamerica.com/

[178] http://www.quackwatch.org/01QuackeryRelatedTopics/DSH/coral.html

[179] Press Release Newswire, October 8, 2006 http://www.prweb.com/releases/2006/10/prweb447583.htm

[180] The Salem News, Vendors: ITV No Longer in Business, Cate Lecuyer, October 3, 2008 http://www.salemnews.com/permalink/local_story_277005230.html

[181] Fusion Power Hour on The Arena Sports Network http://thearenasportsnetwork.com/asn-shows/fusion-power-hour.html

[182] Arena Sports Network Announces Airing of Fusion Power Hour http://www.pr.com/press-release/517797

[183] Warning Letter, April 19, 2004 http://www.casewatch.org/fdawarning/prod/2004/sg.shtml

[184] Federal Trade Commission news release, October 6, 2005 http://www.ftc.gov/opa/2005/10/supreme.shtm

[185] FTC Obtains Preliminary Injunction Against Marketers of Bogus Cancer-Cure "Supreme Greens", July 1, 2004 http://www.ftc.gov/opa/2004/07/dmc.shtm

[186] FTC Charges Marketers of "Weight-Loss Cure" Book with Misrepresenting Book's Contents, October 5, 2007 http://www.ftc.gov/opa/2007/10/weight.shtm

[187] Court finds *Natural Cures' author Trudeau in contempt of 2004 settlement, may be fined again* Christopher S. Rugaber, Associated Press, November 19, 2007 http://www.signonsandiego.com/news/business/20071119-1334-ftc-trudeau.html

[188] Judge finds Beverly company's promise to cure cancer in infomercials 'deceptive', The Salem News, July 19, 2008 http://salemnews.com/punews/local_story_200202510.html

[189] Infomercial creator pleads guilty, will get year for tax fraud, The Salem News, May 3, 2011 http://www.salemnews.com/local/x928074556/Infomercial-creator-pleads-guilty-will-get-year-for-tax-fraud

[190] http://www.cufi.org/site/PageServer?pagename=homepage

[191] http://www.ushmm.org/museum/exhibit/traveling/

[192] http://www.hqr.tv/tag/valentine-at-qvc/

[193] "She Found the Grace to Forgive" http://www.charismamag.com/site-archives/120-features/unorganized/82-she-found-the-grace-to-forgive

[194] "Preacher's First Wife Joins Divorce Battle" http://m.newsok.com/preachers-first-wife-joins-divorce-battle/article/2565747

[195] Infomercial http://www.businessdictionary.com/definition/infomercial.html - Business Dictionary - Copyright©2010 WebFinance, Inc.

[196] Infomercial Definition http://www.yourdictionary.com/infomercial - Your Dictionary - © 1996-2010 LoveToKnow, Corp.

[197] Advertising Media Infomercials Law & Legal Definition http://definitions.uslegal.com/a/advertising-media-infomercials/ - US Legal Definitions - Copyright © 2001-2010 USLegal, Inc.

[198] "Premature poll campaign law can't stop infomercials" http://www.gmanews.tv/story/172527/premature-poll-campaign-law-cant-stop-infomercials - 2007 © GMA Network Inc.

[199] Rudnick, Michael. Char-Broil's First DRTV Effort Gets Grill Sales Sizzling http://www.dmnews.com/Char-Broils-First-DRTV-Effort-Gets-Grill-Sales-Sizzling/article/72763/ DMNews. 16 May 2001.

[200] Fifty years of candy: consolidation, clowns and confidence. *Candy Industry*, August 1, 1994 http://www.allbusiness.com/buying-exiting-businesses/mergers-acquisitions/454710-1.html

[201] DirecTV.com: PAX http://www.directv.com/see/landing/pax.html

[202] Pergament, Alan. Channel 4 returns to the lead, but cable quarrel boosts Channel 7 http://www.buffalonews.com/entertainment/story/497175.html. The Buffalo News. 18 November 2008.
[203] Timothy D. Naegele & Associates Announces Class Action Lawsuit Against Guthy-Renker. http://www.allbusiness.com/crime-law/criminal-offenses-cybercrime/5968871-1.html
[204] 16 CFR PART 255—GUIDES CONCERNING USE OF ENDORSEMENTS AND TESTIMONIALS IN ADVERTISING http://www.gpo.gov/fdsys/pkg/CFR-2012-title16-vol1/pdf/CFR-2012-title16-vol1-part255.pdf
[205] http://www.testimonialshield.net
[206] KSAZ: "Incarcerated TV Pitchman Don Lapre Found Dead", October 3, 2011. http://www.myfoxphoenix.com/dpp/news/justice/incarcerated-tv-pitchman-don-lapre-death-10-2-2011
[207] http://www.politico.com/blogs/bensmith/1008/The_Obama_channel.html
[208] reuters.com http://www.reuters.com/article/rbssTechMediaTelecomNews/idUSN3029152020081030
[209] - "New Nicktoons Show Called Out For Being Just One Huge Skechers Ad" http://consumerist.com/2010/09/new-nickelodeon-cartoon-called-out-for-being-just-one-huge-skechers-ad.html - by Chris Morran on September 15, 2010 – The Consumerist - Shoppers bite back - © 2005-2010 Consumer Media LLC.
[210] "Skechers Puts Promotional Foot Forward Behind Nicktoons' Zevo-3 Series" http://www.multichannel.com/article/453531-Skechers_Puts_Promotional_Foot_Forward_Behind_Nicktoons_Zevo_3_Series.php - by Mike Reynolds - Multichannel News, 8 June 2010 - © 2010 NewBay Media, LLC.
[211] Tom Agee and Brett A. S. Martin (2001), "Planned or Impulse Purchases? How to Create Effective Infomercials" http://www.basmartin.com/wp-content/uploads/2012/05/Agee-and-Martin-2001.pdf, *Journal of Advertising Research*, 41 (6), 35-42.
[212] Brett A. S. Martin, Andrew Bhimy and Tom Agee (2002), "Infomercials and Advertising Effectiveness: An Empirical Study" http://www.basmartin.com/wp-content/uploads/2011/12/Martin-Bhimy-and-Agee-2002.pdf, *Journal of Consumer Marketing*, 19 (6), 468-480.
[213] http://priceonomics.com/the-economics-of-infomercials/
[214] Michael Shermer, " Cures and Cons: Natural scams "he" doesn't want you to know about http://www.sciam.com/article.cfm?id=cures-and-cons," *Scientific American*, March 2006.
[215] http://tammyfaye.com/
[216] The Surreal Life http://www.tv.com/surreal-life/show/12331/summary.html TV.com
[217] Obituary: (UK) newspaper, the Daily Telegraph Issue number 47,317 Monday July 23, 2007 p23
[218] Ex-wife of evangelist Jim Bakker dies http://www.usatoday.com/news/nation/2007-07-21-tammy-faye_N.htm By William M. Welch, USA TODAY
[219] Tammy Faye Messner, ex-wife of disgraced evangelist Jim Bakker, dies at 65 – Associated Press article in Boston Herald – July 22, 2007 http://thetrack.bostonherald.com/moreTrack/view.bg?articleid=1012785&format=&page=2
[220] Bakker marries business friend – North Hills Record – October 5, 1983
[221] Testimony: Baker knew about Hahn being paid off – Associated Press article via Pacific Stars and Stripes – September 16, 1987
[222] PTL link puts church builder Roe Messner in public eye – Kansas City Star via The News-Post Leader – Frederick, Maryland – June 17, 1987 (available of newspaperarchive.com)
[223] Bakker witness says Falwell offered hush money – Associated Press article via The Capital – September 26, 1989
[224] PTL accuses builder of theft conspiracy – Associated Press article via Daily Intelligence/Montgomery County Record – September 10, 1987
[225] Tammy Faye has surgery for colon cancer – Pacific Stars and Stripes – March 22, 1996
[226] Aarthun, Sarah. (2007, June 23). *Tammy Faye is leaving Charlotte area*. The Charlotte Observer http://www.charlotte.com/115/story/170349.html
[227] The Words of Tammy Faye, *Metroweekly* http://www.metroweekly.com/feature/?ak=11
[228] Tammy Faye Messner's Cancer Treatments Stop, Weight Down to Just 65 Pounds http://www.foxnews.com/story/0,2933,271136,00.html Fox News. May 10, 2007
[229] Former Tammy Faye Bakker tells Larry King she has inoperable lung cancer http://www.culteducation.com/reference/bakker/bakker14.html Associated Press/March 19, 2004

[230] FoxNews.com: "Evangelist Tammy Faye Messner Dies of Cancer at 65" http://www.foxnews.com/story/0,2933,290281,00.html July 22, 2007

[231] Public memorial to be planned for Tammy Faye http://www.kansascity.com/news/nation/story/200711.html McClatchy Newspapers – July 22, 2007

[232] Larry King interview with Roe Messner on August 7, 2007 http://transcripts.cnn.com/TRANSCRIPTS/0708/07/lkl.01.html

[233] http://www.sherwoodopendoor.org/

[234] Fdovalina.com http://www.fdovalina.com

[235] 'Gospel According to Tammy Faye' New Musical Reading", *Broadway World News*, December 5, 2007.

[236] Lindsay Wise, "On stage, Tammy Faye lives on: Musical creators say show is a good way to say goodbye", *Houston Chronicle*, July 22, 2007.

[237] New Musical 'Big Tent' Covers Life of Tammy Faye Bakker http://www.broadwayworld.com/viewcolumn.cfm?colid=13810 Broadwayworld.com

[238] Playbill News: Block, Arcelus, Hocking, Stanek and More Set for Tammy Faye Sings Concert http://www.playbill.com/news/article/114554.html

[239] http://www.tammyfaye.com/

[240] http://www.npr.org/templates/story/story.php?storyId=1145322

[241] http://www.emmytvlegends.org/interviews/people/tammy-faye-bakker-messner

[242] http://www.npr.org/templates/story/story.php?storyId=1599635

[243] http://www.imdb.com/name/nm0049176/

[244] http://www.imdb.com/name/nm0883940/

[245] http://www.nancyvalen.com/

[246] https://twitter.com/NancyValenVP

[247] http://www.ftc.gov

[248] http://www.law.cornell.edu/uscode/15/41.html

[249] A Brief History of the Federal Trade Commission http://www.ftc.gov/sites/default/files/attachments/ftc-90-symposium/90thanniv_program.pdf, Federal Trade Commission, 90th Anniversary Symposium.

[250] Republican Party Platform of 1912 http://www.presidency.ucsb.edu/ws/?pid=29633, June 18, 1912, Democratic Party Platform of 1912 http://www.presidency.ucsb.edu/ws/?pid=29590, June 25, 1912, Platform of the Progressive Party http://www.pbs.org/wgbh/americanexperience/features/primary-resources/tr-progressive/, August 7, 1912.

[251] //en.wikipedia.org/w/index.php?title=Template:Competition_law&action=edit

[252] FTC Announces Results of Compliance Testing of Over 300 Funeral Homes in the Second Year of the Funeral Rule Offenders Program http://www.ftc.gov/opa/1998/02/frop-97.shtm, Federal Trade Commission, February 25, 1998

[253] http://www.law.cornell.edu/uscode/15/45.html

[254]

[255]

[256] DHG Healthcare. What hospital executives should be considering in mergers and acquisitions. Available at: http://www.dhgllp.com/res_pubs/hospital-mergers-and-acquisitions.pdf. Accessed November 16, 2014

[257] Federal Trade Commission. In the Matter of Phoebe Putney Health System, Inc., Phoebe Putney Memorial Hospital, Inc., Phoebe North, Inc., HCA Inc., Palmyra Park Hospital, Inc., and Hospital Authority of Albany-Dougherty County. Available at: http://www.ftc.gov/enforcement/cases-proceedings/111-0067/phoebe-putney-health-system-inc-phoebe-putney-memorial. Accessed November 16, 2014

[258] Federal Trade Commission. Administrative Law Judge Upholds FTC's Complaint Against Ohio Hospital Deal, Orders ProMedica to Divest St. Luke's Hospital. Available at: http://www.ftc.gov/news-events/press-releases/2012/01/administrative-law-judge-upholds-ftcs-complaint-against-ohio. Accessed November 16, 2014

[259] Federal Trade Commission. OSF Healthcare System Abandons Plans to Buy Rockford in Light of FTC Lawsuit; FTC Dismisses its Complaint Seeking to Block the Transaction. Available at: http://www.ftc.gov/news-events/press-releases/2012/04/osf-healthcare-system-abandons-plan-buy-rockford-light-ftc. Accessed November 16, 2014

[260] http://www.jstor.org/stable/1902564
[261] https://www.federalregister.gov/agencies/federal-trade-commission
[262] https://www.ftccomplaintassistant.gov
[263] http://www.ftc.gov/os/decisions/index.htm
[264] http://www.ftc.gov/bcp/edu/microsites/idtheft/consumers/filing-a-report.html
[265] //tools.wmflabs.org/geohack/geohack.php?pagename=Food_and_Drug_ Administration&params=39_02_07_N_76_58_59_W_type:landmark_region:US-MD
[266] http://www.fda.gov/
[267] The quoted text from the source indicates "9" but the actual count from the website indicates "14".
[268] Coordinates of FDA Headquarters at White Oak, Maryland:
[269] //en.wikipedia.org/w/index.php?title=Template:Regulation_of_therapeutic_goods_in_the_ United_States&action=edit
[270] 21 CFR 202: Prescription Drug Advertising.
[271] 21 CFR 314.80: Postmarketing Reporting of Adverse Drug Experiences
[272] MedWatch: The FDA Safety Information and Adverse Event Reporting Program http://www.fda.gov/Safety/MedWatch/default.htm. Accessed October 9, 2007
[273]
[274] Regulation of Nonprescription Drug Products http://www.fda.gov/downloads/AboutFDA/CentersOffices/OfficeofMedicalProductsandTobacco/CDER/UCM148055.pdf FDA. Retrieved August 30, 2012.
[275] //en.wikipedia.org/w/index.php?title=Food_and_Drug_Administration&action=edit
[276] FDA/CBER – About CBER http://www.fda.gov/AboutFDA/CentersOffices/OfficeofMedicalProductsandTobacco/CBER/default.htm Retrieved August 30, 2012.
[277] CDRH Mission, Vision and Shared Values http://www.fda.gov/AboutFDA/CentersOffices/OfficeofMedicalProductsandTobacco/CDRH/ucm300639.htm Retrieved August 30, 2012.
[278] FDA Approved Coatings vs. FDA Acceptable Coatings - DECC Company - DECC Company http://www.decc.com/fda-acceptable-vs-fda-approved.php. Decc.com. Retrieved on 2013-10-23.
[279] Does FDA have the authority to regulate tobacco products? http://www.fda.gov/AboutFDA/Transparency/Basics/ucm194423.htm Food and Drug Administration.
[280] Original Text of the 1906 Food and Drugs Act and Amendments http://www.fda.gov/opacom/laws/wileyact.htm
[281] Milestones in U.S. Food and Drug Law History http://www.fda.gov/opacom/backgrounders/miles.html
[282] Report of Congressman Morris Udall on thalidomide and the Kefauver hearings http://www.library.arizona.edu/exhibits/udall/congrept/87th/620817.html.
[283] FDA.gov http://www.fda.gov/ScienceResearch/SpecialTopics/CriticalPathInitiative/default.htm
[284] Innovation or Stagnation: Challenge and Opportunity on the Critical Path to New Medical Products http://www.fda.gov/ScienceResearch/SpecialTopics/CriticalPathInitiative/CriticalPathOpportunitiesReports/ucm077262.htm FDA. Retrieved August 30, 2012.
[285] Retrieved August 30, 2012.
[286] Webcitation.org http://www.webcitation.org/5NkCrjdpd
[287] Books.nap.edu http://www.nap.edu/openbook.php?record_id=11750&page=205 Executive Summary of the 2006 IOM Report *The Future of Drug Safety: Promoting and Protecting the Health of the Public*
[288] Webcitation.org http://www.webcitation.org/5NkCrjdpd
[289] Committee on the Assessment of the US Drug Safety System. (2006). *The Future of Drug Safety: Promoting and Protecting the Health of the Public*. Institute of Medicine. Free full-text http://www.nap.edu/catalog.php?record_id=11750#toc.
[290] http://www.econlib.org/library/Enc1/DrugLag.html
[291] //www.worldcat.org/oclc/317650570
[292] //www.worldcat.org/oclc/50016270
[293] //www.worldcat.org/oclc/163149563
[294] https://www.federalregister.gov/agencies/food-and-drug-administration

[295] http://www.fda.gov/downloads/AboutFDA/CentersOffices/OrganizationCharts/UCM291886.pdf
[296] http://xml.fido.gov/stratml/carmel/FDAwStyle.xml
[297] //tools.wmflabs.org/geohack/geohack.php?pagename=Food_and_Drug_Administration&params=39_02_07_N_76_58_59_W_region:US-MD_type:landmark
[298] John L. McGuire, Horst Hasskarl, Gerd Bode, Ingrid Klingmann, Manuel Zahn "Pharmaceuticals, General Survey" Ullmann's Encyclopedia of Chemical Technology" Wiley-VCH, Weinheim, 2007.
[299] Thomas Hager, *The Demon Under the Microscope* (2006) ISBN 1-4000-8213-7 (cited in "The Saga of a Sulfa Drug Pioneer" http://www.npr.org/templates/story/story.php?storyId=6667754 – NPR *Weekend Edition* 23 December 2006)
[300] NobelPrize.org http://nobelprize.org/nobel_prizes/nobelprize_facts.html
[301] Chemical Heritage http://www.chemheritage.org/women_chemistry/med/rousseau.html Manufacturing a Cure: Mass Producing Penicillin
[302] Antibacterial Agents. Chemistry, Mode of Action, Mechanisms of Resistance, and Clinical Applications. Anderson RJ, Groundwater PJ, Todd A, Worsely AJ. Wiley (2012). ISBN 9780470972458 See Preface material.
[303] Federal Trade Commission Report of Antibiotics Manufacture, June 1958 (Washington D.C., Government Printing Office, 1958) pages 98-120
[304] Federal Trade Commission Report of Antibiotics Manufacture, June 1958 (Washington D.C., Government Printing Office, 1958) page 277
[305] Simons, John. "The $10 billion pill" http://money.cnn.com/magazines/fortune/fortune_archive/2003/01/20/335643, *Fortune* magazine, January 20, 2003.
[306] http://www.outsourcing-pharma.com/Clinical-Development/Pfizer-teams-with-Parexel-and-Icon-in-CRO-sector-s-latest-strategic-deals
[307] Tufts Center for the Study of Drug Development http://csdd.tufts.edu/Research/Milestones.asp
[308] The Pharmaceutical Research and Manufacturers of America (PhRMA) http://www.phrma.org/about/about-phrma
[309] *Has the Pharmaceutical Blockbuster Model Gone Bust?*, Bain & Company press release, December 8, 2003. Press release http://www.bain.com/bainweb/publications/printer_ready.asp?id=14243
[310] Ben Goldacre: The drugs don't work: a modern medical scandal http://www.guardian.co.uk/business/2012/sep/21/drugs-industry-scandal-ben-goldacre/print The Guardian, 2012.
[311] Moynihan R (2003-05- cvc31). Who pays for the pizza? Redefining the relationships between doctors and drug companies. 2: Disentanglement http://www.pubmedcentral.nih.gov/articlerender.fcgi?artid=1126054. *BMJ: British Medical Journal.* Volume 326, Issue 7400, Pages 1193–1196. Retrieved on 2007-10-06.
[312] http://clinicaltrials.gov
[313] Tracy Weber and Charles Ornstein (March 11, 2013) "Dollars for Docs Mints a Millionaire" http://www.propublica.org/article/dollars-for-docs-mints-a-millionaire *ProPublica*
[314] http//www.imshealth.com
[315] http://www.vfa.de/download/SHOW/en/statistics/pharmaceuticalmarket/vfastat_30_en_fa_mt.pdf/vfastat_30_en_sw_mt.pdf
[316] http://www.theguardian.com/business/2014/mar/27/bestselling-prescription-drugs
[317] http://www.drugs.com/stats/top100/2013/sales
[318] Frequently Asked Questions (FAQs) http://www.wipo.int/patentscope/en/patents_faq.html#patent_role
[319] Sanofi Laying Off 1,700 in US http://www.dddmag.com/news-Sanofi-Laying-Off-1700-in-US-101110.aspx
[320] Retail prescription drug sales 1995 to 2006 PDF from www.census.gov http://www.census.gov/compendia/statab/tables/08s0130.pdf
[321] *Bad Pharma*, pp. 274, 287, 303, 311.
[322] Ray Moynihan (2003-05-31). Drug company sponsorship of education could be replaced at a fraction of its cost http://www.bmj.com/cgi/content/full/326/7400/1163. *BMJ: British Medical Journal*, Volume 326, Issue 7400, Page 1163. Retrieved on 2007-10-07.

[323] Koerner BI (March/April, 2003), Dr. No Free Lunch http://www.motherjones.com/news/hellraiser/2003/03/ma_290_01.html. *Mother Jones*, Retrieved on 2007-10-06.

[324] Ray Moynihan and Alan Cassels (2005). *Selling Sickness: How Drug Companies are Turning Us All Into Patients.* Allen & Unwin. New York. ISBN 1-74114-579-1

[325] http://www.nps.org.au/health_professionals/ferh

[326] Medical schools and journals fight drug industry influence http://www.cbc.ca/cp/health/080911/x091102A.html

[327] Cosgrove, Lisa, Krimsky, Sheldon, Vijayaraghavan, Manisha, Schneider, Lisa, Financial Ties between DSM-IV Panel Members and the Pharmaceutical Industry http://content.karger.com/ProdukteDB/produkte.asp?Aktion=ShowAbstract&ProduktNr=223864&Ausgabe=231734&ArtikelNr=91772

[328] Open Payments page in the Centers for Medicare & Medicaid Services website http://www.cms.gov/openpayments/

[329] *Bad Pharma*, p. 123ff.

[330] *Bad Pharma*, p. 143ff.

[331] Sammy Almashat, M.D., M.P.H., Charles Preston, M.D., M.P.H., Timothy Waterman, B.S., Sidney Wolfe, M.D., Rapidly Increasing Criminal and Civil Monetary Penalties Against the Pharmaceutical Industry: 1991 – 2010, Public Citizen's Health Research Group, December 16, 2010

[332] USDOJ: GlaxoSmithKline to Plead Guilty and Pay $3 Billion to Resolve Fraud Allegations and Failure to Report Safety Data http://www.justice.gov/opa/pr/2012/July/12-civ-842.html

[333] http://www.justice.gov/usao/ma/news/Pfizer/Pfizer%20-%20PR%20(Final).pdf

[334] USDOJ: Abbott Labs to Pay $1.5 Billion to Resolve Criminal & Civil Investigations of Off-label Promotion of Depakote http://www.justice.gov/opa/pr/2012/May/12-civ-585.html

[335] #09-038: Eli Lilly and Company Agrees to Pay $1.415 Billion to Resolve Allegations of Off-label Promotion of Zyprexa (2009-01-15) http://www.justice.gov/opa/pr/2009/January/09-civ-038.html

[336] See for example: 't Hoen, Ellen. "TRIPS, Pharmaceutical Patents, and Access to Essential Medicines: A Long Way from Seattle to Doha". *Chicago Journal of International Law*, 27(43), 2002; Musungu, Sisule F., and Cecilia Oh. "The Use of Flexibilities in TRIPS by Developing Countries: Can They Provide Access to Medicines?" Commission on Intellectual Property Rights, Innovation and Public Health, The World Health Organization, 2005.

[337] WTO. "The Doha Declaration on TRIPS and public health", 2001. Available online at http://www.wto.org/english/thewto_e/minist_e/min01_e/mindecl_trips_e.htm.

[338] "Pharmaceutical Manufacturer's Association v. The President of South Africa (PMA)", 2002 (2) SA 674 (CC) (S. Africa).

[339] Helfer, Laurence R. and Graeme W. Austin. "Human Rights and Intellectual Property: Mapping the Global Interface". Cambridge University Press: 2011, pp. 145–48.

[340] http://www.cartercenter.org/healthprograms/showdoc.asp?programID=2&submenu=healthprograms

[341] Pfizer Will Donate Fluconazole to South Africa http://www.aegis.com/pubs/atn/2000/ATN34003.html

[342] http://www.corporatecitizenship.novartis.com Novartis corporate citizenship

[343] //en.wikipedia.org/w/index.php?title=Template:Alternative_medical_systems&action=edit

[344] IOM Report 2005, p. 16–20.

[345] *"Science-based medicine, with its emphasis on controlled study, proof, evidence, statistical significance and safety is being rejected in favour of 'alternative medicine' - an atavistic portmanteau of anecdote, hearsay, rumour and hokum.... Probably the most commercially successful and widely used branch of alternative or complementary medicine is 'phytotherapy'. These are the tablets, powders and elixirs, otherwise known as herbal medicine, that are sold in most countries, through health shops and pharmacies as 'nutritional supplements'.... Only a tiny minority of these remedies have been shown to have mild-to moderately beneficial health effects... So why are affluent, otherwise rational, highly educated people (for*

this is the average user profile) so hungry for phytotherapy?... people still believe that 'natural' equals good and safe despite plenty of evidence to the contrary."... as far as the human body is concerned, 'natural' is meaningless... Equally, what's so safe about consuming substances that need meet no standards of contents? ...", Phytotherapy - good science or big business?, Sara Abdulla, Nature - International Weekly Journal of Science, 5-13-1999 http://www.nature.com/news/1999/990513/full/news990513-8.html

[346] The *Final Report* (2002) of the White House Commission on Complementary and Alternative Medicine Policy states: "The Commissioners believe and have repeatedly stated in this Report that our response should be to hold all systems of health and healing, including conventional and CAM, to the same rigorous standards of good science and health services research. Although the Commissioners support the provision of the most accurate information about the state of the science of all CAM modalities, they believe that it is premature to advocate the wide implementation and reimbursement of CAM modalities that are yet unproven."

[347] According to the Tzu Chi Institute, a Canadian centre established to evaluate complementary and alternative therapies, "alternative therapies are those lacking scientific validation that are excluded from medical school training programs and uninsured by health plans."

[348] "Kessler refers to a lack of efficacy but never pushes back at Hatch by enumerating the dangers that unregulated products pose to the public, the dangers that fill the pages of Offit's book."

[349] O'Connor 1995, p. 2 https://books.google.com/books?id=JXFPb88KLZQC&pg=PA2.

[350] In his book *The Homœopathic Medical Doctrine* Samuel Hahnemann the creator of homeopathy wrote: "Observation, reflection, and experience have unfolded to me that the best and true method of cure is founded on the principle, *similia similibus curentur*. To cure in a mild, prompt, safe, and durable manner, it is necessary to choose in each case a medicine that will excite an affection similar (ὅμοιος πάθος) to that against which it is employed."<ref name="FOOTNOTEHahnemann1833[http://books.google.com/books?id=EnEFAAAAQAAJ&pg=PR3 iii], [http://books.google.com/books?id=EnEFAAAAQAAJ&pg=PA48 48–49]">Hahnemann 1833, p. iii http://books.google.com/books?id=EnEFAAAAQAAJ&pg=PR3, 48–49 http://books.google.com/books?id=EnEFAAAAQAAJ&pg=PA48.

[351] Taylor 2005, p. 109.

[352] Wujastyk 2003, p. xviii.

[353] Mishra 2004, p. 8.

[354] Sagan 1996.

[355] Oxford Dictionary Online http://www.askoxford.com/concise_oed/shaman?view=uk.

[356]

[357]

[358]

[359]

[360]

[361]

[362] IOM Report 2005, p. 19.

[363] The National Cancer Institute's Dictionary of Cancer Terms, states that, "Orthodox medicine [is] ... also called allopathic medicine, biomedicine, conventional medicine, mainstream medicine, and Western medicine"; the same source states that, "Standard medical care" is "[a]lso called best practice, standard of care, and standard therapy."

[364] Harrison's Principles of Internal Medicine 2015, p. 1, chpt. 14-E.

[365] IOM Report 2005, p. 14–20.

[366] Ruggie 2004, p. 20 http://books.google.com/books?id=ViDwi7s2VvMC&pg=PA20.

[367] Mary Ruggie in Chapter 2 of *Marginal to Mainstream: Alternative Medicine in America* said, "By the mid-1990s, the notion that some alternative therapies could be complementary to conventional medicine began to change the status of...alternative medicine. The 21st century is witnessing yet another terminological innovation, in which CAM and conventional medicine are becoming integrative."<ref name="FOOTNOTERuggie2004">Ruggie 2004.

[368] Sointu 2012, p. 13 http://books.google.com/books?id=XC2UUP36bjAC&pg=PA13.

[369] .

[370] Gevitz 1997, pp. 603–33 http://books.google.com/books?id=ZIqk31BXpksC&pg=PA603.
[371] IOM Report 2005, p. 18 http://books.nap.edu/openbook.php?record_id=11182&page=18.
[372] IOM Report 2005, p. 14 http://books.nap.edu/openbook.php?record_id=11182&page=14.
[373] IOM Report 2005, p. 19 http://books.nap.edu/openbook.php?record_id=11182&page=19.
[374] As David J. Hufford, Professor and Director at the Doctors Kienle Center for Humanistic Medicine at the Penn State College of Medicine, has argued: "Simply because an herbal remedy comes to be used by physicians does not mean that herbalists cease to practice, or that the practice of the one becomes like that of the other."
[375] The BMA used the term non-conventional medicine instead of alternative medicine.
[376] .
[377] IOM Report 2005, pp. 17 http://books.nap.edu/openbook.php?record_id=11182&page=17, 196–252 http://books.nap.edu/openbook.php?record_id=11182&page=196.
[378] The Office for Alternative Medicine, part of the National Institutes of Health, was renamed NCCAM in 1998.
[379] IOM Report 2005, p. 17 http://books.nap.edu/openbook.php?record_id=11182&page=17.
[380] IOM Report 2005, p. 17–18.
[381] WHO 2000.
[382] Countercultural Healing: A brief History of Alternavie Medicine in America, James Whorton, PBS, Nov 4 2003, http://www.pbs.org/wgbh/pages/frontline/shows/altmed/clash/history.html
[383] Nature Cures - The History of Alternative Medicine in America, James C. Whorton, Oxford University Press, 2002, http://ir.nmu.org.ua/bitstream/handle/123456789/130555/400a3b078ea853dd93607611eb31561f.pdf?sequence=1
[384] The Rise and Rise of Complementary and Alternative Medicine: a Sociological Perspective, Ian D Coulter and Evan M Willis, Medical Journal of Australia, 2004; 180 (11): 587-589
[385]
[386] The New Age of Alternative Medicine, Why New Age Medicine Is Catching On, Claudia Wallis, Time Magazine, 11-4-1991, http://content.time.com/time/covers/0,16641,19911104,00.html
[387]
[388] Other healers, other cures: A guide to alternative medicine, Helen Kruger, 1974, http://www.amazon.com/Other-healers-other-cures-alternative/dp/0672517086
[389] "A Guide to Alternative Medicine", Donald Law (1975) http://www.amazon.com/Guide-Alternative-Medicine-Donald-Law/dp/B002K530DM/ref=la_B001KIZL82_1_6?s=books&ie=UTF8&qid=1433799261&sr=1-6
[390]
[391]
[392] Trends in alternative medicine use in the United States, 1990-1997: results of a follow-up national survey. Eisenberg DM1, Davis RB, Ettner SL, Appel S, Wilkey S, Van Rompay M, Kessler RC., JAMA. 1998 Nov 11;280(18):1569-75, http://www.anatomyfacts.com/Research/trends.pdf
[393] Edzard Ernst; Singh, Simon (2008), Trick or Treatment: The Undeniable Facts about Alternative Medicine, New York: W. W. Norton, ISBN 0-393-06661-4
[394]
[395]
[396] "OAM's Legislative History," Office of Alternative Medicine Series (OAMS), Office of NIH History Archives, National Institutes of Health, Box 4, Folder 7
[397] "Arizona company agrees to pay $200,000 to settle FTC charges it made false health claims about bee-pollen products," FTC News Notes, December 30, 1992.
[398]
[399]
[400]
[401] Toward an Integrative Medicine: Merging Alternative Therapies with Biomedicine, Hans A. Baer, https//books.google.com
[402] National Center for Complementary and Integrative Health (NCCIH), Skeptics Dictionary, http://skepdic.com/NCCAM.html
[403]

[404] Why the National Center for Complementary and Alternative Medicine (NCCAM) Should Be Defunded, Wallace I. Sampson, M.D, Quackwatch, http://www.quackwatch.org/01QuackeryRelatedTopics/nccam.html

[405]

[406]

[407] Homeopathic Medicine: Europe's #1 Alternative for Doctors, Dana Ullman, Huffington Post, 11-17-2011, http://www.huffingtonpost.com/dana-ullman/homeopathic-medicine-euro_b_402490.html

[408] Homoeopathy booming in India, Prasad R. Lancet, 370:November 17, 2007,1679-80

[409] ECHAMP, Facts and Figures, 2nd edition, 2007 http://www.echamp.eu

[410] Full Committee Hearing, Integrative Care: A Pathway to a Healthier Nation, SD 4-30 (Feb. 26, 2009), United States Senate, http://help.senate.gov/hearings/hearing/?id=03629575-0924-cb2e-13cb-68a8065ababb

[411] Tom Harkin's War on Science, Peter Lipson, Discover Magazine editor's opinion in New York Times, 3-2-2009, https://www.sciencebasedmedicine.org/tom-harkins-war-on-science-or-meet-the-new-boss/

[412]

[413] $34 billion spent yearly on alternative medicine, NBC News, 7-30-2009 http://www.nbcnews.com/id/32219873/ns/health-alternative_medicine/t/billion-spent-yearly-alternative-medicine/#.VY418K_bLIU

[414]

[415]

[416] Legal Status and Regulation of Complementary andAlternative Medicine in Europe; Solveig Wiesener, Torkel Falkenberg, Gabriella Hegyid, Johanna Hök, Paolo Roberti di Sarsina, Vinjar Fønnebø; Forsch Komplementmed 2012; 19(suppl 2):29–36, Nov. 2012, http//www.researchgate.net

[417] NACCIH Charter https://nccih.nih.gov/about/naccih/charter

[418] Peking University Health Science Center (formerly Beijing Medical University) was the first of the kind in China to teach western medicine and train medical professionals.Wikipedia:Citation needed

[419] For an encyclopaedic account of the development of "western" medicine in the period leading up to the reforms in the medical schools of US resulting from the Flexner Report, published at the time of that report, see the article, "Medicine", in the 1911 Encyclopædia Britannica by Thomas Clifford Allbutt.

[420] Bivins 2007, p. 171.

[421] In his introduction to the Flexner Report, Henry S. Pritchett stated, "The fundamental sciences upon which medicine depends have been greatly extended. The laboratory has come to furnish alike to the physician and to the surgeon a new means for diagnosing and combating disease. The education of the medical practitioner under these changed conditions makes entirely different demands in respect of both preliminary and professional training."

[422] Bivins 2007, pp. 164–170.

[423] The earliest occurrence of the term "alternative medicine" in an English language publication was only in 1974, according to the Oxford English Dictionary.

[424] As the medical professor Kenneth M. Ludmerer noted in 2010: "Flexner pointed out that the scientific method of thinking applied to medical practice. By scientific method, he meant the testing of ideas by well-planned experiments in which accurate facts were carefully obtained. The clinician's diagnosis was equivalent to the scientist's hypothesis: both medical diagnosis and hypothesis needed to be submitted to the test of an experiment... Flexner argued that mastery of the scientific method of problem solving was the key for physicians to manage medical uncertainty and to practice in the most cost-effective way."

[425] BMA 1993.

[426] "Evidence based medicine is the conscientious, explicit, and judicious use of current best evidence in making decisions about the care of individual patients"; "Evidence based medicine, whose philosophical origins extend back to mid-19th century Paris and earlier, remains a hot topic for clinicians, public health practitioners, purchasers, planners, and the public. British centres for evidence based practice have been established or planned in adult medicine, child health,

surgery, pathology, pharmacotherapy, nursing, general practice, and dentistry; the Cochrane Collaboration and Britain's Centre for Review and Dissemination in York are providing systematic reviews of the effects of health care".

[427] IOM Report 2005, pp. 17-19 http://books.nap.edu/openbook.php?record_id=11182&page=17.

[428] IOM Report 2005.

[429] //en.wikipedia.org/w/index.php?title=Alternative_medicine&action=edit

[430] In an article in *The British Journal of General Practice* Edzard Ernst et al. stated, *Complementary medicine is diagnosis, treatment and/or prevention that complements mainstream medicine by contributing to a common whole, by satisfying a demand not met by orthodoxy or by diversifying the conceptual frameworks of medicine.<ref name="Ernst1995">*

[431] As a 2010 article in the *New England Journal of Medicine* concluded: *real acupuncture treatments were no more effective than sham acupuncture treatments. There was, nevertheless, evidence that both real acupuncture and sham acupuncture were more effective than no treatment, and that acupuncture can be a useful supplement to other forms of conventional therapy for low back pain.IOM Report 2005, p. 16-20.*

[432] According to the medical historian James Harvey Young:
In 1991 the Senate Appropriations Committee responsible for funding the National Institutes of Health (NIH) declared itself "not satisfied that the conventional medical community as symbolized at the NIH has fully explored the potential that exists in unconventional medical practices.<ref>

[433] The US Internal Revenue Service provides the following definition of medical expenses:
Medical expenses are the costs of diagnosis, cure, mitigation, treatment, or prevention of disease, and the costs for treatments affecting any part or function of the body. These expenses include payments for legal medical services rendered by physicians, surgeons, dentists and other medical practitioners.... primarily to alleviate or prevent a physical or mental defect or illness. Medicines: You can include expenses amounts you pay for prescribed medicines and drugs. A prescribed drug is one that requires a prescription by a doctor for its use by an individual.<ref name= "IRS502">

[434] Cohen 1998, pp. 24, 39, 56, 73, 87.

[435] Cohen 1998, p. 118.

[436] Sir Walton: Science and Technology Committee 2000.

[437] Wujastyk 2003.

[438] WHO 2005.

[439] FDA, *Use Caution With Ayurvedic Products* http://www.fda.gov/ForConsumers/ConsumerUpdates/ucm050798.htm

[440] IOM Report 2005, p. 133 http://books.nap.edu/openbook.php?record_id=11182&page=133.

[441] IOM Report 2005, pp. 135-136 http://books.nap.edu/openbook.php?record_id=11182&page=135.

[442] http://www.iom.edu/Reports/2005/Complementary-and-Alternative-Medicine-in-the-United-States.aspx

[443] http://www.parliament.the-stationery-office.co.uk/pa/ld199900/ldselect/ldsctech/123/12301.htm

[444] //dx.doi.org/10.1037%2F1522-3736.6.1.61a

[445] //dx.doi.org/10.1016%2FS1356-689X%2802%2900077-2

[446] //www.ncbi.nlm.nih.gov/pubmed/12890440

[447] //dx.doi.org/10.1059%2F0003-4819-127-1-199707010-00010

[448] //www.ncbi.nlm.nih.gov/pubmed/9214254

[449] //www.worldcat.org/issn/0094-6354

[450] //www.ncbi.nlm.nih.gov/pubmed/10488264

[451] //www.worldcat.org/oclc/6420468

[452] //www.worldcat.org/oclc/4134656

[453] http://www.csicop.org/si/show/magical_thinking_in_complementary_and_alternative_medicine

[454] //www.worldcat.org/oclc/18616238

[455] http://www.cwru.edu/med/epidbio/mphp439/Sources_of_Healthcare.htm
[456] //www.worldcat.org/oclc/181139440
[457] http://books.google.com/books?id=bZjlC2LEIIC
[458] //www.ncbi.nlm.nih.gov/pubmed/11728302
[459] http://web.archive.org/web/20040206092548/http://www.bsb.mefst.hr/cmj/1999/4001/400102.htm
[460] http://www.bsb.mefst.hr/cmj/1999/4001/400102.htm
[461] http://whqlibdoc.who.int/hq/2000/WHO_EDM_TRM_2000.1.pdf
[462] http://www.who.int/medicines/areas/traditional/Chiro-Guidelines.pdf
[463] http://apps.who.int/bookorders/anglais/detart1.jsp?codlan=1&codcol=15&codcch=614
[464] http://locatorplus.gov/cgi-bin/Pwebrecon.cgi?DB=local&v2=1&ti=1,1&Search_Arg=9502013&Search_Code=0359&CNT=20&SID=1
[465] http://altmedrev.com/
[466] http://locatorplus.gov/cgi-bin/Pwebrecon.cgi?DB=local&v2=1&ti=1,1&Search_Arg=9705340&Search_Code=0359&CNT=20&SID=1
[467] http://www.biomedcentral.com/1472-6882
[468] http://locatorplus.gov/cgi-bin/Pwebrecon.cgi?DB=local&v2=1&ti=1,1&Search_Arg=101088661&Search_Code=0359&CNT=20&SID=1
[469] http://locatorplus.gov/cgi-bin/Pwebrecon.cgi?DB=local&v2=1&ti=1,1&Search_Arg=9308777&Search_Code=0359&CNT=20&SID=1
[470] http://ecam.oxfordjournals.org/
[471] http//locatorplus.gov
[472] http://content.karger.com/ProdukteDB/produkte.asp?Aktion=JournalHome&ProduktNr=224242
[473] http://www.jintmed.org/
[474] http://www.liebertpub.com/products/product.aspx?pid=26
[475] http://www.sram.org/index.html
[476] https://www.dmoz.org/Health/Alternative/
[477] http://nccih.nih.gov/
[478] http://www.cancer.gov/cam/
[479] http://www.vifab.dk/uk
[480] http://www.cancer.org/docroot/eto/content/eto_5_3x_guidelines_for_using_complementary_and_alternative_methods.asp
[481] http://www.umm.edu/altmed/
[482] http://www.fammed.wisc.edu/integrative/modules
[483] http://www.open2.net/alternativemedicine/index.html
[484] http://www.mayoclinic.com/health/alternative-medicine/PN00001
[485] http://www.naturalstandard.com/
[486] http://www.pbs.org/saf/1210/index.html
[487] http://www.pbs.org/saf/1210/video/watchonline.htm
[488] http://www.pbs.org/kcet/closertotruth/explore/show_11.html
[489] http://www.theness.com/index.php/what-is-complementary-and-alternative-medicine/
[490] http://www.skepdic.com/althelth.html
[491] http://www.quackwatch.org
[492] http://metapsychology.mentalhelp.net/poc/view_doc.php?type=book&id=4690&cn=452
[493] http://whatstheharm.net/
[494] //en.wikipedia.org/w/index.php?title=Template:Criminal_law&action=edit
[495] //en.wikipedia.org/w/index.php?title=Template:Tort_law&action=edit
[496] need citation
[497] need citations
[498] *R. v. Olan et al.*, [1978] 2 S.C.R. 1175.
[499] *R. v. Stewart*, [1988] 1 S.C.R. 963.
[500] BBC world service broadcast 29.3.2012.
[501] The Fraud Act 2006 (Commencement) Order 2006 - SI 2006 No. 3200 (C.112) ISBN 0-11-075407-7

[502] "Tax Fraud and the Problem of a Constitutionality Acceptable Definition of Religion". BJ Casino. *American Criminal Law. Rev.*, 1987

[503] Kokenes, Chris (March 19, 2009), "N.Y. lawyer arraigned in alleged $700M fraud" http://money.cnn.com/2009/03/19/news/hedge_fund_fraud/index.htm?postversion=2009031914, CNNMoney.com, retrieved April 10, 2011

[504] Judgement and Statement of Decision http://raklaw.com/pdf/11-15-13-Judgment-Statement-Decision.pdf. Retrieved 27 December 2013.

[505] Nicole Muehlhausen, BIO: Tom Petters http://kstp.com/article/stories/s592708.shtml?cat=63, KSTP.com, September 24, 2008. Retrieved October 8, 2008.

[506] http://www.law.cornell.edu/uscode/18/704.html

[507] http://www.wcl.american.edu/journal/lawrev/48/48-4.cfm

[508] http://www.acpo.police.uk/asp/policies/Data/Fraud%20in%20the%20UK.pdf

[509] http://www.dilloninvestigates.com/index_files/Page390.htm

[510] http://www.acfe.com/

[511] http://www.uscis.gov/propub/ProPubVAP.jsp?dockey=e95bc8f7591b3c6caa51b7cc51f8d255

[512] http://www.fbi.gov/majcases/fraud/fraudschemes.htm

[513] http://justice.gov/criminal/fraud

Article Sources and Contributors

The sources listed for each article provide more detailed licensing information including the copyright status, the copyright owner, and the license conditions.

Kevin Trudeau *Source:* https://en.wikipedia.org/w/index.php?oldid=671850697 *License:* Creative Commons Attribution-Share Alike 3.0 *Contributors:* !dea4u, A bit iffy, Abductive, Aftermath, Albahja00, Amazume, Americus55, AndrewN, Anomalocaris, Anonomous5777, Ardeshir Byromme, Asissono, BDE1982, Barney5327, BarrelProof, Bellerophon5685, Boghog, BrathwaiteKim, BullRangifer, Bunbunsunrise, BuzyBody, Callanecc, Cchambers, Chris1834, Christy747, ClueBot NG, Coinmanj, Collect, CountMacula, Cowandchicken1999, Cyanolinguophile, DanielGinTruth, DarkAudit, Darkwind, Davenru, David in DC, Debresser, Deli nk, Discospinster, DivineAlpha, DoctorJoeE, Donner60, Drmies, Edward, Elseandrew, Essafl, Evanh2008, EvergreenFir, Famspear, Fraggle81, Fyrael, Gobonobo, GoingBatty, Graham1973, Heytherenow, Hmains, Hrhshir, Hullaballoo Wolfowitz, Irtyzx, Jessieswann, Jfmantis, Joalkap, John Cline, Jrrfunding, JzG, KMeyer, Lakun.patra, Lenin and McCarthy, Listmeister, Lukeno94, Markdonn, Materialscientist, McSly, Melopsittacus23, Mr. Stradivarius, MrBill3, Mrschimpf, Mysteryquest, Niteshift36, Non-dropframe, Omnipaedista, Pelecan Shtzu, Pinkadelica, Pluperfectionist2, Poetdancer, Postcard Cathy, Pretzelpaws, Quisqualis, Qwfp, Qwychang, Ravensfire, Rediculousness, Redmack92, Rhododendrites, Rickremember, RickyWho, RoyBoy, Saedon, Sammy109, Scalhotrod, Second Quantization, Severisth, Slightsmile, Sneftel, Solomonfromfinland, Srich32977, Staszek Lem, Strani Beeap, StuHarris, Sussmanbern, Tabris06, Tbhotch, The Interior, TheArguer, Trappist the monk, Vanished user kasjqwii3km4tkid, Vegaswikian, Verdict78, Vincent Lextrait, WLU, Waacstats, WarrenVitcenda, Wbm1058, Widr, Y2kcrazyjoker4, Yobol, Ὁ οἶστρος, 178 anonymous edits 3

MegaMemory *Source:* https://en.wikipedia.org/w/index.php?oldid=610161275 *License:* Creative Commons Attribution-Share Alike 3.0 *Contributors:* Bearcat, ClueBot NG, CwenHoma, Enchanter, FrazerKirkman, Katharineamy, Lenin and McCarthy, Listmeister, Random user 39849958, Sabine's Sunbird, WikHead, Woohookitty, 7 anonymous edits 19

Natural Cures "They" Don't Want You to Know About *Source:* https://en.wikipedia.org/w/index.php?oldid=655589283 *License:* Creative Commons Attribution-Share Alike 3.0 *Contributors:* Alan Liefting, Avb, BeastmasterGeneral, Beginning, Belovedfreak, Bizfixer, Blackmagicfish, Bobo192, Bonadea, Bueller 007, BullRangifer, C6541, Cedders, Chicago god, Clinevol98, ClueBot NG, Consumed Crustacean, CrypticBacon, DARTH SIDIOUS 2, DabMachine, Danelo, Davidmack, Deli nk, Digwuren, Doc James, Dr.simmer, DragonflySixtyseven, Dreier23, Elen of the Roads, Enviroboy, Eternal Sleeper, Five-, Gaius Cornelius, Gerrit, Gilliam, Gwern, Humanintel, Ihavenolife, Irishguy, J04n, JNW, JulietChristieMurray, JzG, Kaori, Kippson, Kristjan Wager, LeContexte, Leon7, Lucid, MER-C, Mahanga, MakeRocketGoNow, MarcusChacoss, Matt122004, Mr. Billion, MrBill3, Mysteryquest, Oatmeal batman, PCock, Pinkadelica, Pjoc99, Plastic editor, Polonium, Portillo, Qirex, RPellessier, Rambone, Remember, Rivcal, Rockfang, Roraem, Router∼enwiki, RoyBoy, Sapphic, Skelly31, Skier Dude, Smith Jones, SoldierOfColbert, Solomonfromfinland, Sticky Parkin, SummerPhD, TKD, The Anome, TheDevilYouKnow, TheRedFear, Thesayerofing, Thomqi, Trancenational, Treygdor, Trivialist, Tyciol, Ubiq, Ukexpat, UnneededAplomb, VoABot II, WLU, Wasaka, Widr, Woohookitty, Xsmasher, 136 anonymous edits 19

The Weight-Loss Cure "They" Don't Want You to Know About *Source:* https://en.wikipedia.org/w/index.php?oldid=672565357 *License:* Creative Commons Attribution-Share Alike 3.0 *Contributors:* 331dot, AnthonyGLee, Barticus88, Bdj, Boghog, Chjoaygame, Crustypie, D6, Deli nk, Dr.simmer, Edward, Gaberdine2, Genesis78941, GregorB, Healthnut1, JFHJr, John, John Vandenberg, JzG, KConWiki, Khazar2, LilHelpa, MastCell, Miamimusic, Mysteryquest, Novangelis, OccamzRazor, Ohnoitsjamie, PCock, Pegship, Pnm, Rhrad, Robofish, Router∼enwiki, S, Saros136, Senorelroboto, Skier Dude, Supertomcom, Sussmanbern, THEN WHO WAS PHONE?, Tamajared, Tobyc75, Tony Sidaway, Treygdor, Trivialist, Wikid77, Yellowcason, Zimbardo Cookie Experiment, 19 anonymous edits 23

Quackery *Source:* https://en.wikipedia.org/w/index.php?oldid=673044462 *License:* Creative Commons Attribution-Share Alike 3.0 *Contributors:* 28bytes, 2over0, Ad Orientem, Adirlanz, Aeusoes1, Alansohn, Alayambo, Alexbrn, Anthony Appleyard, Arthena, Arthur Rubin, Astynax, Audaciter, BD2412, BDD, Ben Ben, Bhny, Bobrayner, Bongwarrior, BullRangifer, Burleigh2, C6541, Camboxer, Citation bot 1, ClueBot NG, Colliric, CoolKoon, Crohnie, Curb Chain, Das48, DavidOaks, Dbachmann, Debouch, Deisenbe, Dewritech, DigitalC, DiverDave, DoorsAjar, Drsjpdc, Dwight Burdette, Eastchester, Enric Naval, Entprasad, Epbr123, Eric Corbett, Espenvh, Eubulides, Everymorning, Faramir1138, Fgnievinski, Fixblor, Fork me, Fred Bauder, Gabbe, GoingBatty, Grayfell, Gronk Oz, Heilige Krieger, Hell in a Bucket, Herbalchocolate1, Herbxue, Hiperfelix, Hmains, Immunize, JDRG, JSLyons, JamesAM, Jarble, Jasper Deng, Jerodlycett, Jimp, JoDonHo, John Paul Parks, JollyrogerMD, Jschnur, JzG, Kay Dekker, Khazar2, Killian441, Kinetik138, Kwamikagami, Lawfriedrich, LeadSongDog, LeisureContributer, Ludwigs2, M. Adiputra, M2545, Mackermer, Maepay123, Magioladitis, MarnetteD, Martin Jambon, Matt Fitzpatrick, Mckburton, Meaghan, Meco, Medicalstaffcc, Mknjbhvgcf, Moreschi, Mprisco824, MrOllie, Mysidia, Naniwako, Objectivesea, Oiyarbepsy, Olivier, Orangemarlin, PBS-AWB, PPdd, Palapa, PerryTachett, Phósphoros, Piledhigheranddeeper, Pingveno, Pnm, Pwjb, QuackGuru, Quercus solaris, Raymondwinn, Rhododendrites, Richard Arthur Norton (1958-), Richard David Ramsey, Riverpa, Rjwilmsi, Rosarino, Roundtheworld, Rrburke, Rsrikanth05, Rumiton, Ryulong, Saedon, Saxophobia, Sbmeirow, SchroCat, Scwlong, Severina123, Shot info, Smk65536, Spyder212, Staszek Lem, Stmrlbs, Susfele, Tabletop, Taksen, Tgeairn, Tha*Lunat!k, Therealbigdave, Thomasdorlo, TippyGoomba, Topbanana, Trappist the monk, Verbal, Vincent Moon, Von Restorff, WhisperToMe, Will Beback, William Avery, Zodon, 122 anonymous edits 26

International Pool Tour *Source:* https://en.wikipedia.org/w/index.php?oldid=640055011 *License:* Creative Commons Attribution-Share Alike 3.0 *Contributors:* Abberley2, Balabushka, BarrelProof, BenRG, Blake Burba, BullRangifer, Charles Matthews, Cholmes75, Chris the speller, ConradPino, Cornerman67, Daniel, Dragquennom, Duncan1800, Dvorak.typist, Epeefleche, EvanCarroll, FoxLad, Funandtrvl, GVOLTT, Huckster88, Infernal Inferno, Islandrave1980, J04n, JakartaDean, Joefromrandb, John of Reading, JoshuaZ, Katana, Ken Gallager, LastBall, LilHelpa, Lquilter, MSJapan, Mahaloth, Meishern, Northamerica1000, Poolwiki, Q11, RailbirdJAM, Rich257, RoyBoy, SMcCandlish, Sandman1142, Slsh, Smith Jones, Tewapack, Weej100, Weej304, Woohookitty, 76 anonymous edits 46

Ed Foreman *Source:* https://en.wikipedia.org/w/index.php?oldid=660223994 *License:* Creative Commons Attribution-Share Alike 3.0 *Contributors:* A bit iffy, Alansohn, Algocu, Americus55, Appraiser, Bearcat, BenKovitz, Betacommand, Billy Hathorn, BrownHairedGirl, Brozozo, CLW, DStoykov, Delaywaves, Donner60, Eggy49er, Fratrep, GHe, Good Olfactory, Ground Zero, HangingCurve, Harryboyles, Hmains, Iheart, JamesReyes, Jevansen, Jwillbur, Karanacs, Khatru2, Koavf, Kumioko (renamed), Lockley, MaxMercy, Mild Bill Hiccup, Reign of Toads, Skywriter, Sun Creator, TexianPolitico, Thismightbezach, Valadius, Wavelength, WereSpielChequers, WilliamJE, 36 anonymous edits 52

Greg Caton *Source:* https://en.wikipedia.org/w/index.php?oldid=643475810 *License:* Creative Commons Attribution-Share Alike 3.0 *Contributors:* 069952497a, 2over0, Bender235, Bgwhite, Black Kite, Carolmooredc, Colonies Chris, Decltype, Delldot, Dyuku, Edgarblythe, Frietjes, GoingBatty, Ground Zero, Jaguar57, Jettparmer, Johnson-Bob, Kitfoxxe, LilHelpa, MastCell, MelanieN, Moe Epsilon, Muhandes, NJA, Off2riorob, Pcap, Perfect64, R'n'B, RL0919, RWJP, Spicewc, Sterling.M.Archer, TenOfAllTrades, Threeafterthree, UnicornTapestry, Verbal, Waacstats, Wavelength, 22 anonymous edits 56

Reno R. Rolle *Source:* https://en.wikipedia.org/w/index.php?oldid=659729459 *License:* Creative Commons Attribution-Share Alike 3.0 *Contributors:* AvicAWB, Bender235, Conquistador2k6, Jamesmcmahon0, Katharineamy, Lambiam, Socialgood, Sonicyouth86, Waacstats, Wadeaminute24, Welsh, 7 anonymous edits 60

Ronald Hoffman *Source:* https://en.wikipedia.org/w/index.php?oldid=604212837 *License:* Creative Commons Attribution-Share Alike 3.0 *Contributors:* ChanceChancellor, Guy M, Hertz1888, Johnpacklambert, Juliaschopick, Lockley, MZMcBride, Mangoe, Mdriver1981, O keyes, Ohnoitsjamie, Waacstats, פאל, עמירם 13 anonymous edits 61

Robert Barefoot *Source:* https://en.wikipedia.org/w/index.php?oldid=632509637 *License:* Creative Commons Attribution-Share Alike 3.0 *Contributors:* Barrystein, BobKawanaka, BullRangifer, Crazytales, Desmond Hobson, Frglz, Garlicdawg, GrahamHardy, Ground Zero, Hmains, Jokestress, Kronos o, Lamro, NimaTheGrateful, Peaceray, Random user 39849958, Rjwilmsi, Ronz, Skyerise, SlamDiego, TheBlueFlamingo, TheGGoose, Troysawyer, Velella, Viewmont Viking, Waacstats, 20 anonymous edits 63

Donald Barrett *Source:* https://en.wikipedia.org/w/index.php?oldid=660457881 *License:* Creative Commons Attribution-Share Alike 3.0 *Contributors:* Alan Liefting, Amystroud, Arjayay, Auntof6, Azumanga1, CKelly, Cliff b adams, Cosprings, David Eppstein, Dbscrewedme, Dr.simmer, Editfromwithout, Greenrd, John of Reading, Kentmoraga, MZMcBride, Malcolma, Marjaliisa, Mattryncarz, Mhoskins, Mysteryquest, O keyes, Orangemike, Palefist, Postcard Cathy, Sandboxer, Skier Dude, Tabletop, Tim!, TravisTX, Waacstats, Wgolf, Xoddf2, Zephyrnthesky, 18 anonymous edits 64

Leigh Valentine *Source:* https://en.wikipedia.org/w/index.php?oldid=658851705 *License:* Creative Commons Attribution-Share Alike 3.0 *Contributors:* Antigravityece, Cerabot∼enwiki, Chris the speller, ClueBot NG, Debbie Do49, Debbieassistant, Debbiedo1949, Debbiedo312, Dobie80, Dravecky, Epbr123, Fæ, Hmains, IlyaKralinsky, Johnpacklambert, MissAmericaGirl, Per Ardua, S2pid80it, Seaphoto, SummerPhD, Teepeewabbit, Tommy2010, Unbuttered Parsnip, UprofitableS, Waacstats, Woohookitty, 52 anonymous edits 66

Infomercial *Source:* https://en.wikipedia.org/w/index.php?oldid=673771463 *License:* Creative Commons Attribution-Share Alike 3.0 *Contributors:* 2buysellstuff, A53collins, Aallasdfa67usgd60, Alan Liefting, Alansohn, Albany NY, Andrewaskew, Aryalive, Athanasius28, Azumanga1, Bgwhite, BiH, Bklimt, BookDen, BornonJune8, Brom 28, Busjack, Chowbok, Chris the speller, Christy747, Chubbles, Chunk5Darth, Closedmouth, ClueBot NG, Corn cheese, DGG, DVdm, Darrel M, DemocraticLuntz, Deskana, Dgrattonwalsh, DiePerfekteWelle, Dougfowkes, Dreadstar, Dsgarnett, Egsan Bacon, Ellinewilliams231, Eyesbomb, Fimatic, Geega127, GoingBatty, Grantbow, Grapesoda22, Graymornings, HappyMidnight, IjonTichyIjonTichy, Indianparttime2, Its snowing in East Asia, Ixfd64, J04n, J4lambert, JMyrleFuller, JamieHill25, JesseAlanGordon, Jimp, John of Reading, JordoCo, Lugnad, M.S.K., Mark Arsten, Mark RBraff, MarkRobbins, Martarius, Martin451, Mastaxkim, May misty456, Mimzy1990, Mogism, Mrschimpf, Msr69er, NP923, NatGertler, Natra Yan, NoseNuggets, Oli Filth, Orangemike, Peachrules14, PhnomPencil, Quicksilvre, RJaguar3, Reconsider the static, Red Jay, Redside, ResearchRave, Richguy77, Robfwb, Rockcenter, Rocknrollrocksout, Ronz, RoyBoy, Samw, Santanaquintas, Santanaquintass, Shoebox2, Shortride, SimonTrew, Smalljim,

Tassedethe, Tentinator, Themfromspace, Trivialist, Tvtonightokc, Vanished user uih38riiw4hjlsd, ViperSnake151, Wavelength, Wcquidditch, Will Beback, WillOakland, Woohookitty, Yamaguchi先生, 202 anonymous edits 68
Big Pharma conspiracy theory *Source*: https://en.wikipedia.org/w/index.php?oldid=668723499 *License*: Creative Commons Attribution-Share Alike 3.0 *Contributors*: Alexbrn, Armaun.sanayei, David Gerard, Froid, Giraffedata, Jeraphine Gryphon, Johnnmillerr, Jonesey95, Niceguyedc, NinjaRobotPirate, Penbat, Sbmeirow, Sunrise, Wavelength, 3 anonymous edits 82
Tammy Faye Messner *Source*: https://en.wikipedia.org/w/index.php?oldid=668664761 *License*: Creative Commons Attribution-Share Alike 3.0 *Contributors*: A Doon, Aboutmovies, Aec is away, All Hallow's Wraith, Allthenamesarealreadytaken, Americasroof, AndreniW, Angr, Anna309411, Aratuk, Asarelah, Astynax, AustinSarrett, Azumanga1, Bacl-presby, Bashereyre, Bbsrock, Bdve, Bearcat, Bobblehead, BornonJune8, Can't sleep, clown will eat me, Canyouhearmenow, Chaheel Riens, Chris-marsh-usa, Cobaltcigs, Coinmanj, Colton Cosmic, Comedyfan1983, CommonsDelinker, Corlier, D6, Dan1025, DandyDan2007, David Unit, Dismas, Dlohcierekim, Donpayette, Doug Weller, Download, Emerson7, Enorton, EstherLois, Fayenatic london, Fire398017, Firsfron, Gaius Cornelius, Good Olfactory, Ground Zero, Guy M, Hail of violence, Hiphats, Horkana, Hydrargyrum, Inks.LWC, Italianlover07, JAF1970, JForget, JGHowes, JackieTeal, Jaldridge86, Jauerback, Jeeny, Jim.Liu, JIspotts, Jnelson09, John of Reading, J〜enwiki, Kaihoku, Kathleen.wright5, Khazar2, Kinu, Koavf, Kurt Shaped Box, Lawikitejana, LorenzoB, M a s, M.S.K., MZMcBride, Maralia, Marteau, Mdann52, Meatsgains, Millionsandbillions, Mlaffs, Mmathu, Monegasque, MykroftM, Nawlin Wiki, Ncasci, Nightscream, Nikkimaria, Nrswanson, Od Mishehu AWB, Oda Mari, Okki, Plastikspork, Pleonic, Pokokitty123, Rich Farmbrough, Rjwilmsi, Rklawton, RobNich, Sabey00, Sabos〜enwiki, Sawblade5, Schetm, Scray, Seeker alpha806, Ser Amantio di Nicolao, SmartyBoots, Smbil58, Socby19, Spencer, Srich32977, StevenKayTrenton, Sugar Bear, TGC55, TJ Spyke, TVFAN24, Taco Viva, Thattherepaul, TheatreKid01, Tinton5, Tirronan, Tony1, Traveliter, Ttonyb1, Ukexpat, Unschool, VKokielov, Vgranucci, Vincelord, WOSlinker, Waacstats, Wikipediatrix, Wikipeterproject, Writergirl26, Wrodina, Xnatedawgx, 162 anonymous edits 84
Nancy Valen *Source*: https://en.wikipedia.org/w/index.php?oldid=664871109 *License*: Creative Commons Attribution-Share Alike 3.0 *Contributors*: A930913, AKGhetto, AN(Ger), American Eagle, Bender235, BizarreLoveTriangle, BornonJune8, Brunothemonkey, Brunothemonkeynvvp, Bunnyhop11, CambridgeBayWeather, CanisRufus, Catapult, Cavarrone, Dobie80, Doncram, Dr. Blofeld, DrStrangeLove, DragonflySixtyseven, Dwscomet, Ebyabe, Eleanor haven, Fly by Night, Freakofnurture, Guat6, Hanksummers, Hmains, Hobophobe, Hullaballoo Wolfowitz, Jason Quinn, Jeffman52001, Jwillbur, Kukini, LittleWink, Magioladitis, Markeer, Monkey32, Pinkadelica, Ponyo, QuasyBoy, RahadyanS, Rjwilmsi, Rms125a@hotmail.com, RobotG, Satinandsteel, Savolya, Ser Amantio di Nicolao, TMC1982, Tassedethe, Tim!, Violetofthevalley, 27 anonymous edits 92
Federal Trade Commission *Source*: https://en.wikipedia.org/w/index.php?oldid=668083282 *License*: Creative Commons Attribution-Share Alike 3.0 *Contributors*: A E Francis, AMuseOfFire, AdamDeanHall, AfeR, Alan Liefting, Alepb42, Anaxial, Apparition11, Arthena, AvnajBevTa, BD2412, Bebestbe, Blondeguynative, Bob Burkhardt, Bonadea, Bongwarrior, Brastein, Briaboru, Brianwc, Brighterorange, Brismile, CanadianLinuxUser, Castrol, CasualObserver'48, CliffC, Clindberg, Closedmouth, CueBot NG, CopperSquare, Courcelles, Crownjewel82, Cryptonymius, Cst17, Cybercobra, Czrisher, DMacks, Darkwind, Devourer09, Discospinster, DocWatson42, Doncram, De Garane, Drboulla, Dthomsen8, Eastlaw, Eddiebeans, Edward, Eep², Epbr123, Epicgenius, Erik Lönnrot, Esmito, FTC OPA, Factsearch, Fashionethics, Fatla00, Freakmighty, Freedomwarrior, Freeheeling, Freewol, Galoubet, Gilliam, GoldRingChip, Grayfell12, Ground Zero, HaggyMac, HappyMidnight, Howcheng, IRP, Illegitimate Barrister, Imperator3733, Int21h, Jarvishunt, Jdebusch, Jerzy, Jojhutton, Jonpatterns, Jordansparks, K6ka, KgLiberty, Lighted Match, Lotje, Lquilter, Magioladitis, Malikashiqui, Masianosp, Materialscientist, Meteor sandwich yum, Minimac's Clone, MrBill3, MrsJJHH, NQC 2736, Neovu79, NetKnight〜enwiki, Neutrality, Non Curat Lex, Noren, Nsaa, Nukeless, Ohnoitsjamie, PJtP, Palosirkka, Peterpkaplan, Puffin, RJaguar3, RM SEO, Rhododendrites, Riffic, Rjensen, Rsrikanth05, STBotD, SaraThustra, Sarah43pr, Sardanaphalus, Scheherazade510, ScheredtherBike, Scriberius, Seth Goldin, Shell Kinney, Shieldforyoureyes, Shirik, Shieldbyrd, Shortride, SirAndrew1, Skittleys, Smallbones, Some jerk on the Internet, Songanto, Stpuidhead, Supreme Deliciousness, Sureshot Auntie, Surfer43, Swliv, The Anome, The Nut, The Thing That Should Not Be, Therequiembellishere, Thewinchester, Tiggerjay, Tim Q. Wells, Tim1965, Ulric1313, VQuakr, Widr, Wtmitchell, 護藍雪, 200 anonymous edits 96
Food and Drug Administration *Source*: https://en.wikipedia.org/w/index.php?oldid=672743416 *License*: Creative Commons Attribution-Share Alike 3.0 *Contributors*: 007bond, 2016matthew, 220 of Borg, 2over0, A520, Abhijeet Safai, Acroterion, Adamhallam, Ajit Basrur, Alarics, Allens, Amorymeltzer, Antony-22, Aristotle Kepler, Arthur Rubin, Asimms3, Athomeinkobe, BD2412, Bgwhite, Bluerasberry, Bolesjohnb, Bryce Carmony, Byelf2007, CapitalR, CaseyNichols, Catlemur, Cerabot〜enwiki, Ceyockey, Cherkash, ChrisGualtieri, Clarkbar10, CueBot NG, Compfreak7, Cullen328, CynicalTurtle, DMacks, DarthNader1942, Dawnseeker2000, Del ink, Dewritech, Doc James, Download, Drayfar, Drphilharmonic, Eaglizard, Edgar181, Editor182, Edward321, Excirial, Flickerd, Funandtrvl, Gareth Griffith-Jones, Gogo Dodo, Ground Zero, Health Canada, Helpsome, Hmains, Hmrox, Hullaballoo Wolfowitz, Indianeskimo, Int21h, J36miles, January2009, Jarble, Jasims3, Jim1138, John, Jphill19, Judicial review171, Jvedude, Kalenmeyer, Kchishol1970, Kirananils, Kkmurray, LN2, LTDinDC, LeadSongDog, Lugia2453, Lybbar12, MacBay7023, Madzane, Magioladitis, Malika42, MariaRegExpert, Marketing Employee, Materialscientist, Mean as custard, Megawyart, MichaelEisele21, Mindmatrix, Mlwmiller, Moabdave, Mr. Granger, MrBill3, MusikAnimal, Mynamestsmart58, Nick Number, Nightscream, Nmemo, Nutster, Nysrtup, Oceanflynn, OracleNayru, Ormistonrocks433, Owen Ambur, Peter James, PinkPolitico80, Poiuytrewqvtaatv123321, Polmandc, Prkkohli, Randy Kryn, Rarian rakista, Rathfelder, Rhuang22, Rjwilmsi, Rod57, SDY, SHJohnson, SantiLak, Scientizzle, Seaphoto, SecondWallo, Servis, SlimVirgin, Snow Blizzard, Sophiaansari, Srich32977, Stepheng3, Terbayang, TheShoeGod, Thsundas, Tom Morris, Trackteur, Twillisjr, Tznkai, Vdubbs, Vegaswikian, Versageek, Viriditas, Way2rach, Wbeadle3, Whywhenwhohow, WildGoose89, Wok787, Woohookitty, Yamastick, Yobol, 141 anonymous edits 106
Pharmaceutical industry *Source*: https://en.wikipedia.org/w/index.php?oldid=672750842 *License*: Creative Commons Attribution-Share Alike 3.0 *Contributors*: Abarros, Achandrasekaran99, Alexbrn, Alfred Bertheim, Anmusna, Anthonyhcole, Asdklf:, Asimms3, Bgwhite, Billposer, BreakfastJr, CaptainMoose1987, Casonova, Chris the speller, ChrisGualtieri, CueBot NG, Contributor2015, Cptbiggsworth266, Daniele Pugliesi, Daweagel, Deli nk, Dewritech, Doc James, DocWatson42, Download, DustBowlTroubadour, Edgar181, Edward, EllenCT, Emreg00, ErikaKelton, FT2, Fraggle81, Gnome de plume, I dream of horses, Intractable, Jakew, Jameshfisher, Jarble, Jerodlycett, John of Reading, Johnfos, Jonesey95, Josh Joaquin, Josve05a, Jytdog, K6ka, Khazar2, LegalTech, Lizia7, Lprd2007, Lukekfreeman, MSL Society, Magioladitis, Marc Bago, Mdsa62, Millbart, Moldeck, Mr P. George, MrBill3, Mrodwin, Myasuda, Neil P. Quinn, Neo Poz, Nipunnayar, Northamerica1000, Noyster, Oceanflynn, Oustseeds, Palosirkka, Petecarney, Pop7x7, Poucquerêl, QuackGuru, Renamed user 51g7z61hz5af2azs6k6, Rjwilmsi, Sahehco, Sanadical, Shanghai Sally, SilverbackNet, SimVirgin, Smalljim, Sofia Lucifairy, Srich32977 0, StarryGrandma, Sunrise, SusanLesch, Swaggity, Tevetu zuluts, TheJJJunk, Toadsoctobus, UseTheCommandLine, Wakebrdkid, Wavelength, Wiki CRUK John, Xancester, گٯ ,ازادﯾ, 116 anonymous edits 125
Alternative medicine *Source*: https://en.wikipedia.org/w/index.php?oldid=673901543 *License*: Creative Commons Attribution-Share Alike 3.0 *Contributors*: AlbertSeole, Bgwhite, BullRangifer, Cyberbot II, El Gatos, Donner60, Evermorning, FiachraByrne, FloraWilde, LeadSongDog, Magioladitis, Mckburton, Mheydari2, Middle 8, Qexigator, QuackGuru, Rhododendrites, Rich Farmbrough, Rjwilmsi, Sunrise, Topbanana, 1 anonymous edits ...151
Fraud *Source*: https://en.wikipedia.org/w/index.php?oldid=672036312 *License*: Creative Commons Attribution-Share Alike 3.0 *Contributors*: 72Dino, ASHaber, AmandaJohnson2014, Amaury, Andrewman327, Andy Dingley, Angelito7, Auric, AzaToth, Babyluvsbaby2, Bearcat, BigDwiki, Bigboy2014, Bkonrad, Bobby230, Bongwarrior, Brantleybcarter, Bromley86, Bulldog73, C.Fred, Calabe1992, Canonlis, Captain Cornwall, ChaosMaster16, ChidemK, Chris the speller, CluBot NG, CommonsDelinker, Cuthbert Pullar, DMacks, DVdm, Dadasathish, DanielBStern, Dapfelba, Djobb, Dmol, Don4of4, Draconiator, ENeville, EcoTort Theatre, Excirial, FDMS4, Fat&Happy, Fginevinski, Flyer22, Folantin, Franea12, Freak412, Free Fro, GR8DAN, Gautehuus, Gogo Dodo, Grafen, GrumpyZОmbie, Gulbenk, HIDECCHI001, HMSSolent, Haeinous, I dream of horses, I-user, JNW, Jack Greenmaven, Jackfork, James Balti, Jdaloner, Jerodlycett, Jim1138, Jo-Jo Eumerus, JoeWhitehead07, KateTheWriter, Kku, Konullu, Lawman4312, Lockendosk, Lotje, LukeSurl, Magioladitis, Matbeeche, MattW93, Mean as custard, Megawyatt, Mike Rosoft, Mindmatrix, Minimac, Mohaski1, MrBill3, MrOllie, Mtking, Navneetkshk111, Nepenthes, NewEnglandYankee, Norman21, Northamerica1000, Nutster, Oluwasangosanya1, Omnipedian, Pane Ellsworth, Paul Wallin, Peterkortvel, Pinethicket, QuackGuru, Raellerby, RafiTadmor, Rider ranger47, Rsrikanth05, Sanya3, SarahLijs, Schaff78, ScottyBerg, Scwlong, Short10113, Skysmith, Sriharsh1234, Stopfraudnow, Strecken, Supdiop, TLAN38, ThePoweroOfX, Thefirstusername, Toched21, Toadsoctobus, Trappist the monk, WPPilot, Webclient101, Wikisawesome, Wikipeli, William (The Bill) Blackstone, Wknight94, Wtmitchell, Yamaguchi先生, לערי ריינהארט, 210 anonymous edits 207

Image Sources, Licenses and Contributors

The sources listed for each image provide more detailed licensing information including the copyright status, the copyright owner, and the license conditions.

Image *Source:* https://en.wikipedia.org/w/index.php?title=File:Padlock-silver-light.svg *Contributors:* User:AzaToth, User:Eleassar 3
Image *Source:* https://en.wikipedia.org/w/index.php?title=File:Kevin_Trudeau_cropped.JPG *License:* Public Domain *Contributors:* Kevin_Trudeau.JPG: RailbirdJAM at en.wikipedia derivative work: – Cirt (talk) 3
Figure 1 *Source:* https://en.wikipedia.org/w/index.php?title=File:KOTH-Orlando.JPG *License:* Public Domain *Contributors:* RailbirdJAM at en.wikipedia 11
Figure 2 *Source:* https://en.wikipedia.org/w/index.php?title=File:WPA_quack_poster.jpg *License:* Public Domain *Contributors:* Max Plattner 27
Figure 3 *Source:* https://en.wikipedia.org/w/index.php?title=File:Marriage_A-la-Mode_3,_The_Inspection_-_William_Hogarth.jpg *License:* Public Domain *Contributors:* Alborzagros, Crisco 1492, Ham II, Julia W 28
Figure 4 *Source:* https://en.wikipedia.org/w/index.php?title=File:Pietro_Longhi_015.jpg *License:* Public Domain *Contributors:* AndreasPraefcke, Auntof6, Bukk, Ecummenic, Emijrp, File Upload Bot (Eloquence), G.dallorto, Leyo, Mattes, Rococo1700, Zhuyifei1999 28
Figure 5 *Source:* https://en.wikipedia.org/w/index.php?title=File:Three_early_medicine_bottles.jpg *License:* Public Domain *Contributors:* Claus Ableiter, Infrogmation, Liftarn, OgreBot 2, The Moose, 1 anonymous edits 31
Figure 6 *Source:* https://en.wikipedia.org/w/index.php?title=File:Snake-oil.png *License:* Public Domain *Contributors:* Cirt, Liftarn, Man vyi, Minery, OgreBot 2, Takeaway, Tangopaso, Ymnes, Zolo 32
Figure 7 *Source:* https://en.wikipedia.org/w/index.php?title=File:Magnetiseur.JPG *License:* Public Domain *Contributors:* BotMultichill, Joseph.valet, SiGarb 33
Figure 8 *Source:* https://en.wikipedia.org/w/index.php?title=File:Electro-metabograph_machine.jpg *License:* Public Domain *Contributors:* Howcheng, Innotata, McGhiever, Zachary 34
Figure 9 *Source:* https://en.wikipedia.org/w/index.php?title=File:Tho-Radia-IMG_1228.JPG *License:* Creative Commons Attribution-Sharealike 2.0 *Contributors:* Rama 35
Figure 10 *Source:* https://en.wikipedia.org/w/index.php?title=File:Scientology_-_The_E-Meter.jpg *License:* Creative Commons Attribution-Sharealike 2.0 *Contributors:* Daniel Spiess 35
Figure 11 *Source:* https://en.wikipedia.org/w/index.php?title=File:Revigorator.jpg *License:* Creative Commons Attribution 2.0 *Contributors:* Andrew Kuchling 36
Figure 12 *Source:* https://en.wikipedia.org/w/index.php?title=File:Anker,_Albert_—_Der_Quacksalber_—_1879.jpg *License:* Public Domain *Contributors:* Ekenaes, FDMS4, Mattes 39
Figure 13 *Source:* https://en.wikipedia.org/w/index.php?title=File:Gerard_Dou_-_The_Quack_-_Google_Art_Project.jpg *Contributors:* Ixtzib, Mattes, Spinster, Vincent Steenberg 39
Figure 14 *Source:* https://en.wikipedia.org/w/index.php?title=File:De_piskijker_door_Jan_Steen.jpg *License:* Public Domain *Contributors:* Bukk, Jan Arkesteijn, Kürschner 40
Figure 15 *Source:* https://en.wikipedia.org/w/index.php?title=File:Jan_Steen_-_De_kwakzalver.jpg *License:* Public Domain *Contributors:* BotMultichill, Bukk, Cbyd, Jan Arkesteijn, Mattes, Vincent Steenberg 40
Image *Source:* https://en.wikipedia.org/w/index.php?title=File:Wikiquote-logo.svg *License:* Public Domain *Contributors:* -xfi-, Dbc334, Doodledoo, Elian, Guillom, Jarekt, Jeffq, Krinkle, Maderibeyza, Majorly, Nishkid64, RedCoat, Rei-artur, Rocket000, 11 anonymous edits 46
Image *Source:* https://en.wikipedia.org/w/index.php?title=File:Commons-logo.svg *License:* logo *Contributors:* Anomie 46
Image *Source:* https://en.wikipedia.org/w/index.php?title=File:Wiktionary-logo-en.svg *License:* Public Domain *Contributors:* Vectorized by , based on original logo tossed together by Brion Vibber 46
Image *Source:* https://en.wikipedia.org/w/index.php?title=File:Wikisource-logo.svg *License:* Creative Commons Attribution-Sharealike 3.0 *Contributors:* ChrisiPK, Guillom, INeverCry, Jarekt, JuTa, Leyo, Lokal Profil, MichaelMaggs, NielsF, Rei-artur, Rocket000, Steinsplitter 46
Figure 16 *Source:* https://en.wikipedia.org/w/index.php?title=File:IPT_Players.JPG *License:* Public Domain *Contributors:* RailbirdJAM at en.wikipedia 47
Figure 17 *Source:* https://en.wikipedia.org/w/index.php?title=File:IPT-NA_Venetian_in_Vegas_129.jpg *License:* Public Domain *Contributors:* RailbirdJAM at en.wikipedia 48
Image *Source:* https://en.wikipedia.org/w/index.php?title=File:Flag_of_the_Philippines.svg *License:* Public Domain *Contributors:* User:Achim1999 51
Image *Source:* https://en.wikipedia.org/w/index.php?title=File:Flag_of_the_United_States.svg *License:* Public Domain *Contributors:* Anomie, Mr. Stradivarius 51
Image *Source:* https://en.wikipedia.org/w/index.php?title=File:Flag_of_Germany.svg *License:* Public Domain *Contributors:* Anomie 51
Image *Source:* https://en.wikipedia.org/w/index.php?title=File:Ed_Foreman.jpg *License:* Public Domain *Contributors:* Delayways, Scooter 52
Image *Source:* https://en.wikipedia.org/w/index.php?title=File:Tammy_Faye_Messner.jpg *License:* Creative Commons Attribution 2.0 *Contributors:* Darwin Bell 84
Image *Source:* https://en.wikipedia.org/w/index.php?title=File:US-FederalTradeCommission-Seal.svg *License:* Public Domain *Contributors:* U.S. Government 96
Image *Source:* https://en.wikipedia.org/w/index.php?title=File:Flag_of_the_United_States_Federal_Trade_Commission.svg *Contributors:* User:Fry1989 96
Figure 18 *Source:* https://en.wikipedia.org/w/index.php?title=File:ApexBuildingHighsmith.jpg *License:* Public Domain *Contributors:* Carol M. Highsmith (born 1946) 97
Image *Source:* https://en.wikipedia.org/w/index.php?title=File:Scale_of_justice_2.svg *License:* Public Domain *Contributors:* DTR 100
Figure 19 *Source:* https://en.wikipedia.org/w/index.php?title=File:EndorsementGuides_0.webm *License:* Public Domain *Contributors:* Simisa, Smallbones 103
Image *Source:* https://en.wikipedia.org/w/index.php?title=File:Food_and_Drug_Administration_logo.svg *License:* Public Domain *Contributors:* U.S. 107
Figure 20 *Source:* https://en.wikipedia.org/w/index.php?title=File:FDA_Bldg_31_-_Exterior_(5161375422).jpg *License:* Public Domain *Contributors:* The U.S. Food and Drug Administration 108
Image *Source:* https://en.wikipedia.org/w/index.php?title=File:Ritalin-SR-20mg-1000x1000.jpg *License:* GNU Free Documentation License *Contributors:* en:User:Sponge 112
Figure 21 *Source:* https://en.wikipedia.org/w/index.php?title=File:FDA_Bldg_51_-_Main_Entrance_(5161374834).jpg *License:* Public Domain *Contributors:* The U.S. Food and Drug Administration 113
Figure 22 *Source:* https://en.wikipedia.org/w/index.php?title=File:FDA_Bldg_62_-_Exterior_(5161375340).jpg *License:* Public Domain *Contributors:* The U.S. Food and Drug Administration 117
Figure 23 *Source:* https://en.wikipedia.org/w/index.php?title=File:Portrait_of_Dr._Harvey_W._Wiley_(FDA_107)_(8203830456).jpg *License:* Public Domain *Contributors:* The U.S. Food and Drug Administration 121
Figure 24 *Source:* https://en.wikipedia.org/w/index.php?title=File:Examining_New_Drug_Applications_(067)_(7184535293).jpg *License:* Public Domain *Contributors:* The U.S. Food and Drug Administration 127
Image *Source:* https://en.wikipedia.org/w/index.php?title=File:Wikinews-logo.svg *License:* Creative Commons Attribution-Sharealike 3.0 *Contributors:* Vectorized by Simon 01:05, 2 August 2006 (UTC) Updated by Time3000 17 April 2007 to use official Wikinews colours and up 127
Figure 25 *Source:* https://en.wikipedia.org/w/index.php?title=File:Glivec_400mg.jpg *License:* Trademarked *Contributors:* D. Meyer 130
Figure 26 *Source:* https://en.wikipedia.org/w/index.php?title=File:Veronal.jpg *License:* *Contributors:* Diannaa, Kopiersperre, OgreBot 2 130
Figure 27 *Source:* https://en.wikipedia.org/w/index.php?title=File:Elixir_Sulfanilamide.png *License:* Public Domain *Contributors:* Anynobody∼commonswiki, DMacks 134
Figure 28 *Source:* https://en.wikipedia.org/w/index.php?title=File:Measles_US_1944-2007_inset.png *License:* Public Domain *Contributors:* 2over0 136
Figure 29 *Source:* https://en.wikipedia.org/w/index.php?title=File:Life_expectancy_by_age_in_1900,_1950,_and_1997_United_States.png *License:* Public Domain *Contributors:* CDC 137
Figure 30 *Source:* https://en.wikipedia.org/w/index.php?title=File:NCP14053.jpg *License:* Creative Commons Attribution 2.0 *Contributors:* Not specified at the source. Uploaded to flickr by Otis Historical Archives National Museum of Health and Medicine. 139
Figure 31 *Source:* https://en.wikipedia.org/w/index.php?title=File:Chiropractic_spinal_adjustment.jpg *License:* Creative Commons Attribution-Sharealike 2.0 *Contributors:* Michael Dorausch from Venice 152

Figure 32 *Source:* https://en.wikipedia.org/w/index.php?title=File:Acupuncture1-1.jpg *License:* Public Domain *Contributors:* Kyle Hunter (= original uploader Kphunter at en.wikipedia) 152
Figure 33 *Source:* https://en.wikipedia.org/w/index.php?title=File:Fallerjfa.JPG *License:* Creative Commons Attribution-Sharealike 3.0 *Contributors:* User:Ramon FVelasquez 153
Figure 34 *Source:* https://en.wikipedia.org/w/index.php?title=File:"Miracle_Cure!"_Health_Fraud_Scams_(8528312890).jpg *License:* Public Domain *Contributors:* FDA graphic by Michael J. Ermarth 153
Figure 35 *Source:* https://en.wikipedia.org/w/index.php?title=File:Botanica.jpg *License:* Public Domain *Contributors:* Original uploader was HouseOfScandal at en.wikipedia 155
Figure 36 *Source:* https://en.wikipedia.org/w/index.php?title=File:LedumPalustre15CH.jpg *License:* GNU Free Documentation License *Contributors:* Leyo, MGA73bot2, Maksim, Xhienne 156
Figure 37 *Source:* https://en.wikipedia.org/w/index.php?title=File:N'anga.jpg *License:* Creative Commons Attribution-Sharealike 3.0 *Contributors:* Hans Hillewaert 156
Figure 38 *Source:* https://en.wikipedia.org/w/index.php?title=File:Xi'an_traditionnal_medecine_market_(18).JPG *License:* Public Domain *Contributors:* User:Vberger 157
Figure 39 *Source:* https://en.wikipedia.org/w/index.php?title=File:Dhanvantari-at-Ayurveda-expo.jpg *License:* Creative Commons Attribution-Sharealike 3.0 *Contributors:* HPNadig 158
Figure 40 *Source:* https://en.wikipedia.org/w/index.php?title=File:ColouredChakraswithDescriptions.jpg *License:* Public Domain *Contributors:* Xxglennxx 159
Figure 41 *Source:* https://en.wikipedia.org/w/index.php?title=File:Tai_Chi1.jpg *License:* Creative Commons Attribution-Sharealike 2.0 *Contributors:* Craig Nagy from Vancouver, Canada 161
Figure 42 *Source:* https://en.wikipedia.org/w/index.php?title=File:Yoga_Class_at_a_Gym.JPG *License:* Attribution *Contributors:* www.localfitness.com.au 161
Figure 43 *Source:* https://en.wikipedia.org/w/index.php?title=File:Manhattan3.jpg *Contributors:* - 162
Figure 44 *Source:* https://en.wikipedia.org/w/index.php?title=File:Hierbas_medicinales_mercado_medieval.jpg *License:* Creative Commons Attribution 2.0 *Contributors:* Raúl Hernández González from Aranda de Duero, Spain 163
Figure 45 *Source:* https://en.wikipedia.org/w/index.php?title=File:Market_Pharmacy_Tana_MS5179.jpg *License:* Creative Commons Attribution-Sharealike 3.0 *Contributors:* Marco Schmidt 163
Figure 46 *Source:* https://en.wikipedia.org/w/index.php?title=File:Traditional_Chinese_medicine_in_Xi'an_market.jpg *License:* Public Domain *Contributors:* User:Vberger 164
Figure 47 *Source:* https://en.wikipedia.org/w/index.php?title=File:Doña_ramona.jpg *License:* Creative Commons Attribution-Sharealike 3.0 *Contributors:* Tomás Castelazo 165
Figure 48 *Source:* https://en.wikipedia.org/w/index.php?title=File:HARKINEAT.jpg *License:* Public Domain *Contributors:* Dhwani1989, Lestatdelc, Monkeybait 173
Figure 49 *Source:* https://en.wikipedia.org/w/index.php?title=File:Prince_Charles_2012.jpg *License:* Creative Commons Attribution-Sharealike 2.0 *Contributors:* Dan Marsh 174
Figure 50 *Source:* https://en.wikipedia.org/w/index.php?title=File:Edzard_ernst.jpg *License:* Creative Commons Attribution-Sharealike 2.0 *Contributors:* Luiyo 177
Figure 51 *Source:* https://en.wikipedia.org/w/index.php?title=File:Use_Caution_With_Ayurvedic_Products_(FDA_October_16,_2008).djvu *License:* Public Domain *Contributors:* Bluerasberry 194
Image *Source:* https://en.wikipedia.org/w/index.php?title=File:Fingerprints_taken_by_William_James_Herschel_1859-1860.jpg *License:* Public Domain *Contributors:* William James Herschel (1833-1917) 207
Figure 52 *Source:* https://en.wikipedia.org/w/index.php?title=File:Workathomead.jpg *License:* Public Domain *Contributors:* Hellno2 (talk) 13:15, 23 August 2009 (UTC). Original uploader was Hellno2 at en.wikipedia 216
Figure 53 *Source:* https://en.wikipedia.org/w/index.php?title=File:White_Van_Speaker_Scam_fraudulent_MSRP.jpg *License:* Creative Commons Attribution-Sharealike 3.0 *Contributors:* Daniel Christensen 217

License

Creative Commons Attribution-Share Alike 3.0
//creativecommons.org/licenses/by-sa/3.0/

Index

Abbott Laboratories, 129, 149
Abbreviated New Drug Application, 115, 127
ABC News, 6
Abigail Alliance v. von Eschenbach, 124
Abuse of process, 211
Academy Award, 93
Access Television Network, 71
ACE inhibitors, 138
Acid reflux disease, 20, 82
Acne vulgaris, 22
Active ingredient, 142
Actress, 92
Acts of Parliament in the United Kingdom, 214
ACT-UP, 123
Actus reus, 207
Acupuncture, 151, 152, 157, 160, 166, 185
Adelphia Communications Corporation, 220
A Devils Chaplain, 188
Adrenalin, 130
Adultery, 208
Adult Swim, 68, 76
Advair, 149
Adverse effect, 41, 201
Adverse effect (medicine), 198
Advertisement, 68
Advertising Standards Authority (United Kingdom), 72
Advice and consent, 108
Aesthetic, 160
AHRQ, 186
AIDS, 20, 22, 63, 82, 123, 150
AIDS denialism, 6, 83
Airport security, 118
Albert Anker, 39
Albert Einstein College of Medicine, 61
Albert T. W. Simeons, 23, 24
Albuquerque, 54
Alcohol, 30, 209
Alexander Fleming, 133
Alexander Glenny, 134
Alexander technique, 193
Alfred Lewis Jones, 181
Alfredo Sáenz Abad, 220
Alienation of affection, 207

Alienation of affections, 211
Alkaline, 21
Allen Stanford, 220
Alley Theatre, 90
Alliance Publishing, 23
Allopathic medicine, 167
Alma mater, 52
Altered state of consciousness, 164
Alternative cancer treatments, 26, 45, 196
Alternative health, 69
Alternative medicine, 3, 5, 29, 43, 62, 63, **151**
Alves Reis, 220
Alzheimers disease, 5
Amazon.com, 25, 225
AM Buffalo, 78
American Broadcasting Company, 8, 76, 78
American Cancer Society, 205
American Civil War, 31
American Dental Association, 41
American Journal of Clinical Nutrition, 7, 25
American Medical Association, 41, 172
American Physical Society, 175
American Revolution, 31
Analytical chemistry, 63
Anaphylactic, 202
Andover, Kansas, 87
Andrew Carnegie, 218
Andrew J. Vickers, 196
Andrew Wakefield, 45
Anesthesia, 158
Angiotensin receptor blockers, 138
Animal Feed, 107
Animals, 209
Animal testing, 140
Annual pharmaceutical drug sales, 146
Anthony Sullivan (pitchman), 80
Anthroposophical medicine, 176
Anthroposophic medicine, 151, 176
Antibiotics, 133, 201
Anti-competitive practices, 101
Antiscience, 154, 155, 201
Antitrust, 41, 96, 100
Antitrust Division of the Department of Justice, 100

Antitrust law, 116
Apostasy, 208
Appeal to nature, 198
Apple Inc., 69
Approved drugs, 141
Archive of American Television, 92
Arizona, 53
Arnold S. Relman, 181
Aromatherapy, 185, 193
Arsenic, 29, 133, 158, 159
Arson, 208
Arsphenamine, 133
Arthritis, 20, 22, 82
Aspartame, 9
Aspergillus terreus, 140
Aspirin, 29, 116
Assassination, 207
Assault, 207
Assault (tort), 210
Assemblies of God, 85
Asset specificity, 215
Assistant Attorney General, 110
Assisted reproduction, 108
Associated Press, 10
Assumption of risk, 210
Asthma, 22, 130
AstraZeneca, 143, 149
Atom, 155
Attempt, 207
Attention deficit disorder, 20, 82, 132
Attorney General of Maryland, 63
Attractive nuisance doctrine, 211
Auctions, 219
Authority, 172
Autoimmunity, 127
Automatism (law), 209
Avastin, 127
Ayurveda, 151, 156, 168
Ayurvedic medicine, 151, 158, 178, 193

Baby boomers, 160
Bachelor of Science, 53
Bacteria, 120
Bad Pharma, 146, 233, 234
Bain & Company, 142, 233
Bait and switch, 21
Bank fraud, 212
Barack Obama, 77, 112, 127
Barbie, 78
Barbie (film series), 78
Bark, 29
Barrie R. Cassileth, 187
Barriers to entry, 101
Barry M. Goldwater, 53
Barry Minkow, 219
Battery (crime), 207

Battery (tort), 210
Battle Creek, Michigan, 43
Bayer, 133
Bayer pharmaceuticals, 132
Bayou Hedge Fund Group, 219
Baywatch, 92, 95
BBC2, 8
BCA Hall of Fame, 47
Beechams Pills, 31
Bee pollen, 173
Behavioral targeting, 102
Beijing Medical University, 38
Beijing National Stadium, 38
Belief, 154
Belo, 79
Ben Cohn, 91
Benedict Lust, 186
Ben Goldacre, 148
Benzedrine, 131
Berkshire Hathaway, 103
Bernard Ebbers, 218
Bernard Madoff, 219
Bernie Friend, 47
Bestiality, 209
Best Pharmaceuticals for Children Act, 126
Best practice, 167
Bestseller, 5
Beta blockers, 138
Better Business Bureau, 34, 74
Better (TV series), 79
Beverages, 122
Beverly, Massachusetts, 10
Bextra, 149
Bid rigging, 101
Bigamy, 207
Big Pharma conspiracy theory, **82**
Billiards, 11
Bill Moyers, 172
Billy Mays, 76, 80
Billy Sol Estes, 53
Biochemistry, 141
Bioelectromagnetism, 160, 186
Biofields, 159, 185
Biography Channel, 93
Biologic medical product, 127
Biologics, 141
Biologics Control Act, 117, 121
Biology, 165, 185
Biomedicine, 151, 165, 169, 199
Biopharmaceutical, 107
Biophysics, 165
Biostatistics, 125
Biotechnology, 141
Birth control movement in the United States, 138
Black Entertainment Television, 72, 77

248

Blackjack, 60
Blackmail, 208
Black Scorpion (TV series), 95
Black Thunder (film), 94
Blasphemy, 208
Blender, 70
Blindness, 10
Bloodletting, 179
Blood transfusion, 107
Blue sky law, 216
Bob Sullivan (journalist), 224
Body work (alternative medicine), 193
Bodywork (alternative medicine), 164
Book signing, 89
Botanica, 155
Bovine spongiform encephalopathy, 119
Boy Meets World, 93, 95
Bradford, 60
Brain pacemaker, 117
Brand, 129, 145
Branson, Missouri, 88
Bravestarr, 77
Breach of confidence, 211
Breach of contract, 212
Breach of promise, 211
Breakfast cereal, 43
Breathing Meditation, 193
Brian M. Berman, 30
Bribery, 208
Bribing, 149
Bristol-Myers Squibb, 149
British Medical Association, 30, 168, 202
British Medical Journal, 172
British National Formulary, 144
Broadcast syndication, 71
Brokered programming, 5, 78
Brooklyn, New York, 92
Broward Community College, 92
Bruce Vilanch, 88
Buffalo, New York, 78
Buffalo Sabres, 220
Buggery, 208
Bupropion, 149
Bureau of Alcohol, Tobacco and Firearms, 58
Bureau of Corporations, 98
Burglary, 208
Business, 53
Business Administration, 66
Business Week, 58

Cacique of Poyais, 219
Caesium chloride, 63
Calculus of negligence, 210
California, 61
Cam (disambiguation), 151
Camphor, 174

Canada, 63, 71, 112
Cancer, 5, 20, 56, 62, 63, 82, 127, 130, 156, 201
Cancer staging, 89
Cansema, 56, 58
Card counting, 60
Cardiovascular, 137
Cardiovascular diseases, 62
Carl Djerassi, 138
Carleton H. Sheets, 71
Carl Sagan, 159, 188, 203
Cartel, 101
Cartoon Network, 76
Caspar Weinberger, 98
Cassie Chadwick, 218
Catch Me If You Can, 218
Catchphrase, 69
Category:Alternative medical diagnostic methods, 154
Category:Alternative medical systems, 151
Category:Biologically based therapies, 151
Category:Energy therapies, 151
Category:Manual therapy, 151
Category:Mind–body interventions, 151
Cathy Mitchell (television personality), 76
Causation (law), 207
CBS, 8, 77
Celebrity Close Calls, 93
Celebrity Ghost Stories, 93
Celia Farber, 83
Cellular phones, 118
Center for Biologics Evaluation and Research, 107, 109, 117, 127
Center for Devices and Radiological Health, 107, 109, 117
Center for Disease Control and Prevention, 41
Center for Drug Evaluation and Research, 107, 109, 114
Center for Food Safety and Applied Nutrition, 107, 109, 118
Center for Tobacco Products, 107, 109
Center for Veterinary Medicine, 107, 109, 119
Chakras, 159, 160
Chapter 7, Title 11, United States Code, 57
Charlatan, 26
Charles Dawson, 218
Charles in Charge, 94
Charles Ponzi, 220
Charlotte metropolitan area, 85
Charlotte Observer, 86
Chasing Farrah, 93
Chemical patent, 145
Chemicals, 172
Chemist, 43
Chemistry, 44, 179
Chemotherapy, 45

Chia Pet, 69
Chicago, Illinois, 227
Chicago Sun-Times, 224
Chicago Tribune, 60
Chickenpox, 134
Child abuse, 192
Child Abuse Prevention and Treatment Act, 192
Child neglect, 192
Childrens Television Act, 78
Chinese Astrology, 157, 186
Chinese martial arts, 162
Chinese numerology, 157
Chinese philosophy, 162
Chiropractic, 41, 43, 79, 151, 164, 179, 185, 190, 194
Chiropractic medicine, 193
Chiropractor, 152
Chlorothiazide, 138
Christian, 164
Christian Broadcasting Network, 85
Christian music, 84
Christian Science practitioner, 192
Christine A. Varney, 99
Christopher Rocancourt, 220
Christopher Wanjek, 5
Chronic fatigue syndrome, 20, 82
Church of Scientology, 43
CIFAS, 214
Cincinnati, 90
CITEREFBivins2007, 237
CITEREFBMA1993, 237
CITEREFCohen1998, 238
CITEREFDawkins2003, 203
CITEREFGevitz1997, 236
CITEREFHahnemann1833, 235
CITEREFHarrison.27s Principles of Internal Medicine2015, 235
CITEREFIOM Report2005, 234–236, 238
CITEREFMishra2004, 235
CITEREFO.27Connor1995, 235
CITEREFRuggie2004, 235
CITEREFSagan1996, 235
CITEREFSir Walton: Science and Technology Committee2000, 238
CITEREFSointu2012, 235
CITEREFTaylor2005, 235
CITEREFWHO2000, 236
CITEREFWHO2005, 238
CITEREFWujastyk2003, 235, 238
Civil action, 212
Civil engineer, 53
Civil engineering, 53
Civil law (common law), 212
Civil penalty, 103
Clayton Act, 96

Clayton Antitrust Act, 98
Clear and convincing evidence, 212
Cleveland Clinic, 128
Clinical practice, 165
Clinical trial, 7, 25, 140, 141, 196
Clinical trials, 115, 141
Clinical trials registry, 142
Cloudbuster, 44
CMJ, 204
CNBC, 71, 74
CNN, 8, 89
CNNMoney.com, 240
Cochrane Collaboration, 158, 169, 183
Cochrane Library, 196
Coercive monopoly, 96, 101
Cognitive bias, 41, 200
Colin Colenso, 47
Colin Mochrie, 76
Collusion, 101
Colon (anatomy), 24
Colon cancer, 88, 89
Colorpuncture, 184
Colostrum, 174
Columbia, Missouri, 66
Commercial broadcasting, 68
Commercials, 66
Commissioner of Food and Drugs, 107–109
Committee on Herbal Medicinal Products, 176
Common cold, 41, 44
Common law, 207, 210, 211
Commons:Category:Federal Trade Commission, 106
Commons:Category:Food and Drug Administration (United States), 129
Commons:Category:Fraud, 221
Commons:Category:Quackery, 46
Communications Act 2003, 72
Communist Party of China, 157
Comparative negligence, 210
Comparative responsibility, 211
Competition law, 100
Competition regulator, 101
Compilation album, 69
Complementary and Alternative Medicine, 37, 41
Complementary medicine, 171
Complicity, 207
Compounding a felony, 208
Compulsory licensing, 150
Computer crime, 215
Comstock law, 208
Comstock laws, 138
Concise Encyclopedia of Economics, 128
Concurrence, 207
Confidential information, 214
Confirmation Bias, 41

250

Conflict of interest, 147
Conflicts of interest, 197
Congress of the United States, 122
Conscious parallelism, 101
Consent, 209, 210
Consent decree, 12
Consent judgment, 101
Consortium, 78
Conspiracy (civil), 211
Conspiracy (crime), 207
Conspiracy theory, 9, 41, 201
Constipation, 22
Consumer Product Safety Commission, 110
Consumer protection, 96
Consumer rights, 74
Contempt of court, 3, 15, 44, 65
Contraception, 208
Contract, 209, 211, 212
Contract research organization, 141
Contributory negligence, 210
Controlled Substances Act, 111
Conventional medicine, 167
Conversion (law), 210
Copper sulfate, 158
Copyright misuse, 101
Coral calcium, 4, 64
Corner Store TV, 71
Corn flake, 43
Coronary artery disease, 137
Corporate abuses, 216
Corporate liability, 207
Corporate manslaughter, 207
Cosmeceutical, 118
Cost effectiveness, 144
Counterculture movement, 172
Craig J. Nevius, 93
Crazy Eddie, 218
Credit card, 215
Credit card fraud, 12
Credit cards, 12
Criminal Code of Canada, 213
Criminal conversation, 208, 211
Criminal history and legal problems, 225
Criminal law, 207, 211, 212
Criminal negligence, 207
Criticism of quackery in academia, 191
Criticism of the Food and Drug Administration, 124, 127
Cruelty to animals, 209
CSI: Crime Scene Investigation, 93
Cultural relativism, 172

Daffys Elixir, 30
Daily Telegraph, 230
Dallas, 79
Dallas, Texas, 52, 53

Damages, 211
Danbury Federal Prison, 44
Dandruff, 22
Daniel Henninger, 128
Data analysis, 217
Datacasting, 73
Dateline NBC, 8
David Gorski, 30, 197
David L Cook, 87
David R. Henderson, 128
David Satcher, 181
Daytime television, 78
D.D. Palmer, 43
Deborah Platt Majoras, 99
Deception, 212, 220
Deep-breathing exercises, 160
Defamation, 27, 211
Defence of property, 209
Defense (legal), 209, 212
Defense of infancy, 209
Defense of others, 210
Defense of property, 210
Degenerative disease, 5
Democratic Party (United States), 53, 98
Demographic, 78
Demonized, 82
Department of Commerce and Labor, 98
Department of Health and Human Services, 108, 109
Department of Health (United Kingdom), 170, 174
Depression (mood), 22, 62, 82
Des Moines, Iowa, 66
Detinue, 210
Developing country, 191
Dewey Decimal Classification, 23
Diabetes, 6, 20, 22, 82, 122, 132
Diagenesis, 63
Diagnostic and Statistical Manual of Mental Disorders, 147
Diana Zuckerman, 128
Dianetics, 43
Dick Thompson Morgan, 97
Dick Van Patten, 94
Dietary supplement, 4, 107
Dietary Supplement Health and Education Act, 174
Dietary supplements, 113
Diet-based therapy, 193
Diethylene glycol, 135
Digital object identifier, 203, 204
Digital on-screen graphic, 71, 74
Diminished responsibility, 209
Diphtheria, 121
Diphtheria antitoxin, 134
Diphtheria toxin, 134

Diphtheria vaccine, 134
Direct marketing, 60, 68
Direct response marketing, 68
Direct response television, 68
Direct-to-consumer advertising, 146
DirecTV, 71
Discovery Channel, 73, 80
Discovery Communications, 78
Discovery Family, 78
Disease, 43, 141, 188
Disease mongering, 147
Disney Channel, 78
Disparities in access to health care, 42
Distrust, 41
Dividing territories, 101
Division of Chemistry, 121
DMOZ, 46, 205
Doha Declaration, 150
Dominant health system, 167
Dominican Republic, 219
Domino effect, 73
Donald Barrett, 10, **64**, 75
Donald Barrett (musician), 64
Don Lapre, 71, 75
Do Not Track, 102
Doshas, 158
Dosing, 141, 143
Double major, 66
Drug, 129, 130
Drug company, 125
Drug development, 141
Drug discovery, 141
Drug Enforcement Administration, 110
Drug Price Competition and Patent Term Restoration Act, 123, 127
Drug safety, 141
DSHEA, 174
Dueling, 208
Dune 2000, 95
Duress, 209
Durham-Humphrey Amendment, 122
Dutch language, 26
Duty of care, 210
Duty to rescue, 210
DVD, 60
Dyazide, 116

Eastern medicine, 166
Eastern New Mexico University, 52, 53
Eastern Time Zone, 77
Eau de Cologne, 30
Ebola, 116
EC, 176
Echinacea, 162, 186
Economic torts, 211
Ector County, Texas, 52

Ecuador, 58
Eddie Antar, 218
Ed, Edd & Eddy, 76
Ed Foreman, **52**
Edith Ramirez, 96, 98
Edmonton, Alberta, 63
Edward Abraham, 135
Edward Davenport (fraudster), 218
Edzard Ernst, 176, 190, 195, 197, 199, 200, 204
Efficacy, 165, 195
Efren Reyes, 47, 51
EGCG, 62
Eggshell skull, 211
Eidetic memory, 10
Eight-ball, 46
Electromagnetic radiation, 107, 118
Electromagnetic therapy (alternative medicine), 186
Electronic program guide, 73
Element (criminal law), 207
Eli Lilly, 143, 149
Eli Lilly and Company, 129, 149
Elixir sulfanilamide, 122, 135
Elizabeth Hanford Dole, 98
El Paso, Texas, 53
E-mail, 36
Embezzlement, 208
E-Meter, 35
Emma Goldman, 138
Encyclopædia Britannica, 106
Encyclopædia Britannica Eleventh Edition, 46
Endocrinologist, 24
End-of-life care, 42
Enema, 43
Energy, 184
Energy medicine, 151, 192
England, 60
England and Wales, 214
Enovid, 138
Enric Durán, 218
Enron, 219
Entertainment Tonight, 88
Entrapment, 209
Enzyme replacement therapy, 127
Ephedrine, 131
Epilepsy, 132
Epinephrine, 130
Equitable jurisdiction, 212
Equitable relief, 102
Eric Wareheim, 76
Erik Estrada, 89
E.S. Johnny Walker, 52, 54, 55
Essential facilities doctrine, 101
Establishment, 171
Estate (law), 211

Estes Kefauver, 139
Ethics, 154
Europe, 68, 81
European Medicines Agency, 144, 176
European Parliament, 176
European Union, 144
Evangelism, 84
Evidence, 151, 170
Evidence based medicine, 167
Evidence-based medicine, 156, 167, 169, 183, 187, 197
Evidence-based practice, 37
Evidence (law), 209, 211
E.W. Scripps Company, 80
Excipients, 114
Exclusive dealing, 101
Exercise, 43
Exhibition game, 47
Exhibitionism, 207
Extortion, 208
Ex turpi causa non oritur actio, 211

Facebook, 17
Face lift, 10
Faith healing, 151, 153, 164
Fallacy, 154, 155, 166, 184, 188
False advertising, 101
False Claims Act, 148, 149
False imprisonment, 207, 210
False light, 211
False pretenses, 208
Family Smoking Prevention and Tobacco Control Act, 119
Fantasia (music), 90
Farhadi, 219
Fashion Merchandising, 66
F. Bam Morrison, 219
FDA (disambiguation), 106
FDA Fast Track Development Program, 116
FDA Warning Letter, 65
Federal Bureau of Investigation, 110
Federal Communications Commission, 70, 87
Federal Food, Drug, and Cosmetic Act, 107, 113, 117, 122, 135, 149
Federal government of the United States, 96, 107
Federal Prison Camp, Montgomery, 3, 17
Federal Register, 106, 129
Federal Trade Commission, 3, 10, 11, 19–21, 23, 37, 74, 82, **96**, 106, 114, 174, 223, 225
Federal Trade Commission Act, 96
Felony, 11, 62, 84, 207
Felony murder rule, 207
Ferdinand Cohn, 44
Fernando Dovalina, 90

Fibromyalgia, 22
Financial crisis of 2007–2010, 73
Financier, 219
Fire and brimstone, 32
First Amendment to the United States Constitution, 3, 4, 12, 14, 120
Fish oil, 62, 162, 186
Flaxseed oil, 162, 186
Flexner Report, 30, 181
Florida, 78
Flovent, 149
Flowbee, 69
Floyd Abrams, 120
Fluconazole, 150
Folk medicine, 166
Food additive, 113
Food and Drug Administration, 3, 20, 37, 41, 44, 56, 57, 65, **106**, 148, 174, 194, 226
Food and Drug Administration (disambiguation), 106
Food and Drug Administration Modernization Act, 126
Food and Drug Administration (United States), 64, 143
Food processing industry, 118
Food safety, 107
Forgery, 212
Form 483, 112
Formaldehyde, 134
Fornication, 208
Fortune Hunter (TV series), 95
Foundation for Integrated Health, 174
Fox Broadcasting Company, 73, 77
Fox Business Network, 74
Fox Sports Southwest, 77
France, 43
Frances Oldham Kelsey, 122, 139
Frank Abagnale Jr., 218
Frank Colton, 138
Franklin Delano Roosevelt, 122
Franklin D. Roosevelt, 216
Frank Mastropolo, 22, 26
Franz Anton Mesmer, 43
Fraud, 3, 12, 19, 75, 101, 154, 166, **207**, 208, 211, 221
Fraud Act 2006, 214
Fraud detection, 217
Fraudulent, 154
Fred Cohen, 221
Frederick Banting, 132
Frederick Emerson Peters, 219
Friends, 93, 95
Fringe Festival, 90
Fringe science, 166
FTC regulation of behavioral advertising, 102
Ft. Lauderdale, Florida, 92

253

Full House, 95
Funding, 168
Funeral home, 102
Funeral Rule, 102
F.W. Woolworth Company, 85

Gambling, 208
Gannett Company, 79
Garfield, 75
Garfield and Friends, 75
Gaston Means, 219
Gaston Ramon, 134
Gauchers Disease, 127
Gay Pride, 88
G.D. Searle & Co., 138
Gemstar-TV Guide International, 73
General Medical Council, 42
Generic drug, 129, 136, 145
Genetically modified organism, 57
Geodon, 149
Geographic coordinate system, 129
George D. Lundberg, 187
George Foreman, 61
George W. Bush, 127
Gerard Dou, 39
Gerhard Domagk, 133
German Medicines Act, 176
Germany, 51
Germ theory of disease, 44, 180
Get-rich-quick scheme, 71, 75
Ginseng, 162, 186
Ginsu, 69
Giuseppe Brotzu, 135
GlaxoSmithKline, 134, 148–150
Glaxo Smith Kline, 129
Gleevec, 130
Glenn Rupel, 22, 26
Glivec, 151
Global Times, 226
Glucosamine, 162, 186
Go-Bots, 77
Gonorrhoea, 33
Good Day L.A., 93
Good manufacturing practices, 140
Good Morning America, 79
Google Book Search, 204
Governor of Florida, 218
Governor of Texas, 53
Grapefruit, 25
Grape therapy, 42
Green Bay, Wisconsin, 79
Green guides, 102
Greg Caton, **56**
Gregor MacGregor, 219
Gregory Pincus, 138
Grocery store, 43

Group boycott, 101
Guayaquil, Ecuador, 56
Guided imagery, 160, 186
Gun control, 77
Guthy-Renker, 71, 80
Gynecomastia, 25

Habeas corpus, 58
Hacker (computer security), 215
Halitosis, 22
Hallandale, Florida, 92
Hallmark Channel, 77
Hamlins Wizard Oil, 43
Hampton Bays, 62
Handbook of Texas, 46
Hardball (1994 TV series), 93, 95
Hard sell, 72
Harold Runnels, 52, 54, 55
Harold Varmus, 175
Harriet A. Hall, 197
Harvey Washington Wiley, 121
Harvey W. Wiley, 121
Hasbro, 78
Headquarters, 108
Heads of Medicines Agencies, 176
Healing, 151
Healing and the Mind, 172
Health Canada, 112
Health care, 151
Health care provider, 154
Health care system, 148
Health Informatics, 109
Health insurance, 125, 183, 185, 201
Health insurance in the United States, 169
Heart attack, 44
Heart failure, 137
Heavy metal poisoning, 159
Help:IPA for English, 3
Helsinki Declaration, 196
Hemostatic, 130
Hepatitis A, 134
Hepatitis B, 134
Herbalism, 185, 193
Herbal medicine, 162
Herbal supplement, 23
Herbert Ley, 18
Herbert Ley, Jr., 6
Herfindahl index, 101
Heritage USA, 84, 86, 87
Hermann Emil Fischer, 132
Herpes, 8, 20, 82
High blood pressure, 25
Hillary Clinton, 77
Hinduism, 160
Hinsdale, Illinois, 46
Hirudo medicinalis, 120

History of alternative medicine, 171, 179
History of competition law, 101
History of medicine, 179
History of the Food and Drug Administration, 121
Hitler Diaries, 219
HIV, 123, 201
Hoax, 212
Hoechst AG, 138
Hoffman Center, 61
Hoffman-La Roche, 129
Holistic, 187
Holistic health, 61
Holistic medicine, 43
Hollywood, 220
Home construction, 74
Home invasion, 207
Homeopathic, 156
Homeopathic remedies, 176
Homeopathy, 43, 151, 155, 175, 176, 178, 185, 198
Home remedy, 184
Home Shopping Network, 61
Homicide, 207
Hood River, Oregon, 90
Horrible Histories (2009 TV series), 76
Hospice care, 89
Hospital Corporation of America, 218
House Energy and Commerce Committee, 115
House of Lords, 203
Houston, 90
Hubert H. Humphrey, 54
Hulda Regehr Clark, 43, 226
Hull High, 93, 95
Human chorionic gonadotropin, 7, 16, 23, 24
Humira, 145
Hu Wanlin, 38
Hydrocarbon, 63
Hydropathy, 185
Hygiene, 181
Hypnotherapy, 160, 185, 193
Hypothalamus, 23

I, 74
Ibuprofen, 116
Identifiers and linked data, 23
Identity theft, 7, 102
Ignorantia juris non excusat, 209
Illinois, 12
Imiglucerase, 127
Imitrex, 149
Imperial Chemical Industries, 138
Imperial Tobacco, 119
Impostor, 218
IMS Health, 145
Incest, 208

Inchoate offense, 207
Incitement, 207
Independent agencies of the United States government, 96
Independent Television Commission, 10
India, 176, 178
Indictment, 214
Indigestion, 22
Inductive reasoning, 41
Industrialized countries, 137
Infinite monkey theorem, 33
Infomercial, 3, 19, 60, 63, 64, **68**, 88, 93
Information, 68
Informed consent, 126
Infraction, 207
Injunction, 211
In re Gateway Learning Corp., 104
Insanity defense, 209
Inside Edition, 8
Institute of Medicine, 125, 127, 169, 195, 202, 232
Insurance fraud, 212
Integrative medicine, 154, 171, 190, 191
Intentional infliction of emotional distress, 210
Intentional tort, 210
Intent (law), 212
Internal Medicine, 61
Internal Revenue Service, 192
International Competition Network, 101
International Falls, Minnesota, 84
International Pool Tour, 3, 11, **46**
International price discrimination, 150
International Standard Book Number, 23, 202–205
International Standard Serial Number, 18, 204
Internet, 215
Internet fraud, 215
Internet Movie Database, 92, 95
Internet radio, 5
Interpol, 59, 110
Interracial marriage, 208
In the Matter of Sears Holdings Management Corp., 104
Intravenous therapy, 158
Invasion of privacy, 211
Investigational New Drug, 143
Invitee, 211
In vitro, 141
In vivo, 141
Ion Television, 71, 73
IPT World Open Eight-ball Championship, 51
Ironmagazine.com, 225
Irving Crane, 50
ITV Direct, 64
ITV (TV network), 72
Ivan Illich, 204

255

J2 Communication, 60
Jack Cox (Texas), 53
Jacques Peretti, 8
Jake Tapper, 8, 17, 22, 26
JAMA (journal), 187
James C. Miller III, 99
James Forsythe, 60
James Paul Lewis, Jr., 219
Jamie Charles Bakker, 84
Jan Crouch, 85
Jane Kaczmarek, 93
Janet D. Steiger, 99
Jan Steen, 40
Japan, 81
Japanese encephalitis vaccine, 134
Japan Prize, 140
Jay Bakker, 85
Jean-Charles Tacchella, 93
Jeffery Self, 91
Jerry Falwell, 86
Jessica Hahn, 86
Jesuits bark, 29
Jewelry, 75
Jim Bakker, 84–86
Jim (horse), 121
Jim J. Bullock, 88
Joe Rogan, 50
Johanna Brandt, 42
John B. Connally, Jr., 53
John Bodkin Adams, 218
John Diamond (journalist), 189
John Harvey Kellogg, 43
John Rigas, 220
Johns Hopkins School of Medicine, 180
Johnson & Johnson, 143, 149
John Spano, 220
John Stonehouse, 220
John Stossel, 22, 26
Joint and several liability, 211
Joint venture, 61
Jokichi Takamine, 130
Jonas Salk, 136
Jon Leibowitz, 99
Jordan Belfort, 218
Joseph Lister, 1st Baron Lister, 181
Joseph M. Jacobs, 175
Joseph von Mering, 132
Joshua D. Wright, 98
Journal Broadcast Group, 80
Journal of the American Medical Association, 7, 25, 177, 182, 187
J. T. Buck, 90
J. Thomas Rosch, 99
J.T. Rutherford, 52, 53, 55
Julie Brill, 98
Justification (jurisprudence), 209

Kama Sutra Records, 91
Kampo, 151
Kanker Sisters, 76
Kansas City, Missouri, 88
Kathy Kinney, 88
Keats Pub, 62
Kefauver-Harris Amendment, 122, 140
Keith McCready, 47
Kenneth Lay, 219
Kenneth Ludmerer, 237
Kevin Trudeau, **3**, 19, 23, 45, 46, 55–57, 60, 62, 63, 65, 75, 82, 88, 93, 220
KGW, 79
Kickback (bribery), 149
Kidnapping, 207
Kiev, 5
Kirk Cameron, 93
Knowledge, 26
Konrad Kujau, 219
Kosher, 60

Laboratory, 108
Lady Bunny, 88
Laetrile, 124, 196
Lamictal, 149
Land flip, 71
Larceny, 3, 12, 208
Larry King, 88
Larry King Live, 89, 90
Las Cruces, New Mexico, 52, 53
Laser, 118
Lasker Award, 138
Lasker-DeBakey Clinical Medical Research Award, 140
Last clear chance, 211
Las Vegas, Nevada, 47, 51
Las Vegas Valley, 11
Law, 208, 212
Law of attraction (New Thought), 7
Laying of hands, 153
Lead, 159, 162, 185
Lee Majors, 94
Legal drug trade, 129
Legal issues, 209
Legal liability, 126
Legal malpractice, 210
Legitimation, 180
Leigh Valentine, 8, **66**
Lentil, 29
Leprosy, 150
Lewd, 208
LGBT rights movement, 88
Libertarianism, 128
Library of Congress Classification, 23
Library of Economics and Liberty, 128
Licensee, 211

Light therapy, 184
Linezolid, 149
LIN Media, 79
Linus Pauling, 44
Lions Gate Entertainment, 88
Listen to Me (film), 93, 94
List of CEOs, 219
List of forms of alternative medicine, 154
List of herbs with known adverse effects, 197
List of largest pharmaceutical settlements in the United States, 148
List of pharmaceutical companies, 130
List of questionable diagnostic tests, 26
List of questionable diseases, 26
List of United States federal agencies, 107
List of World Eight-ball Champions, 50
Liver, 24
Liverpool School of Tropical Medicine, 181
LiveScience, 5
Lobbyists, 146
Loch Lloyd, Missouri, 84, 88
London School of Hygiene & Tropical Medicine, 181
Long Beach Island, 61
Longjack, 25
Loree Jon Jones, 47
Lorillard, 119
Lorraine Day, 64
Los Angeles, 92
Los Angeles Times, 93
Los Angeles Valley College, 56
Lotronex, 149
Lou Harry, 69
Louis Pasteur, 43, 133, 180
Lou Pearlman, 219
Lovastatin, 140
Loverboy (1989 film), 93, 94
Lovisa Åhrberg, 42
L. Ron Hubbard, 43
Lupus, 82
Lupus erythematosus, 20
L Word, 93
Lyme disease, 174
Lymphatic filariasis, 150
Lynchburg, Virginia, 86
Lyndon B. Johnson, 53
Lyndon LaRouche, 77
Lynn, Massachusetts, 3, 4

Madagascar, 163
Magnesium sulfate, 62
Magnetic healing, 160
Magnétisme animal, 43
Magnet therapy, 184
Mail and wire fraud, 215
Mainstream medicine, 164, 167

Major depressive disorder, 20
Malaria, 29, 151
Malfeasance in office, 208
Malicious prosecution, 211
Malpractice, 210
Manhattan, 62, 162
Manipulative therapy, 164
Manslaughter, 207
Mao Zedong, 157
Marc Dreier, 218
Marcia Angell, 170
Margaret Hamburg, 108
Margaret Sanger, 138
Market concentration, 101
Marketing, 60, 201
Market power, 101
Market share liability, 211
Mark Nigrini, 217
Marlon Manalo, 51
Marriage à-la-mode (Hogarth), 28
Martin Frankel, 219
Mary Dennett, 138
Mascara, 122
Masonic lodge, 54
Massage, 185
Mass marketed, 172
Mass media, 101
Mattel, 78
Matthew Lesko, 75
Matthews, North Carolina, 87
Matt the Knife, 219
Maureen K. Ohlhausen, 98
Maurice Hilleman, 134
Mayhem (crime), 207
Mayo Clinic, 204, 206
McGraw-Hill, 62
Measles, 134
Médecins Sans Frontières, 150
Media General, 78, 80
Medical degree, 194
Medical device, 107, 117
Medical diagnosis, 168, 237
Medical doctor, 43
Medical education, 168, 182
Medical literature, 168
Medical maggots, 120
Medical malpractice, 210
Medical marijuana, 124
Medical research, 179
Medical school, 147
Medical school in the United States, 169, 181
Medical schools, 154, 182
Medical science, 165–167
Medicare fraud, 149
Medicare (United States), 148, 218
Medication, 129, 141

Medications, 141
Medicine, 26, 61, 151, 155, 165, 167, 169, 237
Medicines and Healthcare products Regulatory Agency, 144, 148
Medicines and Related Substances Control Amendment Act, 1997, 150
Meditation, 160, 168, 186, 193
Meditation (alternative medicine), 193
MedWatch, 115
MegaMemory, **19**
Mehmet Oz, 45
Meningitis, 134
Mens rea, 207
Mentally challenged, 10
Mental retardation, 137
Mercatus Center, 128
Merck and Co., 138
Merck and Company, 134
Merck & Co, 140
Merck & Co., 129, 148, 150
Merck Sharp & Dohme, 136
Mercury (element), 29, 159
Meredith Corporation, 79
Merger, 100
Merger control, 101
Meta-analysis, 195
Metabolic pathway, 141
Metabolism, 62, 186
Miami, Florida, 92
Miami Vice, 92–94
Miasm, 43
Michael Aldrich, 72
Michael H. Cohen, 193, 202
Michael Monus, 219
Michael Pertschuk, 99
Michael Sabo, 220
Michael Shermer, 18, 21, 22, 26, 230
Michigan, 12
Microbiology, 43, 44, 181
Microsoft, 69
Microwave oven, 118
Middle Ages, 26
Mike Sigel, 47, 51
Mimi Bobeck, 88
Mimis Day Parade, 88
Mind-body intervention, 168, 194
Mind-body interventions, 192
Mind-body medicine, 160
Minister (Christianity), 85
Minneapolis, Minnesota, 85
Miscarriage of justice, 208
Misdemeanor, 207
Misprision of felony, 208
Miss Missouri USA, 66
Missouri, 88
Mistake (criminal law), 209

Mistake of law, 209
MMR vaccine controversy, 45
Mnemonic, 19
Mobile medical apps, 127
Model home, 74
Mohammad Usman of Madras, 181
Molecular biology, 141, 165
Molecule, 155
Molly Ringwald, 93
Monopolization, 101
Monopoly, 101
Monosodium glutamate, 9
Montgomery, Alabama, 3
Morbidity, 137
Morphine, 129, 158
Mortality rate, 137
MSNBC, 77, 224
Muckraker, 121
Multi-level marketing, 4, 12, 56
Multiple sclerosis, 20, 82
Mumps, 134
Murder, 207
Murder She Wrote, 93
Murder, She Wrote, 94, 95
Muscular dystrophy, 20, 82
Musical theatre, 90
Mylan Laboratories Inc., 115
My Little Pony, 77
Myocardial infarction, 125
Myside bias, 41
Mysticism, 201

Name-brand, 115
Nancy Valen, **92**
Nanga, 156
Napoleonic wars, 33
Narcolepsy, 131
Narrative, 68
NASA, 224
NASDAQ, 56
Natasha Korecki, 224
National Board of Health (Denmark), 171
National Cancer Institute, 205
National Center for Complementary and Alternative Medicine, 168, 176, 188, 191
National Center for Complementary and Integrative Health, 178, 188
National Center for Toxicological Research, 107, 109
National Fraud Authority, 214
National Health and Medical Research Council, 170
National Health Service, 144
National Health Service (England), 170, 193
National Hockey League, 71

National Institute for Health and Care Excellence, 144
National Institute of Health, 173
National Institutes of Health, 117, 168, 188, 205
National Lampoon, Incorporated, 60
National Prescribing Service, 147
National Research Center for Women and Families, 128
National Rifle Association, 77
Natural Causes, 58
Natural Cures They Dont Want You to Know About, 3, 5, 14, **19**, 24, 62, 82
Natural monopoly, 101
Natural science, 165
Naturopath, 43
Naturopathy, 42, 151, 155
Naval Ordnance Laboratory, 109
NBC, 8, 70, 77, 78, 90
NBCSN, 71
NCCIH, 184
NCCIH classifications, 151
Necessity, 209
Necessity (tort), 210
Negligence, 210
Negligence in employment, 210
Negligent entrustment, 210
Negligent homicide, 207
Negligent infliction of emotional distress, 210
Nelson Mandela, 17
Nermal, 75
Netherlands, 30
Network marketing, 64
Neutral reportage, 211
Nevada, 11, 60
Nevirapine, 83
Nevis, 8
New Age, 20, 159, 166, 201
New age movement, 172
New chemical entity, 142
New Drug Application, 114, 143
New England Journal of Medicine, 30, 143, 172
New Jersey, 61
New Mexico, 52–54
New Mexicos 2nd congressional district, 52, 53, 55
New Mexico State University, 52, 53
New York, 62, 78, 92
New York City, 61, 92
New York Islanders, 220
New York State Consumer Protection Board, 14, 21
New York Stock Exchange, 220
New York Times, 5, 18, 175, 224
NHL, 220

Nickelodeon, 78
Nick Leeson, 219
Nicktoons (TV channel), 78
Nightline (U.S. news program), 8
Nine-ball, 46
NNDB, 19
Nobel Prize, 44
Nobel Prize in Physiology or Medicine, 133
No Free Lunch (organization), 147
No medical training, 225
Non-maleficence, 190
Nonsense, 154
Non-steroidal anti-inflammatory drug, 125
Norfolk, Virginia, 79
Norman Gevitz, 202
Norman Vincent Peale, 54
Normative, 169
North America, 70
North Central University, 85
Northern Alberta Institute of Technology, 63
Northern Ireland, 214
Norway, 5
Not sold in stores, 69
Novartis, 130, 150
NPR, 233
Nuisance, 210
Nutrition, 43

Obesity, 20, 82
Obscenity, 208
Obstruction of justice, 208, 221
OCLC, 128, 204
Odessa, Texas, 52, 53
Ofcom, 72
Offence against the person, 207
Office for the Study of Unconventional Medical Practices, 173
Office of Alternative Medicine, 173
Office of Criminal Investigations, 107, 110
Office of Global Regulatory Operations and Policy, 109
Office of Regulatory Affairs, 107
Off-label, 115
Off-label use, 149
Ojai, California, 16, 61
Olanzapine, 149
Olive Leaf Extract, 62
Omega-3 fatty acid, 162, 186
Onanism, 33
One Punk Under God, 90
Online shopping, 72
Opium, 29, 30
Opportunity cost, 142, 199
Opt-out, 102
Oregon, 79
Organic synthesis, 130

259

Orgone, 44
Orgone Accumulator, 44
Orlando, Florida, 47, 51, 87
Orphan drug, 144
Orphan Drug Act, 144
Orrin Hatch, 174
Orson Swindle, 99
Orthodox medicine, 167
Orthomolecular medicine, 44, 193
Oskar Minkowski, 132
Osteopathic manipulative medicine, 164, 179
Osteopathic medicine in the United States, 164, 168
Osteopathy, 151, 164, 168, 185
Osteoporosis, 62
Over-the-counter drug, 107
Over-the-counter drugs, 112
Oxford English Dictionary, 237

Pacific Time Zone, 77
Packaging and labeling, 113
Paid Programming (TV pilot), 68, 76
Pain tolerance, 158
Palliative care, 42, 193
Palm Springs, California, 87
Pamela Jones Harbour, 99
Panic attack, 89
Parade (magazine), 89
Parade Magazine, 59
Parallel imports, 150
Paranoia, 44
Parke Davis, 130
Parliament of the United Kingdom, 203, 214
Paroxetine, 149
Par Pharmaceutical, 116
Party Political Broadcast, 72
Pasteurization, 44
Pasteurized, 120
Patent, 129, 196
Patent medicine, 30, 31, 159
Patent misuse, 101
Pathogen, 141
Pathophysiological, 182
Patrick Dempsey, 93
Patrick Manson, 181
Pat Robertson, 85
Paula Zahn, 8
Paul Berg, 175
Paul Crouch, 85
Paul Ehrlich, 133
Paul Kurtz, 183
Paul Offit, 29, 184
Paul Rand Dixon, 98
Paxil, 149
Payola, 208
PBS, 236

Pediatrician, 126
Peking Union Medical College, 180
Peking University Health Science Center, 237
Penicillin, 133
Penn State Milton S. Hershey Medical Center, 236
Penny stock, 218
Pentecostal, 84
Peoples Republic of China, 38
Peripheral arterial disease, 137
Perjury, 208
Permian Basin (North America), 53
Personal development, 70
Perverting the course of justice, 208
Pet, 108
Peter Popoff, 72
Petters Group Worldwide, 220
Pfizer, 129, 135, 148–150
PGA Tour, 46
Pharmaceutical, 129
Pharmaceutical Benefits Advisory Committee, 144
Pharmaceutical companies, 19
Pharmaceutical drug, 107
Pharmaceutical formulation, 141
Pharmaceutical fraud, 148
Pharmaceutical industry, 3, 82, 111, **129**
Pharmaceutical marketing, 142
Pharmaceutical medications, 41
Pharmaceutical Research and Manufacturers of America, 142
Pharmacokinetics, 123, 143
Pharmacology, 130
Pharmacopoeia, 33
Phar-Mor, 219
Phenobarbital, 132
Philip Elman, 98
Philippines, 51
Phobia, 20, 82
Phone fraud, 215
Physician, 12, 17, 61, 116
Physicians in the United States, 182
Physics, 160
Physiology, 165, 188
Phytotherapy, 162
Pickpocketing, 208
Pierre Paul Émile Roux, 134
Pietro Longhi, 28
Piltdown Man, 218
PitchMen, 80
Pitch People (1999 film), 73
Pituitary, 23
Placebo, 154, 183, 190
Placebo Effect, 38, 190
Political convention, 68
Polytetrafluoroethylene, 118

Ponzi scheme, 218, 220
Pool (cue sports), 46
Porkys Revenge, 93, 94
Portal:Criminal justice, 209
Portales, New Mexico, 52, 53
Portal:Law, 209, 211
Portland, Oregon, 79, 90
Portmanteau, 68
Portsmouth, Virginia, 85
Portuguese escudo, 220
Possession of stolen goods, 208
Post hoc, ergo propter hoc, 200
Postmarketing surveillance, 115, 143
Poverty, 191
Prayer, 153, 164, 168
Pre-clinical development, 141
Predatory pricing, 101
Preface, 1
Pregabalin, 149
Pre-owned vehicle, 73
Prescription drug, 107, 122
Prescription Drug Marketing Act (PDMA), 146
Prescription drugs, 112
President of the United States, 108, 112, 216
Price fixing, 101
Primatene Mist, 131
Prime Minister of Canada, 112
Prime time, 68, 71
Prince Charles, 174, 190
Prize, 196
Product bundling, 101
Product design, 60
Product engineering, 60
Product liability, 210
Professional certification, 26
Profit motive, 8
Progressive Era, 96, 121
Progressive relaxation, 160, 186, 193
Prohibition, 209
Prontosil, 133
Propaganda, 166
Property law, 209, 211
ProPublica, 143
Prosperity gospel, 72
Prostate cancer, 174
Prostitution, 208
Protein, 127
Providence, Rhode Island, 79
Provocation (legal), 209
Proximate cause, 210
P. Roy Vagelos, 140
Pseudonym, 57
Pseudoscience, 8, 154, 155, 166, 184
Pseudo-science, 33
Psychiatry, 143
Psychological, 62

PTL Club, 86
Publication bias, 195
Public Broadcasting Service, 206
Public Broadcasting System, 172
Public health, 107
Public Health Service Act, 108, 111, 117
Public indecency, 207
Public nuisance, 210
Publishers Weekly, 24, 25
PubMed Identifier, 204
Puerperal fever, 44
Puerto Rico, 108
Pumbaa, 75
Pure Food and Drug Act, 34, 43, 121
Pure Food and Drugs Act, 135
Pyramid scheme, 4, 12

QALY, 144
Qi, 157, 160, 162, 186
Qigong, 157, 162
Qi gong, 160, 186
Quack, 46
Quackery, **26**, 46, 154, 155, 171, 179
Quackwatch, 6, 16, 27, 37, 184, 189, 206
Quantitative property, 68
Quasi-tort, 210
Quinine, 29, 129
Qui tam, 149
QVC, 75

Rabies, 44
Rabies vaccine, 134
Racketeering, 116
Radiation therapy, 45
Radioactive, 122
Radioactive quackery, 35
Radio syndication, 61
Ramón Báez Figueroa, 219
Rancho Mirage, California, 87
Randomized clinical trials, 175
Randomized controlled trial, 195
Rape, 207
R. Barker Bausell, 190
R&D 100 Awards, 60
Rebecca Grant (American actress), 46
Recreational drug use, 209
Reflexology, 185, 193
Refusal to deal, 101
Regional sports network, 77
Regression Fallacy, 41, 195
Regulation, 107
Regulation and prevalence of homeopathy, 194
Regulation of alternative medicine, 194
Regulation of food and dietary supplements by the U.S. Food and Drug Administration, 113

Regulations, 127
Reiki, 159, 160
Relative risk, 138
Relativism, 169
Relator (law), 149
Relevant market, 101
Religion, 154, 166, 184
Religious broadcasting, 72
Renal disease, 137
Reno, Nevada, 11, 50, 51
Reno R. Rolle, **60**
Replevin, 210
Republican Party (United States), 52, 98
Requiem for a Dream, 77
Rescue doctrine, 210
Res ipsa loquitur, 210
Restraint of trade, 211
Revalenta arabica, 29
RFD-TV, 74
RHEMA Bible Training Center, 66
Richard C. White, 52, 55
Richard Dawkins, 188, 203
Richard Mulligan, 93
Richard Nixon, 54, 157
Richard Whitney (financier), 220
Rick Scott, 218
Right of self-defense, 209, 210
Risk factor, 137
River blindness, 150
R.J. Reynolds, 119
Robbery, 207, 208
Robert Barefoot, **63**
Robert Koch, 44, 181
Robert Pitofsky, 99
Robert Tilton, 8, 67, 72
Robert Wagner, 94
Robert William Gettleman, 15
Robot Chicken, 76
Rodney Morris, 51
Roe Messner, 84, 87
Ronald Hoffman, **61**
Ron Jeremy, 89
Ron Popeil, 76
Röntgen ray, 181
Roosevelt County, New Mexico, 52, 53
Rose Shapiro, 6
Rosiglitazone, 149
Ross Perot, 77
Rotary International, 54
Rovi Corporation, 73
Royal Assent, 214
Royal College of Physicians, 42
Roy Porter, 202
Rubella, 134
Rulemaking, 102
Ryan J. Davis, 91

Ryans Hope, 92, 94
Ryan Stiles, 76
Rylands v Fletcher, 210

Safety monitoring, 141
Salicylic acid, 29
Sally Mayes, 91
Salon.com, 60
Salton, Inc., 60
Salve, 26
Samantha Thomas, 92
Same-sex marriage, 88
Samuel Hahnemann, 43, 202, 235
Samuel Hopkins Adams, 34
Samuel Israel III, 219
Sanatorium, 43
San Diego, California, 70
San Fernando Valley, 56
Santa Fe Natural Tobacco Company, 119
Santo Golds Blood Circus, 75
Saturday morning cartoon, 73
Saturday Night Live, 76
Saved by the Bell, 93, 95
Scandinavian Simvastatin Survival Study, 140
Science, 154, 165
Science based medicine, 29
Science-based medicine, 167, 172, 191
Science fiction, 43
Science Museum of Minnesota, 34, 46
Science policy of the United States, 120
Scientific American, 18, 22, 26, 230
Scientific American Frontiers, 206
Scientific evidence, 154, 165, 184, 195
Scientific fraud, 215
Scientific literacy, 201
Scientific method, 151, 154, 165, 170, 184, 192, 195
Scientific Review of Alternative Medicine, 184
Scientific skepticism, 159, 188
Scientific validation, 154, 184, 195
Scientology, 35
Scottish Medicines Consortium, 144
Scott W. Rothstein, 220
Screen Actors Guild, 66
Scurvy, 62
Sean McDaniel, 91
Secretary of Health and Human Services, 108
Security (finance), 216
Seduction (tort), 211
Self-help, 23
Self-published, 5
Senescence, 62
Sentence fragment, 140
Serendipity, 141
Serial killer, 218
Serious Fraud Office (United Kingdom), 214

Seth Kalichman, 83
Seven Sundays, 94
Seventh Circuit Court of Appeals, 4, 16
Sexual assault, 207
Shaman, 165
Shamanism, 151, 164
Sherwood, Arkansas, 90
Shiatsu, 193
Shop America, 60
Shopkeepers privilege, 210
Shriners, 54
Sic, 198
Siddha medicine, 151
Side effect, 172
Sign-off, 68
Silk Stalkings, 95
Silver, 29
Silver Spring, Maryland, 109
Similia similibus curentur, 235
Simon Singh, 204
Simvastatin, 140
Sinclair Broadcast Group, 80
Skechers, 78
Skeptical Inquirer, 204
Skeptics Dictionary, 206
Skill, 26
Skinny Bitch, 25
SkitHOUSE, 76
Small but significant and non-transitory increase in price, 101
Smith, Kline and French, 131
Smuggling, 208
Snake oil, 32, 187
Soap opera, 70
Sodium sulfate, 38
Sodomy, 209
Solicitation, 207
Somatotypes, 44
Sonora, Mexico, 165
South Africa, 150
South America, 81
South Carolina, 85
Southeast Asia, 81
South Park, 76
Spamming, 36
Specific performance, 212
Sperm donation, 108
Spin City, 93, 95
Spiritual healing, 185
Sponsor (commercial), 68
Standard medicine, 167
Standard of care, 210
Standard Oil Co. v. United States, 97
Stanley Cup playoffs, 71
Stanley Ho, 50
State attorney general, 3

Statute of limitations, 210
Statutory rape, 207
Stefan Santl, 47
Stephen Barrett, 16, 22, 27, 184, 189, 206
Stephen Harper, 112
Stephen Ostroff, 107, 108
Stephens College, 66
Steve Jobs, 69
Steven Novella, 187, 206
Steve Novella, 82
Steven Salzberg, 188
St. Johns Wort, 9
St. Louis, Missouri, 66
St. Marys High School (Lynn, Massachusetts), 4
Stockbroker, 216
Stock market, 216
Streptococci, 133
Stress (medicine), 22
Strike action, 209
Stroke, 137
Subculture, 169
Subdivision (land), 74
Subject-matter jurisdiction, 14
Suckers: How Alternative Medicine Makes Fools of Us All, 6
Suicide, 75, 209
Sulfanilamide, 134
Sulfonamide, 133
Sulfur, 158
Sulfuric acid, 32
Summary conviction, 214
Sunscreen, 6
Supernatural, 154, 155, 166, 184
Superstition, 154, 166, 184
Super Tuesday, 77
Supreme Court of Canada, 214
Surgeon General of the United States, 181
Surgery, 41
SV40, 136
Synonyms, 166
Syntex, 138
Syphilis, 133
Systematic review, 158

Tachyphylaxis, 138
Tai chi, 160, 185
Talk show, 61, 68
Tammy Faye Messner, 8, 18, **84**
Tampa, Florida, 78
Tanning booth, 118
Tax evasion, 208
Tega Cay, South Carolina, 86
Telebrands, 80
Telemarketing fraud, 100
Televangelist, 84

Televangelists, 72
Television, 118
Television advertisement, 68
Television commercial, 68
Television format, 68
Television producer, 92
Television program, 68
Television station, 68
Template:Alternative medical systems, 151
Template:Competition law, 101
Template:Criminal law, 209
Template:Fraud, 215
Template:Regulation of therapeutic goods in the United States, 112
Template talk:Alternative medical systems, 151
Template talk:Competition law, 101
Template talk:Criminal law, 209
Template talk:Regulation of therapeutic goods in the United States, 112
Template talk:Tort law, 211
Template:Tort law, 211
Teratogenic, 139
Terrell McSweeny, 98
Terry Calvani, 99
Testimonial, 166
Testosterone, 25
Têtes à Claques, 76
Texas, 13, 52, 53, 77
Texas 16th congressional district, 52, 55
Texass 16th congressional district, 53
Thalidomide, 122, 139
The 1993 Snake Oil Protection Act, 175
The 700 Club, 66
The Big Picture (1989 film), 94
The Cat in the Hat (film), 75
The Demon-Haunted World, 188, 203
The Drew Carey Show, 88
The Dr. Oz Show, 45
The Early Show, 8
The establishment, 172
The Eyes of Tammy Faye, 88
Theft, 208
Theft Act 1978, 214
The Gospel According to Tammy Faye, 90
The Heavenly Kid, 93, 94
The Independent, 189, 200
The Lancet, 45
The Lion King 1½, 75
The Love Boat: The Next Wave, 95
The Magic Clown, 70
The Men Who Made Us Thin, 8
The National Council Against Health Fraud, 36, 184
The New England Journal of Medicine, 170
The New Yorker, 89
The New York Times, 24, 25, 226

The New York Times Best Seller list, 60
Theodore Roosevelt, 121
The Oprah Winfrey Show, 93
Theoretical definition, 169
The PTL Club, 84, 91
Therapy, 168
Thermos-Grill2Go, 69
The Smoking Gun, 18
The Surreal Life, 84, 89
The Times, 176
The Transformers (TV series), 77
The Wager (2007 film), 94
The Washington Post, 188
The Weight-Loss Cure They Dont Want You to Know About, 3, 7, 16, **23**
The Young Riders, 95
Thomas Allinson, 42
Thomas Clifford Allbutt, 237
Thomas G. Morris, 52, 55
Thomas Hager, 233
Thomas Harkin, 173
Thomas Petters, 220
Thorsten Hohmann, 51
Tie-in, 77
Tijuana, 70
Tim and Eric Awesome Show, Great Job, 76
Time Inc, 204
Timeline of medicine and medical technology, 181
Time magazine, 172
Time (magazine), 64, 226, 229
Time-value of money, 142
Tim Heidecker, 76
Timothy Muris, 99
Tincture of benzoin, 33
Tinnitus, 62
Tiny Toon Adventures, 75
Title 15 of the United States Code, 96, 103
Title 16 of the Code of Federal Regulations, 97
Title 18 of the United States Code, 110, 221
Title 21 of the United States Code, 111
TiVo, 73
Tobacco products, 107, 119
Today (NBC program), 8, 90
Today (U.S. TV program), 79
Tongkat ali, 25, 225
Too Many Cooks (short), 76
Toothbrush, 117
Tort, 209, 210, 212
Tort (conflict), 211
Tortious interference, 211
Toxicity, 143
Toxin, 179
Traci Bingham, 89
Trade secret, 214

Traditional Chinese medicine, 38, 151, 156, 157, 168, 178
Traditional Korean medicine, 151
Traditional medicine, 151, 156, 163, 184, 191
Traditional Mongolian medicine, 151
Traditional Tibetan medicine, 151
Transferred intent, 210
Trespass, 210
Trespasser, 211
Trespass to chattels, 210
Trespass to land, 210
Tribune Media Services, 73
Trick or Treatment, 204
Tricyclic antidepressants, 131
Trinity Broadcasting Network, 66, 85
TRIPS, 150
Trishelle Cannatella, 89
Tropical medicine, 181
Trover, 210
Trust (19th century), 96
Trust-busting, 96
Trust law, 211
Trusts and estates, 209
Tuberculosis, 62, 122, 151
Tulane University School of Public Health and Tropical Medicine, 181
Turkish Taffy, 70
Turlingtons Balsam, 30, 31
TV Guide, 93
TV One (US TV network), 77
Twitter, 95
Ty Bollinger, 45
Tying (commerce), 101

UK, 147
Ukraine, 5
Ultrahazardous activity, 210
Unani, 151
Unethical, 154
United Kingdom, 10
United Methodist, 53, 54
United States, 27, 43, 51, 52, 61, 68, 70, 111, 112, 136
United States Congress, 107, 113
United States Court of Appeals for the Seventh Circuit, 15
United States Department of Agriculture, 110, 119
United States Department of Health and Human Services, 107, 170
United States Department of Justice, 100
United States Department of Transportation, 54
United States district court, 15
United States District Court for the District of Columbia, 14

United States District Court for the Northern District of Illinois, 13
United States dollar, 111
United States federal court system, 110
United States federal executive departments, 107
United States government, 19
United States House of Representatives, 52, 53, 55, 173
United States Medical Licensing Examination, 182
United States National Academies, 202
United States National Do Not Call Registry, 100
United States Navy, 43, 53
United States Penitentiary, Lewisburg, 44
United States presidential election, 1912, 97
United States presidential election, 2008, 77
United States Senate, 108
United States v. American Tobacco Co., 97
United States Virgin Islands, 108
University of Berlin, 181
University of Calgary, 6, 17
University of Florida, 92
University of Maryland, Baltimore, 182, 206
University of Wisconsin, 206
Univision, 77
Unsupported attributions, 25, 60
Upjohn, 129
Upton Sinclair, 121
USA Today, 24, 25
U.S. Customs and Border Protection, 110
USDA, 107
U.S. Department of Justice, 100
U.S. Food and Drug Administration, 194, 198
US National Center for Complementary and Alternative Medicine, 196
US Navy, 56
U.S. Securities and Exchange Commission, 12, 116, 216
U.S. Senator, 53
U.S. state, 108
US Supreme Court, 124
Uta Hagen, 92

Vaccination, 156
Vaccine, 44, 107
Vaccine Act of 1813, 121
Valdecoxib, 149
Valproic acid, 149
Valtrex, 149
Vanilla Ice, 89
Vegan, 60
Vegetarianism, 43
Vehicular homicide, 207
Vereniging tegen de Kwakzalverij, 30

Veronal, 132
Vertical integration, 141
Vertical restraints, 100
Veterinary medicine, 107
VH1, 89
Vicarious liability, 211
Vicarious liability (criminal), 207
Victimless crimes, 208
Vioxx, 125
Viper (TV series), 95
Viral video, 76
Visualization (cam), 193
Vital energy, 160
Vitalism, 5, 43, 156, 186
Vitamin C, 44
Vitamin C megadosage, 44
Vitamin D, 62
Vitamix, 70
Volenti non fit injuria, 211
Voyeurism, 207

Waldron, Kansas, 90
Walker, Texas Ranger, 95
Wallace Sampson, 183
Wall Street Journal, 24, 25
War of 1812, 31
Warren Buffett, 103
Warren G. Harding, 219
Warts, 41
Washington, D.C., 96, 97, 110
Washington Metropolitan Area, 109
Wayne Brady, 76
Wayne Jonas, 175
Webster Kehr, 45
Weekend Edition, 233
Weekend Marketplace, 73
Weight loss, 23
Weird Al Yankovic, 76
Weird Al Yankovic in 3-D, 76
Wellbutrin, 149
Western medicine, 166
West Texas, 53
Wetumka, Oklahoma, 219
WFAA-TV, 79
WFLA-TV, 78
What information to include, 184, 195
Wheel series, 72
Whistleblower, 149
White Oak, Maryland, 108
Whose Line Is It Anyway? (U.S. TV series), 76
Wichita, Kansas, 87, 88
Wickenburg, Arizona, 63
Wikinews:Category:Food and Drug Administration, 129

Wikinews: Obama calls food safety system a hazard to public health, 127
Wikipedia:Citation needed, 10, 14, 27, 42, 48, 50, 54, 56, 64, 65, 70, 71, 73, 85–87, 94, 119, 124, 140, 158, 181, 196, 215, 237
Wikipedia:Citing sources, 157
Wikipedia:Disputed statement, 169, 184, 191
Wikipedia:Please clarify, 4, 9, 18, 131
Wikipedia:Verifiability, 43, 128
Wikisource, 106
Wikt:enigma, 183
Wikt:hawker, 26
Wikt:pseudo-medicine, 26
Wildlife smuggling, 209
Wilhelm Reich, 44
Wilk v. American Medical Association, 41
William Herbert Sheldon, 44
William Hogarth, 28
William H. Welch, 180
William Kovacic, 99
William Osler, 180
William Radam, 32
William Shatner, 94
Willie Mosconi, 50
Will Keith Kellogg, 43
Will (law), 209, 211
Willow, 29
Windmill Entertainment, 93
Wine, 32
Wisconsin, 79
Wizard Oil, 43
WKBW-TV, 78
WLUK-TV, 79
WNAC-TV, 79
Woodrow Wilson, 96, 97
Works Progress Administration, 27
WorldCom, 218
World Health Organization, 41, 171
World Net Daily, 57
World Trade Organization, 150
World War II, 133, 135
Wushu (term), 160
WVBT, 79

XETV-TDT, 70
Xploration Nation, 74
X-ray, 181

Y2K, 57
Yeast infections, 22
Yoga, 185, 193
Yoga (alternative medicine), 193
Yoga as exercise or alternative medicine, 160

Zevo-3, 78

Zimbabwe, 156
Ziprasidone, 149
ZMapp, 114
Zofran, 149
Zyprexa, 149

www.ingramcontent.com/pod-product-compliance
Lightning Source LLC
Chambersburg PA
CBHW071248230426
43668CB00011B/1635